Honecker's Germany

Also by David Childs:

The GDR: Moscow's German Ally (1983)

Honecker's Germany

Edited by
David Childs
University of Nottingham

London
ALLEN & UNWIN
Boston   Sydney

Allen & Unwin (Publishers) Ltd,
40 Museum Street, London WC1A 1LU, UK

Allen & Unwin (Publishers) Ltd,
Park Lane, Hemel Hempstead, Herts HP2 4TE, UK

Allen & Unwin, Inc.,
8 Winchester Place, Winchester, Mass. 01890, USA

Allen & Unwin (Australia) Ltd,
8 Napier Street, North Sydney, NSW 2060, Australia

First published in 1985

British Library Cataloguing in Publication Data

Honecker's Germany.
Germany (East) – Social conditions
I.   Childs, David
943.1087'8   HN460.5.A8
ISBN 0-04-354031-7

Library of Congress Cataloging in Publication Data

Honecker's Germany.
Bibliography: p. 188
Includes indexes.
1. Germany (East) – Addresses, essays, lectures.
2. Honecker, Erich – Addresses, essays, lectures.
I. Childs, David, 1933–
DD287.H66   1985   943.1   85-9064
ISBN 0-04-354031-7 (alk. paper)

Set in 10 on 11 point Times by Ann Buchan (Typesetters),
Walton-on-Thames, Surrey and printed in Great Britain by
Billing and Sons Ltd, London and Worcester

Contents

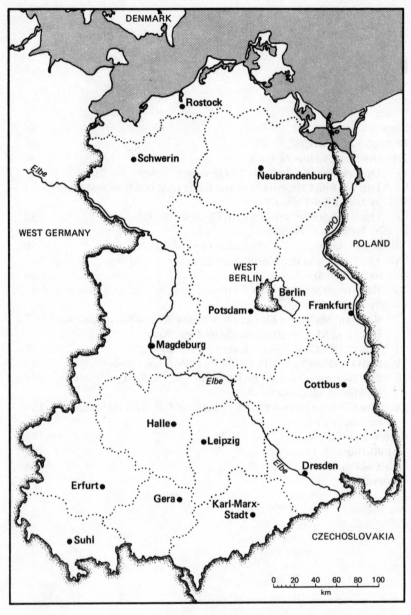

DENMARK

● Rostock

● Schwerin

● Neubrandenburg

Elbe

WEST GERMANY

POLAND

Oder

Neisse

WEST
BERLIN

Berlin

Potsdam ●

● Magdeburg

● Frankfurt

Elbe

Cottbus ●

Halle●

● Leipzig

Elbe

Dresden ●

Erfurt●

Gera ●

Karl-Marx-
Stadt ●

● Suhl

CZECHOSLOVAKIA

0   20   40   60   80   100
km

Bezirk

1 Berlin	6 Gera	11 Neubrandenburg
2 Cottbus	7 Halle	12 Potsdam
3 Dresden	8 Karl-Marx-Stadt	13 Rostock
4 Erfurt	9 Leipzig	14 Schwerin
5 Frankfurt	10 Magdeburg	15 Suhl

The administrative regions of the GDR

Preface

It was decided to call this book *Honecker's Germany* because it concentrates on the GDR since 1971. Some contributors have, however, felt obliged to say something about the period before that date as well. This matters little as right from the start Honecker played a key role in the SED's efforts to create a socialist state between the Elbe and the Oder, first as head of the Free German Youth, 1946–55, and then in the higher councils of the party itself. Finally, from 1971 Erich Honecker has served as first/general secretary of the SED and from 1976 as head of state as well.

This collection of essays attempts to deal, in the main, either with topics not covered in my earlier *The GDR: Moscow's German Ally*, or with topics which could not be discussed at length. This is particularly true of the chapters on the churches, youth, Christa Wolf and Irmtraud Morgner, the GDR Navy, GDR relations with the USSR, and, even more, GDR relations with the USA. As for the other chapters, they deal with subjects important enough to merit further discussion from a different perspective from the one I originally chose. I hope that, in some small measure, the new book will do justice to the growing body of research on the GDR being undertaken in Britain and North America. Our only contributor who is not working in an English-speaking state is Professor Hermann Weber. Herr Weber has spent virtually the whole of his adult life researching German communism, the SED and the GDR. At some time or other we have all made use of his publications. I would like to take this opportunity to thank him, and his colleagues, for arranging the first Anglo-West German study conference on the GDR at the University of Mannheim in September 1984. The discussions at the ninth annual conference of the Association for the Study of German Politics, with Hermann Weber, led to both the conference and the book.

I would like to thank Tony Millson and Roland Smith of the British Military Government, Berlin, and Tim and Josiane Evernard and the staff of the British Embassy (GDR) for their hospitality during my visit in 1984. I should also like to thank Brian Quigley and Greg Sandford of the US Embassy to the GDR for giving me their impressions of US–GDR relations, and Stefan Heym for receiving me into his home.

Readers should note that 'billion' follows American, not German, usage throughout, that is it denotes 1,000 millions. Finally, I must emphasize that the views expressed in this book are those of the individual authors alone.

David Childs,
University of Nottingham,
May 1985

Introduction

DAVID CHILDS

The last decade and a half has been an exciting one for the foreign-policy-making elite of the German Democratic Republic (GDR). In 1969 the GDR, despite its economic, educational and military development, was almost totally isolated diplomatically. It was desperately happy to receive a few backbench parliamentarians from anywhere west of the Elbe. To a considerable extent it was the abandonment of the Hallstein doctrine by Bonn, its diplomatic sanctions against any state outside the Soviet bloc taking up relations with the GDR, which paved the way for the worldwide recognition of Honecker's German state in the 1970s. No one can accuse the GDR's leaders of failing to take full advantage of the new situation. They had a ticket to ride and they rode! Since then they have shown no tendency to develop travel sickness or jet lag! Erich Honecker is an enthusiastic traveller and he sets the tone. The fact that the GDR's most crucial relations are with Bonn and, above all, with the USSR, has obscured its relations with the rest of the world. With Bonn, relations, despite ups and down, have been far better than most Western commentators and politicians would have believed possible in 1969. More surprisingly, the change of government in Bonn in 1982, from a left of centre to a right of centre coalition, has led to no worsening of relations between the two German states. Any serious West German politician, whatever his party, feels obliged to visit the GDR. This mirrors public concern about the maintenance of close relations with the other half of Germany. Equally, the politicians of the GDR know that they must strive for better relations with Bonn because of the expectations of their people. It seems that the process of inter-German *détente*, resulting from the *Ostpolitik* pursued since 1969, has taken on a momentum of its own which the politicians could not resist even if they wanted to. The credits from Bonn negotiated by the GDR in 1983 and 1984 will give further momentum to this process because they help to secure the human ties between the citizens of the two states. The DM 1 billion (£270 million) credit West German banks granted the GDR in summer 1983 led to the GDR lifting the minimum exchange requirement demanded from children visiting from the West. The DM 950 million (£257 million) credit announced in July 1984 led to a reduction of the minimum exchange requirement for pensioners from the West visiting the GDR, and some other concessions. After falling for several years from the 3,124,000 peak in 1975 visits by West Germans to the GDR have risen since 1981:

1981	2,088,000
1982	2,218,000
1983	2,219,000

During the same period, 1981–3, roughly 1,120,000 West Germans annually have visited East Berlin from West Berlin on a daily basis. The number of West Berliners visiting the GDR annually over the same period is 1,720,000. In 1983 the number of GDR pensioners visiting West Germany and West Berlin actually fell from 1,553,873 in 1982 to 1,462,949 in 1983. But the number of GDR citizens under pensionable age visiting the West on urgent family business went up from 45,709 in 1982 to 64,025 in 1983. The number of telephone calls from West Germany to the GDR remained over 23 million in 1983 and the number of calls in the other direction went up from 7.9 million in 1982 to 10.2 million in 1983. It will be remembered that the population of the GDR is only about 16.9 million. These millions of encounters between Germans from East and West obviously posed a continuing challenge for the ruling Socialist Unity Party (Sozialistische Einheitspartei Deutschlands – SED).

This process of *détente* between the two German states can, at present, only go so far. Just how far nobody knows. The USSR has expressed its doubts about the agreements over the West German credits and accused West Germany of attempting, according to *Pravda* (2 August 1984), to disturb the stability of the GDR with the aim of reunification. It claimed that the expansion of human contacts was merely an attempt to get new channels for political and ideological influence. Clearly the SED leadership cannot simply ignore Moscow's views. The GDR is heavily dependent on the USSR for its fuel supplies. It is heavily dependent on the same source for its trade. It has a massive Soviet military presence within its frontiers and the Soviet security service, the KGB, has a network of agents throughout the GDR. As Herr Ulbricht found out in 1971, the leader of the SED is very vulnerable to the consequences of Soviet lack of confidence in him. No doubt Herr Honecker and his colleagues have been doing some special pleading in Moscow. They will mention their support for the Soviet line on Poland and Afghanistan. They will emphasize their decision to withdraw from the 1984 Olympics, a very big sacrifice indeed for the GDR, as a sign of their continuing solidarity with the Soviet leadership. They will remind their Soviet colleagues of the increase in their defence capacity in line with Soviet policy. They will point out that they need more relaxed relations with Bonn in order to promote their own domestic stability. Such ties help the GDR to maintain its standard of living and make its people less desperate psychologically. The SED leaders will argue that if there is a serious internal crisis in the GDR this would have severe consequences for the socialist systems of Poland and Czechoslovakia. One further argument put forward by SED leaders is that by presenting a more acceptable image to the West they are helping the 'peace forces' in the Bonn republic and elsewhere. By these, they mean the green movement and the left-wing of the Social Democratic Party (Sozialdemokratische Partei Deutschlands – SPD) but also certain elements in the Free Democratic Party (Freie Demokratische Partei – FDP) and even in the Christian Democratic Union (Christlich-Demokratische Union – CDU). By presenting a more acceptable face of socialism they can improve their relations with the other Western states thus helping the peace–defence strategy of the Warsaw Pact as a whole. If state visits mean anything, they can claim some successes in this direction.

In 1984 Erich Honecker was pleased to welcome on GDR soil the prime ministers of Italy (Bettino Craxi), Greece (Andreas Papandreou) and Sweden (Olof Palme). Oskar Fischer, the GDR Foreign Minister, was received by Queen Beatrix of the Netherlands while on an official visit in July, Horst Sindermann has hosted a parliamentary delegation from Belgium and Kenneth Clarke, the British Minister of Health, had talks with Willi Stoph, chairman of the Council of Ministers and number two in the GDR hierarchy. Certainly in Greece, the Netherlands, Belgium and Britain controversy reigns about defence policy and Sweden needs constant reassurance that its neutrality is not in danger from the Warsaw Pact. When Werner Felfe, member of the Politburo and a deputy head of state, visited Britain in June, no doubt he discussed more than just agriculture with his hosts. The GDR leaders will be proud to remind their Soviet colleagues of their relations with states outside of Europe. They will mention the hero's welcome they laid on for Kim Il Sung, the wayward communist king of North Korea, and the talks they had with the Chinese Minister of Health in July. In the same month a delegation of the Arab League was in the GDR and the GDR has continued to engage Iran in dialogue, despite that state's anti-communist position. The GDR has continued to support Nicaragua and has maintained good relations with Mexico. The SED leaders can also mention in their own favour their quiet diplomacy, especially in the Third World. Here I am thinking of the training and education offered by the GDR to foreign students. According to *Foreign Affairs Bulletin* (bulletin of the GDR Foreign Ministry, 23 May 1984),

In the years from 1976 to 1980 alone, approximately 11,000 foreigners were trained and further trained, and from 1981 through 1983 a total of some 7,600 finished their studies in the German Democratic Republic. Some 10,000 foreigners from 106 countries are now studying at GDR universities, colleges and specialized schools. They come above all from the People's Democratic Republic of Yemen, Libya, Ethiopia, Nicaragua, Afghanistan, Angola, Mozambique and Algeria.

The GDR thus can present itself as a significant factor in international diplomacy. Surely there are some in Moscow who are wise enough to understand this?

To his own people Honecker stresses his attempts to improve relations with the West despite the escalation of the arms race and the stationing of the new US rockets on West German soil. He will point out that he is prepared to talk to any Western politician despite ideological differences. In the case of West Germany even Herr Franz Josef Strauss, leader of the Christian Social Union (Christliche-Soziale Union – CSU) has not been beyond the pale. Honecker can contrast the continuing unemployment in the West with the full employment in the GDR, and the modest improvements in social welfare in the GDR with the cuts in benefits in West Germany and elsewhere. He will claim that his party and its allies in government are doing everything within their means to improve the physical appearance of the GDR's towns and cities. The reopening of the virtually rebuilt Leipziger Gewandhaus, das Deutsche Schauspielhaus and the Friedrichstadtpalast are just three proud examples of this. The improvements in housing over the last decade are also part of the picture.

Very many GDR citizens remain sceptical and unmoved by all this. They still feel their standard of living is lower than they have a right to expect. (Queues and shortages are still a common feature of GDR life.) They still resent the many restrictions on their personal freedom and they still resent the arrogance of officialdom. They still await more candour and less cant from their media and from their politicians. They do not welcome new US weaponry on German soil, but many of them feel either that Soviet actions have provoked this development or that they, and the rest of Europe, are the victims of the great power mania of Moscow as well as of Washington. In general, the image Moscow projects appeals to them less than that projected by Washington. The Olympic Games have strengthened these respective images. By joining in the Soviet boycott of the Los Angeles games Honecker threw away a great opportunity for improving the GDR's image among its own people. Unconvinced by Soviet arguments, many East Germans saw Honecker exposing himself as being merely Moscow's satrap rather than acting as the head of a sovereign state. His decision not to go to Bonn confirmed this view.

The continuing undercurrent of scepticism, frustration and even downright opposition is clear from the many thousands who have been allowed to go in the first half of 1984 to West Germany, and the many times that number who have applied to leave. It is remarkable that there are those who are prepared to get themselves arrested and to spend around two years in jail just in order to get to the West. Some even more desperate try to jump the queue by jumping the frontier. The following cases reported in the *Guardian* (4 October 1983) were typical.

A 20-year-old East German escaped into West Germany uninjured by climbing a border fence and avoiding mines and automatic firing devices, West German border police said yesterday. They said that the man, a mechanic, escaped into West Germany early on Saturday, to become the fourth East German to flee the country in two days . . . On Thursday, two East Germans, aged 22 and 25, escaped into West Germany by climbing border fences. On Wednesday, an East German border guard escaped to the West after climbing a border fence.

These were the lucky ones. Since the building of the Wall in August 1961, 73 deaths have been recorded in West Berlin of those attempting to climb over it. In the same period 110 East Germans have died trying to cross the main East-West dividing line (*Süddeutsche Zeitung*, 11–12 August 1984). Nearly 200,000 East Germans have taken risks and successfully fled the GDR, nearly 300,000 have left legally (some after imprisonment). They are from all social and age groups. They range from the humblest pensioner to those who have given up a great deal to get out. Franz Loeser was one of the latest of these. As a professor of philosophy at Humboldt University and a member of the Presidium of the Peace Council of the GDR he enjoyed a privileged and not uninteresting life. On a private visit to the USA in 1983 he decided he did not wish to continue to support the policies of the SED and decided, therefore, not to return to the GDR. Despite their genuine attempts to placate their own people the leaders of the GDR know that there are others like Herr Loeser in their party, and many more outside it, who never had any commitment to the GDR. That is why they must maintain this ugly frontier in the heart of Germany.

1

The Socialist Unity Party

HERMANN WEBER

The Socialist Unity Party of Germany (Sozialistische Einheitspartei Deutschlands – SED) is, with 2.2 million members, not only the biggest party in the two German states but, with the exceptions of the Soviet Communist Party, the Romanian Communist Party and the British Labour Party, in the whole of Europe as well. In addition, it is a party whose claim to leadership in the state is constitutionally secured. The 1974 constitution of the German Democratic Republic (GDR) proclaims that the state is led by the working class and its Marxist–Leninist party (article 1). Thus it is written down that the SED is the state party of the GDR. But its claims go further. The SED aims to control all areas of public life. Thus it is both the leader of the entire social life of the GDR and is responsible for the whole system of political, ideological, scientific, technical, economic and cultural work.[1]

   This SED claim to total leadership, which the party has tried to achieve since the 1950s, primarily means the domination of the GDR political system. Because the non-communist parties, allowed in 1945, have officially recognized the SED's claim to leadership,[2] because the mass organizations – such as the trade unions, the Free German Youth (Freie Deutsche Jugend – FDJ), the Democratic Women's Federation (Demokratischer Frauenbund Deutschlands – DFD), and so on – are totally dependent on the SED, and, finally, because state policy is determined by the SED, the party is the leading political organ of the GDR. Because of this role numerous factors, with which the GDR has got to deal continuously, become the SED's problems. There are two main problems in this connection, problems which for decades have created difficulties for the GDR. First, the GDR is only a part or constituent state (*Teilstaat*) of the German nation. It has evolved from a common history and, in addition, it remains with its gaze always fixed on West Germany. Secondly, in the 1950s the Stalinist system of the

USSR was transplanted to the GDR. But Stalinism, a centrally directed state economy and political dictatorship (including the violence of despotic arbitrary rule), had grown out of the USSR's backwardness. The GDR was thus formed from a model which, in Marx's terms, emanates from a lower socio-economic formation, which stood in contradiction to Germany's socio-economic development.

In accordance with these two basic problems the SED's strategy was to concentrate first on German unity. Since the end of the 1960s, on the other hand, it has striven for 'demarcation' (*Abgrenzung*) *vis-à-vis* West Germany. Basically, the function, programme and structure of the SED was modelled on the Communist Party of the Soviet Union (CPSU). Admittedly, the historical development of the SED did not run in a straight line; there were breaks in the continuity.

Continuity and Change

The present-day SED can only be correctly understood if its growth over nearly four decades is taken in account. Tradition still has a considerable influence on SED policy, and its leadership's way of acting is now, as ever, stamped by its origins and experience. A look at the history of the SED enables us to discern five periods in which the SED (at first under the direction of, and with the support of, the Soviet occupying power) erected a Soviet-style 'socialist' system. Through radical changes to the economic, social and political structures the old propertied and ruling strata were expropriated and deprived of power. In their place a new ruling stratum under the direction and control of the SED appeared. The five phases were:

(1)   From 1945 to 1948 structures were changed and the preconditions for a new society were created by various reforms (land reform, educational reform, reform of the judiciary and industrial reform). The political and, above all, the party system remained strongly oriented towards the traditions of the Weimar Republic. The transformation of the SPD into the communistic SED produced an organization which was still not a cadre party in the Leninist sense, but was a mass party in which the former Social Democrats had parity with the Communists in its leading committees. It wished to follow a German road to socialism and did not identify itself with the Soviet model.

(2)   Between 1949 and 1955 the GDR took over the Stalinist system of the USSR. Total power in political life and society was exercised by the SED (which itself had been transformed into a Stalinist 'party of a new type'), albeit under the direction of the USSR. The party ran and controlled society with bureaucratic-

dictatorial methods and was opposed by the majority of the population (proved by the numbers of refugees and the revolt of 17 June 1953).

(3) In the period between 1956 and 1961 the SED carried out a half-hearted deStalinization. In the GDR further structural changes, such as the collectivization of agriculture, were carried through and the Stalinist base was conserved. The SED had more room for manoeuvre in shaping its own policy, but under Ulbricht the GDR remained a loyal ally of the USSR.

(4) From 1961 to 1970 the economic stabilization of the GDR was carried out. Due to deStalinization, on the one hand, and the demands of modern industrial society, on the other, the SED transformed its methods of ruling. It switched more and more from terror to the neutralizing and manipulation of the masses. The new aim of rationalizing and modernizing the economic system pushed the efficiency of the economy to the centre of party activity and consequently the role and function of the SED was changed. In the 'socialist' achievement (*Leistung*)[3] and consumer society the SED began a process of transformation from a bureaucratic *Apparat* party to a state party with a technocratic style of leadership. The SED also attempted to free itself from an uncritical acceptance of the Soviet model and the total predominance of Soviet policy.

(5) After the removal of Ulbricht in May 1971 the SED under Honecker revised its efforts at independence. The GDR remained, however, the junior partner of the USSR. Internally, the SED turned away from a technocratic emphasis and gave priority once again to ideology. It was felt that flexible methods of leadership would strengthen the power of the state party and enforce its claims to leadership.

In considering these stages of the SED's development and the GDR's history three turning-points are of particular significance. The first was in 1948–9 when the SED was transformed into a 'party of a new type', with which the Social Democratic traditions, structures and influences were to be overcome. The special German road to socialism was abandoned. The party was centralized and transformed into a communist party to enable it to play its role as the state party of the GDR. The second turning-point was in 1961 when the SED reached its goal of transforming the GDR according to the Soviet model and, by building the Berlin Wall, sealing it off. But now the party faced a new situation. Up until 1961 ideological norms and programmatic aims had determined the SED's policy of changing the structures of the GDR according to the Soviet model, but by that date the changed reality of GDR society had more influence on the SED and the weight of facts forced the SED to change its policies within a system which had become 'conservative'. The end of the Ulbricht era in 1971 brought about a third significant change. The SED, under its new first secretary (from 1976 general secretary), Erich Honecker, again recognized the leading role of the USSR and the Soviet model as absolutely binding. Even if this did not signify a repeat of the total dependence of the GDR as in the 1950s, it had to subordinate itself to the general strategy and tactics of the USSR. Because of increasing difficulties with the more self-confident working class in communist-ruled states (the Polish disturbances of 1970 were an extreme example), the methods of leadership had to be changed. Under Honecker the social concerns of the lower-income groups were more seriously taken into account through 'social measures', the style of party work became more businesslike. Attempts were made to encourage participation from below in order to solve the increasingly complicated problems of the GDR. This did not mean, in any way, a reduction of the SED's 'leading role' for, on the contrary, the party continued to extend its dominating role in politics, society and the economy. All sectors of public life were to be more strongly regulated and controlled, admittedly with more flexible methods.

At the same time, the SED underlined the change of 1971 by concealing Ulbricht's role, indeed turning him into a 'non-person'. (Only in the last two years has Ulbricht been given greater prominence again.) Nevertheless the changes in the years since 1971 have not been as great as the continuity in the SED's development. A comparison of the changes in the SED since 1971 with the complete development of the party indicates that continuity has been maintained in its approach to decisive questions.

Problems under Honecker

In 1971 Honecker replaced Ulbricht. The most recent phase, therefore, already comprises a third of the SED's history. The SED leadership under Honecker has loudly proclaimed that democracy has been realized in the GDR and socialism is being built. Now, as before, the legend is maintained that the SED is carrying out the aims of the German working-class movement. Yet in the most recent period under Honecker the SED has not taken a single step in the direction of democracy and socialism. As in 1970, before the fall of Ulbricht, the GDR is once again in a state of crisis. Although the GDR has managed to become one of the twelfth largest industrial states in the world and has reached the highest living standard of any of the communist-ruled states, and although its citizens are materially better off than before, there has been an increase in dissatisfaction. This is connected, first, with the fact that the hopes of bettering material standards, awakened by Honecker, have not been fulfilled (also because of the world economic crisis). In addition, the living standard of the East Germans is still only about half as high as in West Germany. Because of the orientation of the citizens of the GDR towards West Germany, as well as the stagnation of living standards in 1977–9, this has remained a ground for continuous dissatisfaction.

The crisis was, however, not only sparked off by economic difficulties. New unrest among artists, intellectuals and young people had already begun after Wolf Biermann was deprived of his GDR citizenship in 1976, which signalled the end of the period of liberal cultural policy. So once again, nearly thirty-five years after its founding, the GDR proved itself to be a state whose stability was based not on the broad support of its citizens but on the instruments of power, guaranteed by the USSR, *vis-á-vis* the population. The SED's answer to this new crisis was, and is, measures of repression, reprisals against writers, the arrest or expulsion of opponents, the perfecting of the surveillance state (*Überwachungsstaat*), or preventive regimentation such as the amendment of the criminal code by which every critical word can be suppressed.

During the course of its history the GDR had, by taking over the Soviet model, fully established the rule of the Communist Party, the SED. On the other hand, numerous reforms were carried through. Some of these reforms were, without doubt, of a progressive nature. These social achievements indicated the rudiments of a society based on solidarity, but the political dictatorship, the regimentation of all areas of life by the SED, the attempt to stamp out any nonconformism, are indications of just how much the GDR swings between modernity and outmoded methods of ruling.

SED: Way of Working and Structure

According to its own view of itself the SED is 'the conscious and organized vanguard of the working class and of the working people of the GDR'.[4] The structure of the party is based on 'democratic centralism'. According to a still-valid interpretation by a leading SED member this principle means: a united party programme, strategy and tactics being decided by the party congress as its highest organ; between congresses the Central Committee (ZK) determines the party line; the decisions of higher bodies are absolutely binding on lower ones; the elective principle for all leading bodies from top to bottom and the accountability of party organs to their organizations; strict party discipline and subordination of the minority to the majority. 'Conscious party discipline is for all comrades equally binding.'[5]

The SED is, however, a party ruled by a party *Apparat*, that is, by full-time functionaries. There can be no talk of either free democratic elections or of the accountability of these functionaries in decisive political questions. Moreover, many full-time officials are not elected. Even formally, only the members and candidates of the leading organs (from the ZK down to the basic organizations) and the secretaries are elected. Directors and other employees of the departments of the party *Apparat* at all levels, instructors and party organizers, editors, teaching staff at party schools, functionaries of the mass organizations and the state apparatus nominated by the party, are appointed, not elected, and are only accountable to higher, not lower, bodies. The structure of the party (*Bezirk, Kreis, Ort*, that is, the organization at regional, small town and village level respectively) is not built up from below but, on the contrary, instructions are issued from above. The party organization is regimented through a strict, but in no way democratic, centralism.

For the most important leading positions in the *Bezirke* and *Kreise* only obedient, disciplined cadres are selected and employed in appropriate functions from which they can be removed at any time by those higher up. In this way a core of functionaries is created which attempts to carry out the decisions of the leadership and to influence the members and lower functionaries in the spirit of the party leaders. This is executed without reference to the members, under the sole direction of the authoritative, full-time *Apparat*. Members of the SED are thus virtually powerless, for within the party organization they can scarcely go beyond the boundaries set by the leadership and the *Apparat*'s activities cannot be checked by them.

Because the SED, as the leading organ of the GDR, asserts its right to total leadership, a united and powerful party organization is in fact decisive and the inner party structure essential. The iron discipline of party members and the strict hierarchical centralism are, for that reason, the true principles underlying party structure.

Because the party under Honecker asserted with renewed emphasis the role of the working class, this ought to be reflected in its social structure which has considerably altered between the Ulbricht era and today. Between 1966 and 1981 the proportion of workers rose from 45 per cent to 57.6 per cent and the proportion of the intelligentsia from 12 per cent to 22 per cent. At the same time the proportion of white-collar employees and farmers declined. Of the party members and candidates, 34 per cent are graduates of either a university or a *Fachschule* (primarily concerned with training technicians). Among full-time functionaries the main trend is towards employing graduates. For instance, 64 per cent of all party secretaries, including all secretaries in the *Bezirk* and *Kreis* leaderships, were graduates in 1981 according to Honecker in his report to the Tenth Party Congress. The claim to control all fields forces the SED leadership, therefore, to be more 'objective' in its methods and to require its officials to have better professional qualifications. Only in this way can it exercise strict centralism within the party and realize its claim to the leading role in all fields.

The SED leadership can enforce its internal party regime and its centralized decision-making because of three factors. In the first place there is the voluntary discipline and subordination of the members and, above all, the functionaries, and the way they fall into line. This is supposed to be strengthened by the claim that the SED is a 'voluntary league of struggle of the likeminded' and the rank and file's limited right to be heard is supposed to encourage the comrades' trust in each other, their sense of belonging and unity in thought and action. It was not by chance that Honecker emphasized, at the Eighth Party Congress, that the strength of the SED lay in the activity of its basic units. Therefore, the work of convincing people (*Überzeugungsarbeit*) and the petty political work (*politische Kleinarbeit*) were at the core of its activity. Increased ideological training should strengthen the belief that political aims can only be achieved with a united party of struggle (*Kampfpartei*), which presupposes unconditional party discipline. Where voluntary subordination to this hierarchical shaping of policy is not forthcoming, the leadership is equipped with repressive means to enforce it. Because every contradiction of the line laid down by the leadership is regarded as deviation, which is prosecuted by the Party Control Commission, an opposition (even more so an organized faction) is now, as ever, impossible.

The second factor of the centralized party structure is the power of the full-time *Apparat*. It selects the functionaries, deploys them, removes them and prepares the 'elections'. As well as deciding personnel policy the *Apparat* controls the entire life and activity of the party through decisions, directives and instructions. The numerous instructors and party organizers, who individually or in brigades lead the organization on behalf of the leadership, secure the carrying through of uniform policy. The leadership – Politburo, Secretariat, central party apparatus – decide which problems they will deal with themselves and which questions will be delegated to lower organs. The lower organs do not concern themselves with decisions, directives, or orders from the leadership (and certainly not with the political line), but only with their realization. Of course, even the most highly centralized system needs 'feedback' and in its decision-making the SED leadership must consider the mood, possibilities and operational style of its base. The SED has for a long time attempted to apply scientifically established methods of management, as Erich Honecker claimed in 1970, 'to the entire leadership and management process of the party', from 'analysis, through prognosis and decision-making to its execution'. This presupposes a suitably trained and selected class of functionaries.

The selection and training of cadres is the third factor ensuring internal party structures and guaranteeing the unity of the SED. The fact that the selection and planning of cadres is carried out by the higher levels of the *Apparat* proves that it is not the 'elections' at different party levels which decide who carries out what functions. They establish what the 'long-term and far-sighted' demand for cadres will be, so that at the appropriate time suitable cadres from the working class, with the necessary knowledge, abilities and experience in party work are available. Cadre development plans and the *nomenklatur* (that is, party lists of offices staffed directly or indirectly by party nominees) of cadres enable the leadership to operate a 'long term and purposeful cadre development'.[6]

At the Tenth Party Congress in 1981, Honecker emphasized that 'the continuous increase of the leading role of the party in all spheres of society is an objective necessity'. The SED leadership starts from the proposition that the 'cadre question' is decisive and that, therefore, the best way of securing the 'leading role' is by training loyal cadres.[7] These must show, above all, devotion to the party, unconditional recognition of the leadership, have qualifications and undergo ideological instruction. Nearly all the middle and higher functionaries have for years been indoctrinated at party schools, now, very largely, the same has been achieved for the lower functionaries. Of the 80,230 party secretaries of the 78,677 basic organizations of the SED, over 80 per cent have spent more than a year at a party school and 64.5 per cent are graduates of universities or *Fachschulen*. The tasks of these cadres were clearly defined at the Tenth Party Congress (and have been since). Once again the leadership emphasized that 'the decisive field of struggle of the party's, and every communist's, revolutionary action, is, and remains, the economy'. According to Horst Dohlus, writing in the ZK's organ, *Neuer Weg*, 'A raising of the level of the work of [party] management' is necessary in order to achieve 'scientifically based strategy and tactics'.[8] At the Tenth Party Congress Honecker himself declared that there were three main directions in which party work was to be 'further qualified'. First, a high level of effective leadership was reached when the ZK's decisions were put into practice in a uniform and united manner in the party groups and in every working collective (*Arbeitskollektive*). This was meant to underline once again the strict centralism of the party. Any loosening of 'democratic centralism' was unacceptable to the SED leadership, only 'ideological and organizational unity and consistency' counted. Secondly, Honecker emphasized that because the decisive field of struggle (*Kampffeld*) for the party remained the economy, party organs must ensure a big increase in efficiency. An efficient economy is aimed at neutralizing the population and thus stabilizing the rule of the SED. Thirdly, Honecker called for a high level of work among the masses in order to consolidate the political consciousness of the working people. The party should not, therefore, be inward-looking but should actively influence the population.[9]

Voluntary discipline, the power of the *Apparat* and cadre selection are still in Honecker's era the basis of the inner party structure. The top leadership, Politburo and Secretariat, can secure in this way internal party stability, the precondition for the SED's 'leading role' in the GDR. Even if in the period since 1971 voluntary subjection to the party has been more strongly emphasized, the power of the *Apparat* and cadre selection remain decisive elements in the hierarchical structure which the SED exhibits as a communist party of the Soviet type and as a relic of Stalinism. The party statute conceals these facts more than it reveals them. Nevertheless, it is worthy of mention that in its new statute, agreed at the Ninth Party Congress in 1976, the SED normalized its role as a party to the extent that new members can resign (something for which there had been no provision since the 1950s).

The party's most important connecting link remains the Marxist–Leninist ideology. The central dogma of the SED remains unchanged even today: it is that the party puts Marxism–Leninism into practice, that the party is therefore scientific, that it is therefore always right. The party's claim to absolute leadership in society derives from this. Even in the Honecker era, therefore, ideology retains an overriding significance. In the SED, Marxism–Leninism of the Soviet type determines the norms of conduct, serves to guide social and political action, and, through the development of consciousness, tries to achieve the integration of the leadership elite. A significant function of ideology is the concealment and justification of the existing power relations. Compared with the Ulbricht era, the role of ideology has grown. It is not without significance that when the unity of ideology, politics and economy is proclaimed, ideology is put first. The constant linking together of these three factors is defined, since the Ninth Party Congress, as a characteristic of the style of party work.[10] Even when Honecker at the Tenth Party Congress in 1981 changed the order and spoke of the unity of politics, economy and ideology, he still emphasized the significance and the 'superiority of our Marxist–Leninist ideology'.[11]

For the ruling elite, ideology in fact plays the role of an integrating and mobilizing force. In the hierarchically structured SED, power lies with the Politburo, the Secretariat and with the departments of the *Apparat* of the ZK in East Berlin. The Politburo decides all fundamental questions, the Secretariat carries out the selection of cadres and the *Apparat* checks and controls the lower party organs.

Table 1.1 *Politburo of the SED at the End of 1983*

	Age	Trained as	1933–1945	Full-time Official (no. of years)	Joined SED/KPD
Erich Honecker[a]	71	roofer	10 years in detention	52	1929
Paul Verner[a]	72	turner	10 years abroad	51	1929
Willi Stoph	69	brick-layer	in Germany	39	1931
Heinz Hoffman[b]	73	mechanic	10 years abroad	50	1930
Erich Mielke[b]	76	worker	12 years abroad	52	1925
Erich Mückenberger	73	mechanic	4 years in detention	38	1927 (SPD)
Hermann Axen[a]	67	journalist	5 years in detention	41	1932
Kurt Hager[a]	71	journalist	9 years abroad	49	1930
Horst Sindermann	68	journalist	11 years in detention	36	1929
K Gerhard Schürer[b]	62	mechanic	–	34	1948
Horst Dohlus[a,b]	58	hair dresser	–	33	1946
Werner Felfe[a,b]	55	white-collar worker	–	35	1945
Joachim Herrmann[a,b]	55	journalist	–	32	1946
Werner Krolikowski[b]	55	white-collar worker	–	31	1946
Konrad Naumann[b]	55	worker	–	33	1945
Harry Tisch[b]	56	mechanic	–	33	1945
Dr Günther Mittag[a]	57	economist	–	30	1946
K Dr Werner Jarowinsky[a]	56	economist	–	23	1945
K Günter Kleiber	52	graduate engineer	–	16	1950
K Margarete Müller	52	graduate agriculturalist	–	18	1951
K Egon Krenz[b]	46	teacher	–	22	1955
K Inge Lange[a,b]	56	tailor	–	29	1945
K Günter Schabowski[b]	54	journalist	–	28	1952
K Werner Walde[b]	57	white-collar worker	–	33	1946
Alfred Neumann	74	carpenter	4 years in detention	50	1929

[a] = secretary   [b] = elected since 1971   K = candidate

The Politburo holds, through its members, all the decisive positions in the state and society in its hands. In addition, and unlike the CPSU, all SED secretaries of the ZK belong to the Politburo. As elected at the Tenth Party Congress it was made up of 25 members – 17 full and 8 candidates (see Table 1.1).

The leadership's inner circle – Honecker, Verner, Stoph, Hoffman, Mielke, Mückenberger and Neumann – have travelled a similar road through life and therefore hold similar basic views which are founded on common experiences. Today, all about 70 years old, they have carried on a working-class occupation but have been for decades full-time party officials. Apart from Mückenberger (a Social Democrat until 1946) they all joined the KPD before Hitler came to power and either spent long years in prison (or camp) or lived abroad. Axen, Hager and Sindermann had a similar development but were not originally workers. In contrast to these, a second group – Dohlus, Felfe, Herrmann, Krolikowski, Naumann and Tisch – only became communists in or after 1945. They also come from a working-class background, were too young to be persecuted by Hitler and have long years of *Apparat* experience. Another group – Mittag, Jarowinsky, Kleiber, and Müller – are trained experts who came into the leadership under Ulbricht. Apart from Mittag their role has been relatively small. The last group to enter the Politburo, as candidates – Krenz, Lange, Schabowski and Walde – have also had typical *Apparat* careers. It is interesting that half of the members and candidates of the Politburo were promoted after Ulbricht's departure and that many of them had worked with Honecker earlier in the FDJ.

Twelve years after taking over the party leadership, Honecker – who due to the cult of personality stands out from the rest of the leadership – is attempting to continue, on the one hand, his domination of the party and, on the other, the modernization of society. Now, as before, three levels of power are used to carry out these aims:

(1) the party apparatus itself – that is, the full-time officials and their voluntary, unpaid helpers;
(2) the state apparatus – that is, the government, administration, judiciary, political police (SSD – State Security System), army, media, and so on;
(3) the mass organizations and other parties which, as 'transmission belts', form contacts with all sections of the population and direct them.

Basically, the SED as the state party uses, to secure its rule, three methods that it took over from the USSR of Stalin and still uses today:

(1)   Opponents of the regime are put down by terror. The state security service and the political judiciary move against any minority which actively tries to alter the system or opposes party rule. Yet it is potential rather than actual terror which holds society in check. Today, 'normal' means of repression are enough and the SED's rule remains intact even with considerably limited terror, at its disposal, as deStalinization showed.

(2)   As a method of exercising power 'neutralization' is coming increasingly to the fore. It is felt that many citizens who have no wish to take part in politics, the so-called non-political individuals who are neither opponents nor supporters of the regime, can be kept passive through growing prosperity and having a little room for personal manoeuvre. If the leadership succeeds in eliminating from everyday life the bureaucratic excesses and dictatorial over-enthusiasm which cause the East German people more annoyance and are more likely to excite opposition than are big political issues, then its rule will be stabilized through neutralization. Naturally the use of this method depends, in the first place, on the economic efficiency of the system and, therefore, on the degree of affluence.

(3)   Ideology, which serves both as a justification for the SED's rule and as an instrument for its concealment, does not only function as a connecting link with the ruling elite. In addition, through education and the development of consciousness, it is meant to help win new supporters, above all from the ranks of youth. The SED is thus striving both to neutralize opponents and to persuade those neutralized to accept its ideology.

Because of this role ideology gains an additional significance. It can become the starting-point of internal communist opposition. In this case, it is a matter of a numerically small opposition of intellectuals, writers, and so on. The example of Czechoslovakia in 1968 indicates that from such a democratic communist opposition a change in the regime can be achieved. This is connected with the fact that the stability of a communist system depends, in the first place, on the smooth functioning of its *Apparat*. It demands unconditionally that the leadership is united and that functionaries in the hierarchically organized *Apparat* fall into line. Opposition in the party or the *Apparat* appears threatening, so that the leadership must prevent 'deviations'. Party and *Apparat* are, however, more susceptible to an inherent opposition than to any other deviation. For that reason an internal communist opposition is a real danger. That is why the SED leadership in both the past and present swiftly resorts to repression in order to smash every trace of such opposition.

Already by the 1950s there existed the 'third way' opposition, which, citing Marx, sought a change in the political system and a 'human' socialism, a 'third way' between Soviet Communism and West German Social Democracy. The Wolfgang Harich group and similar 'national communist' groups were persecuted and their members arrested. But the contradictions within the GDR made continual criticism inevitable. The political, social and national situation again and again produced internal communist opposition. Individuals such as Robert Havemann represented this opposition and articulated its ideas. Such theoretical ideas, from Harich to Havemann, have the same starting-point. They test the reality of the communist-ruled states against Marxist theory and point out the contradictions between theory and practice, between claim and reality. This leads to a demand for the bureaucratic dictatorship to be overthrown. The aims of this internal communist opposition are freedom of information, of discussion and, ultimately, of organization to carry through the will of the majority. It wants a combination of the communist socio-economic order with elements of democratic co-determination and an institutionalized rule of law. Admittedly, the effectiveness of this opposition should not be overestimated. As long as dictatorial-bureaucratic communism continues to function in the USSR, there is little chance of fundamental changes in the GDR. Although the history of the GDR up to the present indicates that opposition movements keep on appearing, the ruling system has shown itself to be firmer than is often thought to be the case in the West.

Up to now, the SED has kept the form of a centralized organization with powers concentrated in the leadership, but attempts at modernization follow their own laws. The striving to make the economy efficient under Ulbricht led to technocratic tendencies and to a distancing from the Soviet model. Even before this, the improved educational system and ideological training produced the 'third way' opposition. It is possible that the more managerial style of leadership (*Versachlichung des Führungsstils*), the emphasis on the party's social responsibility, or the encouragement of initiative by the party base will produce unexpected results, for example, more self-confidence and social demands from the working class or a striving for genuine political participation from below. These could be the beginnings of the transformation of the SED into a 'reform party' and a movement towards 'reform communism'. This would mean that the SED would concede a weakening of its right to absolute leadership, a loosening of its domination of the parliamentary bodies and its monopoly of the media, would pay more attention to the social interests of the working class and allow internal party democracy. Such a change is not to be expected in the near future, it is only conceivable as a process of transformation. When considering the future it should not be overlooked that the party will – as in the past – bear the imprint of the real state of affairs, even if its sets itself against a democratic development.

Notes: Chapter 1

This chapter was translated by David Childs.

1 Horst Dohlus, *Der demokratische Zentralismus – Grundprinzip der Führungstätig-keit der SED bei der Verwirklung der Beschlüsse des Zentralkomitees* (Berlin, 1965), p. 6.
2 Hermann Weber, *DDR Grundriss der Geschichte 1945–1981* (Hanover, 1982).
3 Here is meant a society in which the rewards, in material terms, distributed to individuals are supposed to be related to their efforts (translator's note).
4 *Statut der SED*, 1976.
5 Dohlus, *Der demokratische Zentralismus.* p. 10.
6 Walter Assmann and Gunter Leibe, *Kaderarbeit als Voraussetzung qualifizierter staatlicher Leitung* (Berlin, 1972), p. 79.
7 *Protokoll* [Official reports of the SED congresses], Vol. 1, p. 132.
8 *Neuer Weg*, no. 9 (1981).
9 *Protokoll*, Vol. 1, p. 137.
10 *Neuer Weg*, no. 17 (1976), p. 750.
11 *Protokoll*, Vol. 1, p. 137.

2

The Written Constitution – The Basic Law of a Socialist State?

INGE CHRISTOPHER

The Constitution of 1949

The GDR's present written constitution is very different from the one adopted in October 1949 when the GDR was founded. The first constitution, largely based on an SED draft of September 1946, and intended for a united Germany, stemmed from a time when the USSR, for a variety of reasons, had not yet decided to establish a socialist republic in its Zone of Occupation. Particularly the section on human rights, including the right to strike (article 14) and to emigrate (article 10), retained features of a liberal *Rechtsstaat*. In the economic sphere, the 1949 constitution represented a mixture of elements of a private and a state economy. While the economic freedom of the individual was guaranteed within an economic order conforming to the principles of social justice (article 19), the future development along socialist lines was facilitated by provisions which called on the state to establish a 'public economic plan' (article 21) and demanded the transfer of all natural resources, the steel industry, power stations, and so on, to public ownership. Expropriation with or without compensation – the latter in case of misuse of property 'to the detriment of the public good' (article 24) – was envisaged.

With regard to the organization of the state, the GDR's first constitution resembled, at least superficially, the *Grundgesetz* (Basic Law) of West Germany. There were, however, considerable differences in the legislative process, with the East German Länderkammer, which was to represent the interests of the individual regions, occupying a much weaker position than its West German counterpart. Another important difference concerned the formation of the government. According to article 92 all parties with at least 40 seats in the People's Chamber (Volkskammer) which then had a total of 400 members, had a right to be represented in the government. This, on the one hand, was in keeping with the SED's Marxist 'alliance policy' which means that in order to achieve its aims the party of the working class must initially work with and through other parties; on the other hand, it ensured that if ever the SED were to find itself in a minority position – perhaps in preparation for German unification – its continued influence in government would be safeguarded. An assured share in government for any parliamentary party which commanded at least 10 per cent of the total number of mandates, could also be seen as a clever device to prevent the formation of any meaningful opposition within the Volkskammer.

The GDR's first constitution was a compromise. It could either serve as a basis upon which to build socialism in the years to come, or it could lead to a Western-type, all-German republic. Critics will, of course, point out that the absence of an independent constitutional court reduced the constitution to a rather worthless document. Indeed, as time progressed, the GDR authorities did not seem to set much store by the accuracy of the constitution. Thus in spite of the great changes which took place during the eighteen and a half years this constitution was in force, only three amendments were made. These related to the inclusion of the military service clause; the abolition of regional parliaments; and, upon the death of the GDR's first president, Wilhelm Pieck, the replacement of the office of president by the Council of State (Staatsrat).

Why a New Constitution in 1968?

The GDR is not the only socialist state to have replaced its original constitution with a new one. During the past three decades or so, Yugoslavia, Hungary, Romania, Czechoslovakia and Poland have had two or more constitutions and the USSR adopted a new constitution as recently as October 1977. This conforms with the Marxist–Leninist belief in the progression of history and the role of the working class, led by its party, which uses the state as its main instrument in achieving its goal, that is, a socialist and eventually a communist society. As the GDR was not established as the outcome of a true revolution, it was necessary to bring about a 'revolution from above'. GDR historians see the history of their republic as a series of periods of transformation from its 'capitalist, imperialist and fascist' past through various stages of socialism which will eventually lead to communism. The Marxist belief in progress, in the dynamism of historical development, thus finds expression in the changed constitutions of the GDR.

While the 1950s were marked by the 'building of socialism', first officially propagated in 1952, the 1960s witnessed political and economic consolidation. The creation of the Council of State in 1960, with Ulbricht as chairman, strengthened not only the personal position of the then first secretary of the SED but also the role of the party. The building of the Berlin Wall, effectively stemming the damaging outflow of often highly skilled labour, and the introduction of the New Economic System of Planning and Managing the Economy in 1963 led to economic success. As the GDR climbed into twelfth place among the industrial powers of the world, West German observers began to talk of a 'red economic miracle'.[1] With political consolidation, economic success and the development, mainly amongst the younger generation, of a good measure of pride in their 'socialist fatherland' – fanned also by considerable achievement in the field of sport – the desire to establish a separate identity as a state increased. As an early form of demarcation (*Abgrenzung*) from West Germany, the GDR adopted its own Education Bill, Family Code, Penal Code and Code of Criminal Procedure. Of particular significance in the quest for identity was the Nationality Bill of 1967 which was to emphasize the fact that the GDR was a separate state in its own right. Despite its obvious contradiction with article 1 of the still-valid 1949 constitution, which not only calls Germany 'indivisible' but also goes on to say 'there is only one German nationality', no amendment was made. When its West German neighbour, during the period of the Grand Coalition (1966–9), began to look for *rapprochement* with the East, the GDR leadership reacted with great suspicion. Contrary to earlier plans for a confederation, the Seventh SED Party Congress in 1967 declared West Germany to be 'unworthy' of a confederation. In preparation for this change of policy an article had appeared in *Neues Deutschland* in January 1967 praising socialist achievements and deriding capitalist West Germany, with its continued exploitation of the worker, as 'medieval'.[2]

Against this background of the GDR's emergence as a proud socialist state, Ulbricht announced at the party congress in April 1967 that a new 'appropriate' constitution would soon be drafted. He admitted that 'for some time it has been apparent that the present constitution . . . obviously no longer corresponds to the conditions of the socialist order and the stage of historical development' (*Neues Deutschland*, 18 April 1967). A Committee for the Drafting of a Socialist Constitution was set up under the chairmanship of none other than Walter Ulbricht who at that time occupied the three most important positions in the GDR: first secretary of the SED, chairman of the Council of State, and chairman of the National Defence Council (Nationaler Verteidigungsrat). This committee's work progressed swiftly as a detailed draft, based on guidelines issued by the Politburo, had been prepared in advance.

It was realized that the new socialist constitution had great propaganda potential. Many articles extol the virtues of socialism and make unequivocal claims as to its success. For example, article 9 which deals with socialist ownership of the means of production, states: ' . . . By breaking the power of the monopolies and big landowners, and by abolishing the capitalist profit economy, the source of war policy and the exploitation of man by man was swept away. Socialist ownership has stood the test.' (These claims were deleted in the amendment of 1974.) Every household received a copy of the draft constitution by post and a big campaign of public discussion meetings was launched. This was to familiarize GDR citizens with the new constitution, encourage them to participate in the building and further shaping of socialism, and give them a feeling that they had a real say in the running of their society. Thus more than 750,000 meetings took place and a great many suggestions were made. The only important amendments resulting from these discussion, however, were – in reply to pressure from the churches – the inclusion of the guarantee of 'freedom of conscience and freedom of belief' in article 20 and the inclusion of the second sentence of article 33 which states that no GDR citizen may be extradited to a foreign power. Thus, in spite of the public discussions and the plebiscite of 6 April 1968 when 94.5 per cent of the population entitled to vote gave their 'yes' to the new constitution, it was very much a product of the SED.

Principles of the Socialist Constitution

Whereas in 1949 any reference to 'socialism' had been carefully avoided, the 1968 constitution leaves us in no doubt that it was to be the basic law of a socialist state. Already the preamble announces proudly that 'the people of the German Democratic Republic . . . have given themselves this socialist constitution'. According to the official GDR reference work, *Kleines Politisches Wörterbuch*, socialism is

> the first [lower] phase . . . of communism; it is based on the public ownership of the means of production, the political rule of the working class, the alliance with the class of co-operative farmers, the intelligentsia and other sections of the working population as well as on the leading role of the Marxist–Leninist party.'[3]

These main principles and other elements nowadays normally understood by socialist states to be characteristics of a socialist society, such as a planned economy, full employment based on the right to work, socialist internationalism, democratic centralism and the concentration of power, socialist legality, form the basis of the 1968 constitution and were either left unaltered or strengthened, particularly as concerns the special relationship with the USSR, in the amendments of 1974.

While the definition of 'socialism' in the *Kleines Politisches Wörterbuch* puts the public ownership of the means of production first, the constitution accords top priority to the leading role of the working class and its communist party. The very first article describes the GDR as a socialist state and as 'the political organization of the working people in town and countryside who are jointly implementing socialism under the leadership of the working class and its Marxist–Leninist party' (1968 version). Although the SED is not mentioned by name, this enshrining of its leadership role is fundamental to an understanding of the GDR's political structure. Thus elections cannot bring about a change in government but serve to affirm the SED's position. According to Marxist–Leninist teaching, the working class, led by their party, once having gained power must maintain a firm grip on the organization of the state and must use the state as an instrument towards their goal. Whereas this idea is not explicit in the constitution, section II (c) of the SED social programme of 1976 talks of the necessary 'further strengthening of the socialist state' and describes the same as 'the main instrument of the working people, led by the working class, in the shaping of the developed socialist society and on the road to communism'. Since the Eighth Party Congress of 1971 and even more so since the Ninth Party Congress of 1976 it has been stressed that the leading role of the SED is further increasing. The new programme prepared for the Ninth Party Congress maintains: 'The more far-reaching and complicated the tasks of management and planning of all aspects and forms of social processes become, the more the role of the political leadership . . . of the Marxist–Leninist party increases' (section IV). The constitution does not explain why the working class and their party occupy this special position. However, according to Marxist ideology, the three most important reasons for the leading role of the working class are: (1) the working class represents numerically the largest part of the population; (2) the workers are the most productive part of the population; (3) the working class has a historical mission, and thus a right and duty to lead the state in the period of transition to communism.

Another important element of the 1968 constitution is the socialist economic order. According to article 9 the national economy is based upon 'socialist ownership of the means of production' and it 'serves the strengthening of the socialist order, the constantly improving satisfaction of the material and cultural needs of the citizens, the development of their personality and their socialist relations in society'. Article 9 also contains the principle of the 'socialist planned economy'. Whereas in 1968 central planning and management was to be combined with 'the individual responsibility of the socialist commodity producers', the 1974 version dropped the idea of the factory managers sharing so much responsibility. The term *Waren-produzenten* was replaced by *Betriebe* (enterprises) and the 'initiative of the working people' was added. No doubt the 1968 formulation had been influenced by the New Economic System which gave the individual factory manager more responsibility. In the late Ulbricht era the economy was allowed a certain autonomy *vis-à-vis* the political leadership, a trend which was to be reversed under Honecker. Article 10 is concerned with socialist and article 11 with personal ownership. Three forms of socialist property are distinguished: (1) nationally owned property of society as a whole; (2) joint co-operative property of collectives of working people, which means agricultural co-operatives and various trade co-operatives; (3) property of social organizations of citizens. This refers to the property of the SED, the Free German Trade Union Federation (Freier Deutscher Gewerk-schaftsbund – FDGB), and so on. Article 10 also emphasizes that 'it is the duty of the socialist state and its citizens to protect and increase socialist property'. Personal property which 'serves to satisfy the material and cultural needs of citizens' is guaranteed, as is the right of inheritance of such property. The constitution reminds citizens that 'property and the rights of authors and inventors shall not be used in a way contrary to the interests of society' (article 11) and that 'private economic associations for the establishment of economic power are not permitted' (article 14). Whereas the GDR's first constitution provided for expropriation and socialization without compensation, the socialist constitution of 1968 stipulates that an 'appropriate compensation' would have to be paid (article 16). This is, however, of no great significance as by 1968 no major property was left for expropriation and the citizen would have had little redress if he did not agree with what was considered 'appropriate'.

The constitution also contains the principle of the concentration of power. Socialist democracy rejects the Western idea of the division of power, that is, the separate powers of the legislature, the executive and the judicature, as first elaborated by the French philosopher Montesquieu in 1748. Thus we find in *Kleines Politisches Wörtbuch*: 'The socialist state knows no division of power; the sovereignty of the people includes the executive and the judicature.'[4] According to the constitution (article 47) the rights of the people, represented by the Volkskammer must not be curtailed and the Volkskammer implements the principle of the unity of decision and enforcement' (article 48). It goes without saying that in a highly centralized state without an equivalent of the West German Bundesrat or an upper chamber like the British House of Lords, any check on power by a second chamber is impossible.

No less than eighteen articles are devoted to the Volkskammer which is described as 'the supreme organ of state power in the German Democratic Republic. It decides in its plenary sessions the 'basic questions of state policy'. Thus the Volkskammer, the GDR's parliament, enjoys constitutionally a wealth of power, but a Western critic nevertheless described it, and in my opinion rightly so, as 'the most meaningless organ in the decision-making process'.[5] Although there are a number of standing committees, plenary sessions, which are supposed to decide 'basic questions of state policy' (article 48), are a rare occurrence. Their frequency has steadily decreased since the 1950s when they averaged about ten a year; since 1978 two one-day sessions per year have become the norm. The number of laws passed is small compared with Western democracies. As there is no opposition, the members of the Volkskammer are not confronted with opposing views and cannot decide between alternatives. Decisions are nearly always taken unanimously but in 1972 a small number of CDU members voted against the Abortion Bill. The Volkskammer can be called an *Akklamationsorgan*, that is, after the reasons for the proposed legislation have been explained, the members give their assent to decisions which have in reality been taken in advance. It is obvious that this could not be different in a socialist state where both ideologically and constitutionally the Marxist–Leninist party has an unassailable leadership function. It must not be forgotten that the other four parties do not exist in opposition to, or in competition with, the SED, but as 'allies'. All parties and the 'mass organizations' which also hold seats in the Volkskammer declare in their statutes that they are contributing, under the leadership of the SED, to the shaping of a socialist society. The idea that there is no room for opposition is not explicitly stated in the constitution but it is implied in article 3 which declares that 'the political parties and mass organizations pool all forces of the people for joint action for the development of a socialist society'.

The real decisions are thus taken by the SED, and as this party is organized on the principle of democratic centralism this means by the effective head of the SED power structure, the Politburo. According to the SED statute (III, 23) democratic centralism includes the ruling that 'all decisions of the higher party organs are binding on subsequent organs, and the minority, as also the individual, have to subordinate themselves in a disciplined manner to the decisions of the majority'.

According to article 90 'the administration of justice serves to implement socialist legality, protect and develop the German Democratic Republic and its state and social order'. The constitution does not explain what 'socialist legality' means but the *Kleines*

Politisches Wörterbuch and other GDR sources make it quite plain that the law is considered subordinate to politics. Socialist law, according to *Marxistisch–Leninistische Staats–und Rechtstheorie* is 'the expression of the will of the working class led by its Marxist–Leninist party'.[6] Thus law and the administration of justice have a role to play in the transformation of society. Law is not expected to be impartial but to have 'class character'. It seems an anachronistic remnant from the 1949 constitution that the socialist constitution still adheres to the principle of judges being 'independent in their administration of justice' (article 96). Since the division of power is decried as a bourgeois idea which is incompatible with the sovereignty of the working people, and the working people are, in turn, led by the working class and their Marxist–Leninist party, judges cannot really be independent in their administration of justice. For one thing, many judges are members of the SED and are therefore bound by the party statute to carry out party resolutions. The constitution itself curtails the idea of judicial independence by stipulating that 'only persons loyally devoted to the people and their socialist state . . . may be judges' (article 94). Moreover, all GDR judges, including lay judges and members of social courts, are elected and are accountable to those by whom they were elected (article 95). They can also, in certain circumstances, be relieved of their office by those who have placed them there. All this, together with the fact that many GDR laws contain political statements in their preambles, underscoring the political purpose of the law, makes the idea of the independence of the judges incompatible with the ideology and practice of the GDR. It remains to be seen whether a further revision of the constitution will purge it of this *Rechtsstaat* feature.

The GDR's highest court, the Supreme Court, 'directs the jurisdiction of the courts on the basis of the constitution, the laws and other statutory regulations . . . It ensures a uniform application of the law by all courts' (article 93). This court thus has a directive function which goes far beyond that of supreme courts in Western systems. At the lower level, socialist democracy gives the citizens a considerable opportunity to participate in the administration of justice. There are two types of social courts *(gesellschaftliche Gerichte)* where only lay people adjudicate. Disputes commissions exist mainly in factories and in institutions of health care, education, culture and so on. They deal with all disputes arising in the world of work to which the Labour Code applies. Their rulings are binding for the individuals and the managements concerned but contestants have a right to appeal to the district courts. Arbitration commissions have been set up on housing estates and in rural communities to deal mainly with quarrels between neighbours. In addition, social courts are responsible for handling less complicated civil law cases and minor offences referred to them by the

People's Police (Volkspolizei – VP) and other public authorities. Social courts can impose fines up to a certain ceiling, issue reprimands, or oblige the person in question to repair the damage caused or do other socially useful work. GDR sources stress that members of social courts 'exercise the right to participation responsibly' and that 'they make citizens aware that enjoying one's own rights necessarily implies respect for the rights of the community and of fellow citizens'.[7]

Rights and Duties of the Individual

The 1968–74 constitution devotes articles 19–40 to 'basic rights and basic duties of the citizens'. In a Western democracy basic rights are understood not as rights granted by the state but as rights which exist a priori, as innate human rights given by God, not by man. GDR ideologists, however, stress that the concept of basic rights in a socialist democracy is quite different as 'socialist basic rights emanate from socialist social conditions'. Therefore 'there is no continuity between the bourgeois and the socialist rights of man . . . Only the political and material institutions and aims of socialist society ensure freedom, dignity and personal development of the human being'.[8] According to *Kleines Politisches Wörterbuch* there are no 'eternal, innate human rights'; they reflect the interests of the ruling class and therefore have 'historical character'. It is the fundamental significance of the teachings of Marx, Engels and Lenin, so it is maintained, that they showed that in spite of bourgeois revolutions, in spite of declarations of human rights, suppression and exploitation of man continued and human rights were not realized in practice. This situation, according to the GDR constitution, now has changed fundamentally, for 'the exploitation of man by man has been abolished for ever' (article 2). While in Western democracies human rights are often seen as rights against the authority of the state, as rights which ensure for the citizen a sphere which is free from interference by the state, such rights, it is believed, would no longer make sense in the GDR as the socialist state is an instrument of the working class and their party. Moreover, according to article 2, 'man is the centre of all efforts of socialist society and its state'. This does not mean that the stress lies on the interests of man as an individual. According to Marxist–Leninist teaching there is fundamental agreement between the interests of society and the interests of the individual. More recently it has, however, been acknowledged that the harmony of interests is not absolute and that occasionally conflicts of interest of a personal nature can occur. But it is expected of the individual that he integrate himself into society voluntarily, and it is an important function of socialist education, from the crèche upwards, to teach the individual to realize the necessity of this integration.

Rather than God-given 'human rights', the socialist basic rights are primarily seen as rights granted by the state to its citizens so that the individual may develop his personality for the good of society and himself. Such rights are often referred to as *sozialistische Persönlichkeitsrechte*. Thus we find in article 19: 'Free from exploitation, oppression and economic dependence every citizen has equal rights and manifold opportunities to develop his abilities to the full extent and to unfold his talents in socialist society unhindered . . . for the welfare of society and for his own benefit.' Great emphasis is laid on the citizen's right and duty to participate in the shaping of socialist society. This is mainly expressed in the very lengthy article 21 which contains the exhortation: 'Participate in working, in planning, and in governing!' That 'rights' imply 'duties' is made clear later in the same article: 'The implementation of this right is at the same time a high moral obligation for each citizen.' GDR commentators go to some lengths to explain the unity between socialist rights and socialist duties: 'It is necessary for society that the citizen recognizes and implements his rights in an inseparable unity with his responsibility towards society and his duties as a citizen.[10] Thus, apart from the 'moral obligation' to participate in socialist democracy, the constitution contains a number of instances where duties are either mentioned on their own or coupled with rights. These include the duty 'to protect and increase socialist property' (article 10); to defend 'peace and the socialist homeland and its achievements' (article 23); to engage in 'socially useful activity' (article 24); to 'learn a vocation' (article 25). According to article 38, 'it is the right and the supreme duty of parents to educate their children to become healthy, happy, competent, universally educated and patriotic citizens'.

True to the socialist character of the 1968–74 constitution, certain rights have been given more emphasis and are set out in greater detail than was the case in 1949. Thus article 20 which deals with 'equal rights and . . . the same legal status' (of men and women) adds that the 'promotion of women, particularly with regard to vocational qualification, is a task of society and the state'. Mother and child now 'enjoy the special protection of the socialist state' and support through 'special measures' is promised to large families and single-parent families (article 38). Similarly, the socialist constitution pays greater attention to physical and mental health. The citizen's right to the protection of his health and working capacity is 'guaranteed by the planned improvement of working and living conditions . . . the promotion of physical culture . . . sports activities and tourism' (article 35). Much space is given to 'the right to education' in article 25 which, containing six paragraphs, is one of the longest in the whole constitution. As was the case in 1949, the 1968 constitution declares that 'militarist and revanchist propaganda in all forms, war mongering and the manifestation of hatred against creeds and nations are punished as crimes' (article 6). What is important here is the interpretation of terms like 'revanchist propaganda'. In short, any criticism of the GDR-style socialist system could fall into this category of 'crime'.

Certain rights and freedoms proclaimed in 1949 which were to prove an embarrassment once the building of socialism got underway, were dropped in 1968. The right to strike (1949: article 14) was an obvious victim. Such a right, it is argued, can only apply to a capitalist society where workers have to defend themselves against exploitation. In a socialist system workers would only be striking against themselves. Strikes in publicly owned factories, it can be claimed, would also violate article 10 of the socialist constitution which calls it the duty of the socialist state and its citizens 'to protect and increase socialist property'. Nor is it surprising that the right to emigrate has been eliminated. It is, of course, still possible to emigrate legally from the GDR but applications of citizens below the age of retirement are dealt with tardily and more often than not refused. As it is expected of every citizen to make a personal contribution to the strengthening of the socialist state, an application to emigrate can be viewed as a hostile act and can thus lead to discrimination.

While article 30 declares the inviolability of the 'person and liberty' of every citizen of the GDR, it is interesting to note that the official commentary envisages a restriction of this liberty not only in cases where a person's action would infringe the legal order but also where 'socialist morals' (*sozialistische Moralnormen*) would be offended.[11] In some articles the restriction of freedoms becomes quite clear. Thus the GDR citizen does not have an absolute right to express his opinion freely and publicly, but he may do so only 'in accordance with the spirit and the aims of this constitution' (article 27). This means that there is no room for opinions which question the socialist state in general or the leading role of the SED in particular. The *Verfassungskommentar* declares that any criticism has to be 'constructive' and that there can be no freedom for 'anti-socialist propaganda'.[12] Moreover, the 1979 amendment to the Penal Code extended the catalogue of culpable actions in this context and raised the punishment for such crimes to a maximum of eight years' imprisonment for individuals acting on their own and ten years for those who collaborate with organizations or persons whose activities are directed against the GDR. Unlike the Basic Law of West Germany where article 5 guarantees not only free expression of opinion but also the right for people to inform themselves freely from generally accessible sources, the GDR constitution recognizes no such right.

Phrases like 'in accordance with the spirit and aims of this constitution' occur in several articles referring to the right to peaceful assembly, the right to form associations, the freedom of churches, and so on. In the absence of an independent constitutional court it is difficult to ascertain what such phrases mean in practice. The citizen who feels deprived of his constitutional rights can submit petitions, grievances, and so on to the 'elected bodies and their deputies, or to state and economic organs' (article 103) but he has no access to an independent arbitrator. And it is the Volkskammer itself which decides 'in case of doubt on the constitutionality of legal regulations' (article 89).

The Amendments of 1974

In 1968 Ulbricht had maintained that the new constitution 'will be the most democratic constitution which ever existed in Germany' and that the 'principles of the socialist state and society, and thus of socialist democracy, formulated in it, correspond to the conditions of historical developments in the coming decades'.[14] And yet, in September 1974 Honecker declared in a statement to the Volkskammer that 'it has become necessary to amend the present constitution'.[15] However, this does not contradict Ulbricht's view that the socialist principles, as formulated in 1968, would be of relevance for many years to come. The 1974 amendments do not change the basic socialist order but take account of important developments which occurred after Honecker had replaced Ulbricht as first secretary of the SED in May 1971.

The 1968 constitution contained a number of references to the German nation. Not only did the GDR describe itself, in article 1, as a 'socialist state of the German nation' but in the preamble the people of the GDR had also felt 'imbued with the responsibility of showing the whole German nation the road to a future of peace and socialism'. While the 1968 preamble blamed the West for having split Germany 'in order to build up West Germany as a base of imperialism and of struggle against socialism, contrary to the vital interests of the nation', article 8 declared that the GDR and its citizens 'strive . . . to overcome the division of Germany imposed upon the German nation by imperialism, and support the step-by-step rapprochement of the two German states until the time of their unification on the basis of democracy and socialism'.

In the early 1970s, as a result of the West German *Ostpolitik* which led to the signing of the Basic Treaty *(Grundlagenvertrag)* in 1972, the relationship between the two parts of Germany changed fundamentally and the concept of the 'German nation' took on a new significance. As the Basic Treaty speaks of 'normal good-neighbourly relations' it was only natural that all hostile references to West Germany were eradicated from the constitution. And as the two German states also promised to respect each other's 'independence in internal and external affairs' it could have been construed as interference if the GDR had persisted with its perceived responsibility of showing the whole German nation the road to socialism. But there was a more compelling reason for the GDR to drop all references to the German nation: as Bonn was preparing to recognize the GDR as a separate German state, the then Federal Chancellor Willy Bandt evoked the concept of the German nation as the bond around the divided Germany (Report on the State of the Nation, 14 January 1970). The more West Germany stressed that the people on both sides of the border had a feeling of belonging together *(fortdauerndes Zusammengehörigkeitsgefühl)* and that the German nation would not be split by the recognition of the GDR – Brandt spoke of 'two states within one nation' – the more the GDR emphasized its separateness. As the West increasingly promoted *Annäherung (rapprochement* or 'getting closer to each other'), this term, still used in article 8 of the 1968 constitution, was quickly dropped by the GDR leadership and replaced by *Abgrenzung* (demarcation), which stressed the ideological differences between the two Germanies. Consequently the 1974 amendments which eliminated all references to the German nation can be seen as the constitutional manifestation of this policy of demarcation. Instead of describing the GDR as a socialist state of the German nation, article 1 now proclaims that 'the German Democratic Republic is a socialist state of workers and farmers'. Despite the ruling in article 65 that drafts of major new laws have to be submitted to the people for discussion, the GDR citizens were only informed of the 'Law amending the Constitution of the GDR' the day after it had been passed unanimously by the Volkskammer. This is in marked contrast to the publicity which had surrounded the adoption of the first socialist constitution. While in West Germany much attention was paid to the 'deGermanization' of the constitution (*Entdeutschung der Verfassung,* a term used in *Die Zeit,* 4 October 1974), neither Honecker's statement to the Volkskammer nor the East German press made any direct reference to the erasure of the German nation from the constitution. One can only assume that at that time the SED leadership wanted to avoid a public debate on the delicate question of whether or not the people of the GDR were part of the German nation. There seems to have been a certain amount of consternation and uncertainty amongst the population, for on 12 December 1974 Honecker found it necessary to say in a speech to the Central Committee: 'There is no room for any uncertainty when filling in questionnaires. . . . The answer is simple and clear and without any ambiguity: *Staatsbürgerschaft – DDR, Nationalität – deutsch.'*

In the months and years following the constitutional amendment, politicians, ideologists and lawyers went to considerable lengths elaborating a theory of nation and nationality. According to this, the citizens of the GDR, although being of German nationality – which means that ethnically they are Germans – no longer belong to the German (that is, bourgeois) nation as it survives in West Germany. In the GDR, it was argued, a new, fundamentally different, socialist nation was developing. While at the Ninth Party Congress in 1976 Honecker thus spoke of a 'developing socialist nation', the Tenth Party Congress (1981) was told that a 'socialist German nation' had constituted itself in the GDR. This means that by 1981 the process of development had been considered completed and that after a few years of careful avoidance the adjective 'German' was once again employed.

Although Ulbricht had to give way to Honecker as first secretary in 1971, he still remained chairman of the Council of State (Staatsrat) until his death two years later. As Ulbricht was by then clearly out of favour, the role of the Council of State was diminished in order to strip him of the power to which he was still trying to cling. This was achieved by strengthening the Council of Ministers (Ministerrat), and particularly its chairman, *vis-à-vis* the Council of State on the basis of a law (*Gesetz über den Ministerrat der DDR*) passed in October 1972. When the constitution was amended in 1974 the changes in the articles referring to the Council of Ministers and the Council of State thus primarily amounted to setting the record straight two years after the event. The new version of article 76 calls the Council of Ministers the 'government' of the GDR, which had not been the case in 1968. Honecker also put his stamp on the amended constitution by eliminating the idea of the 'socialist community of man' from article 18. This concept, which had gained currency in the Ulbricht era and which implied a harmonious classless society, was rejected by Honecker who stresses that class struggle still exists. All articles which had referred to the 'management and planning of the economy' were amended to read 'planning and management'. Under Ulbricht the economy had been allowed a certain measure of independence, thus management had priority over planning; with Honecker greater emphasis has once again been laid on central planning.

At Honecker's first party congress as first secretary (1971) the raising of the standard of living, both in material and cultural terms, was declared to be a major task. With the amendments of 1974 this was incorporated into the constitution as 'the decisive task of the advanced socialist society' (article 2). Not only was the concept of the 'advanced socialist society' new to the constitution, but in the amended preamble we now find that the citizens of the GDR are 'imbued with the will . . . to continue unswervingly along the road of socialism and communism'.

The Role of the Constitution

Like the written constitutions of Western democracies, the constitution of the GDR contains certain rules concerning the structure of the state, the functions of the various organs of the state, the rights and duties of the citizen, the administration of justice, and so on. As a socialist constitution it also devotes much space to the 'socialist social order'. However, the GDR constitution can in certain respects be considered incomplete. For instance, it mentions only the principle of the leading role of the Marxist–Leninist party without clarifying how this role is exercised in practice. Let us illustrate this omission with an example: the meeting in the GDR in December 1981 between Erich Honecker and Helmut Schmidt was described as a German summit meeting. No doubt Schmidt, then federal chancellor, and Honecker, chairman of the Council of State and general secretary of the SED, were the politically most powerful men in their respective countries. If we wished to establish how this position of power is derived it would only be natural to refer to the written constitutions of the two German states. In the case of West Germany it will be found that according to article 65 of the Basic Law the federal chancellor determines general policy and is responsible for it. But what does the constitution of the GDR say about the positions which Honecker holds? Articles 66–75 deal with the Council of State, a collective head of state. However, Honecker met with the West German head of government, not with the head of state, that is, the federal president. Thus Honecker took part in the German summit meeting primarily not as chairman of the Council of State, but as general secretary of the SED, a position which in practice means that he is the most powerful man within the party and consequently the most powerful politician in the GDR. But if we search the constitution for a description of the role of the general secretary of the SED we shall draw a blank. In order to find out more about the party whose leading role has been constitutionally superimposed upon the GDR we must resort to the programme and statute of the SED. But as concerns the general secretary, there is no mention in the party programme and the statute (section 42) simply states that 'the Central Committee elects . . . the general secretary', without clarifying his role.

The GDR's socialist constitution does not only have the function of codifying existing law and practice, but it also has a programmatic and educative role. Some of its long articles are not legalistic but explain what the GDR claims to have achieved (for example, article 2: 'The exploitation of man by man has been abolished for ever'); elsewhere it exhorts the citizen to do things (article 21: 'Participate in working, in planning, and in governing') and sets tasks for the present and future. The constitution is written in an uncomplicated, propagandistic style and is intended to get through to the man in the street. It extols the advantages of a socialist society and aims to contribute to the development of the socialist personality. Whereas the GDR citizen rarely appeals to the constitution in order to defend his rights – in the absence of an independent constitutional court this would be to little avail – certain articles of the constitution are often quoted in textbooks or by functionaries in order to illustrate how the socialist state encourages the citizen to participate in socialist democracy and in cultural life, how the state promotes education and further training, how mother and child are guaranteed the special protection of the state, and so on.

It is true that little attention was paid to the accuracy of the constitution in the years leading up to April 1968 when the first socialist constitution was adopted, but since then much more care has been taken to avoid a situation where critics from within or without could point at obvious discrepancies between theory and practice. And if the Western critic, for example, queries whether elections are really 'free . . . and secret' (article 54), the official GDR answer will be that there is no breach of the constitution as the citizen has the right to abstain (that is, there is no actual fine if he wishes to do so) and has the right to cross out names of candidates and to cast his vote in secret, even if the very great majority choose to hand in their voting papers unaltered and openly. The main reason, however, why there is now no longer such a gap between *Verfassungsrecht* and *Verfassungswirklichkeit* (that is, theory and practice) is that many articles contain principles rather than details, that certain rights can only be exercised 'in accordance with the spirit and aims of this constitution' (for example, article 27) and that the inclusion of the leading role of the working class and its Marxist-Leninist party gives the SED the constitutional right to stay in power, unchallenged by elections, and to have the final say in state and society. Thus the present written constitution can be seen as a true 'basic law' of the GDR.

Notes: Chapter 2

1   F. Schenk, *Das rote Wirtschaftswunder* (Stuttgart, 1969).
2   H. Weber, *Von der SBZ zur DDR* (Hanover, 1968), pp. 324–5.
3   *Kleines Politisches Wörterbuch* (Berlin, 1978).
4   ibid., p. 321.
5   J. Weber *et al.*, *DDR – Bundesrepublik Deutschland* (Munich 1980), p. 174.
6   *Marxistisch–Leninistische Staats– und Rechtstheorie*, ed. by Institut für Theorie des Staates und des Rechtes der Akademie der Wissenschaften der DDR (Berlin, 1980), p. 405.
7   C. Heinze *et al.*, *Recht im Dienste des Volkes* (Berlin, 1979), p. 106.
8   ibid., p. 93.
9   *Kleines Politisches Wörterbuch*, p. 577.
10 E. Poppe *et al.*, *Grundrechte des Bürgers in der sozialistischen Gesellschaft* (Berlin, 1980), p. 80.
11 *Verfassungskommentar: Verfassung der Deutschen Demokratischen Republik. Dokumente – Kommentar* (Berlin, 1969), Vol. 2, p. 121.
12 ibid., Vol. 2, p. 107.

13 S. Mampel, *Die sozialistische Verfassung der Deutschen Demokratischen Republik* (Frankfurt-on-Main, 1982), pp. 707–8.
14 *Verfassungskommentar*, Vol. 1, p. 53.
15 *Statement in Support of the Law Amending the Constitution of the GDR* given by E. Honecker to the Volkskammer, 27 September 1974. English edition by Panorama-DDR-Auslandsagentur.

All quotations in English from the GDR constitution (1968–74) are from the authorized translation by Intertext, Berlin.

3

The Economy of the German Democratic Republic

STEPHEN F. FROWEN

Introduction

The first part of this chapter provides a brief outline of the economic development of the GDR during the postwar period, its economic problems and achievements, and the main areas of difficulty during the 1980s. The second part concentrates on the GDR's foreign trade and, in particular, on the links between the GDR and West Germany.

By all objective standards the economic achievements of the GDR during the postwar period have been quite outstanding, considering the particularly difficult development problems the GDR economy had to face. Despite these adverse economic circumstances (the major ones are briefly outlined below), the GDR is now, according to the World Bank in Washington, the twelfth most important industrial country in the world. Among socialist countries, the GDR has the highest per capita income ($US 6,622 in 1982), with the USSR and Czechoslovakia taking second and third place respectively. Even if we exclude the unsettled first decade of the postwar period, the per capita income of the GDR in real terms still quadrupled between 1955 and 1982. Since 1970 alone, the rise in GDR real per capita income amounted to 75 per cent, that is, an annual growth rate of over 6 per cent – well above the growth rates achieved by most Western industrial countries during this period (see Table 3.1).

The Postwar Economic Development

Population and Employment

The GDR has a population of nearly 17 million, which is only just over

Table 3.1   *GDR National Income at 1980 Prices*

Year	Total Marks billion	Per head of the population Marks thousand	Per employed in the productive sectors
1950	29.3	1.6	4.5
1955	54.3	3.0	7.9
1960	76.7	4.4	11.4
1965	91.0	5.3	13.8
1970	117.4	6.9	17.7
1975	152.8	9.1	22.9
1980	187.1	11.2	27.4
1981	196.1	11.7	28.7
1982	201.1	12.0	29.4
1983	210.1	12.6	30.4
		1960 = 100	
1965	119	120	122
1970	153	155	156
1975	199	204	201
1980	244	251	241
1981	256	263	252
1982	262	271	258
1983	274	283	268
		1970 = 100	
1975	130	132	129
1980	159	162	155
1981	167	170	162
1982	171	175	166
1983	179	183	172

Source: Statistisches Jahrbuch der Deutschen Demokratischen Republik (Staatsverlag der Deutschen Demokratischen Republik, Berlin, annual publication).

one-quarter of the population of West Germany (including West Berlin). However, the area of approximately 42,000 square miles it covers amounts to 43.5 percent of that of West Germany (including West Berlin). Thus, the population density of the GDR compared with that of West Germany is relatively low, although within the GDR there are considerable regional differences between its northern (mainly agricultural) and its southern (chiefly industrial) areas.

By 1982 the population of the GDR had reverted to this region's pre-1939 level of 16.7 million, after having reached a peak of 19.1 million in 1948, the latter being due to the influx of refugees from Eastern Europe. The main decline of approximately 2 million occurred during the period leading up to the building of the Berlin Wall in 1961 and was caused principally by emigration to West Germany.

However, steady (though minor) declines continued from 1967 onwards. Among the present population females outnumber males by 1 million.

At over 50 per cent, the number of employed as a percentage of the total GDR population is one of the highest in the world. This is largely due to the fact that nearly one half (47 per cent in 1982) of all females form part of the labour force. On average, more than 50 per cent of the employed labour force are women. Their share in employment in some sectors (such as trade, posts and telecommunications as well as in the non-productive sections of the economy) amounted to almost 75 per cent. But even in industry alone, the proportion of females employed amounted to over 40 per cent. Elaborate training schemes ensure the training of both men and women. In fact, three-quarters of the total labour force have completed a vocational training. Of these, nearly one-quarter are graduates of universities or technical colleges. Of the total labour force, no less than two-fifths are absorbed by the industrial sector. Every citizen of working age has a constitutional right to a job and there is no unemployment in the GDR.

The Structure of the GDR Economy

The economy of the GDR, being a socialist country, is centrally planned and virtually the entire means of production are publicly owned. The change of ownership of the means of production after the Second World War obviously led to far-reaching structural changes in the GDR economy, which is still confronted by serious problems despite its remarkable achievements in recent decades.

The most important planning instruments are the medium-term economic plans from which the annual economic plans are abstracted. The first economic plan covered the second half of 1948 and was followed by the two-year plan for 1949–50, two five-year plans for 1951–5 and 1956–60, two seven-year plans for 1959–65 and 1964–70 and three further five-year plans for 1971–5, 1976–80 and 1981–5.

By far the largest sector of the GDR economy is the industrial one, which, as a percentage of total net output, has shown a steady increase from 59.9 per cent in 1960 to 69.8 per cent in 1982. During the same period, the 'agriculture and forestry' sector registered a decline from 16.9 per cent to 7.8 per cent (see Table 3.2). This trend is not dissimilar to that of West Germany.

One of the GDR's chief economic problems is its lack of raw materials and sources of energy. It therefore depends heavily upon foreign trade. Most raw materials have to be imported, and in exchange the GDR exports mainly industrial products.

Table 3.2   *GDR Sector Net Output and National Income Produced at 1980 Prices (in Marks billion)*

Sector	1960	1970	1980	1981	1982	1983
Industry	48.0	80.5	136.1	143.7	148.6	156.6
Construction	4.5	8.2	11.7	12.3	12.4	13.0
Agriculture and forestry	13.5	14.9	16.6	17.1	16.7	17.2
Other sectors	14.0	21.2	33.6	34.8	35.4	36.4
Net output of all sectors	80.0	124.8	198.0	207.9	213.1	223.2
Adjustments for productive consumption	3.3	7.4	10.9	11.8	12.0	13.1
National Income	76.7	117.4	187.1	196.1	201.1	210.1
As a percentage of net output						
Industry	59.9	64.5	68.7	69.1	69.7	70.2
Construction	5.6	6.5	5.9	5.9	5.8	5.8
Agriculture and forestry	16.9	12.0	8.4	8.2	7.8	7.7
Other sectors	17.6	17.0	17.0	16.8	16.5	16.3
	100.0	100.0	100.0	100.0	100.0	100.0

Source: *Statistisches Jahrbuch der Deutschen Demokratischen Republik* (annual).

Phases of Economic Development

When analysing the postwar economic development of the GDR, we can distinguish four distinct periods:

(1)   The period of reparation payments: 1945–53.
(2)   The period of population decline until 1961.
(3)   The period of reforms: the 1960s.
(4)   The period of increasing external economic difficulties until the early 1980s.

(1)   *The Period of Reparation Payments: 1945–53* The economic improvements in the GDR since 1945 have been achieved against a background of considerable initial difficulties. The Second World War left the GDR with a loss of productive capacity of only 15 per cent against a loss of 21 per cent suffered by West Germany. However, the dismantling of plant and machinery by the USSR in the GDR was more than double that carried out by the Western Allies in West Germany (26 per cent and 12 per cent respectively). Considering that the remaining plant at partially dismantled factories was in most instances useless, the total loss of productive capacity in the GDR has been estimated at approximately 50 per cent of the 1939 figure.

In addition, the GDR had to make reparation payments to the USSR out of current output until the USSR-GDR Agreement of 1953. During the first four postwar years these deliveries to the USSR absorbed as much as 15 per cent of the GDR's real national income, which was more than the share of gross investment. In contrast, West Germany, after the initial dismantling of plant and machinery, actually received new equipment, raw materials and food free of charge through the Marshall Plan and other US-aid programmes which were of decisive importance during the period of postwar reconstruction.

The reparation obligations of the GDR *vis-à-vis* the USSR had, of course, rather adverse effects not only on the level of consumption but also on the volume of new investment urgently required to compensate for the dismantling of factories by the USSR. A further aggravating factor for the GDR derived from the division of Germany. The sources of raw materials and half-finished products were mainly located in the Western parts of Germany. These goods, essential to the GDR's industrial sector, could not be obtained from the USSR or other Eastern bloc countries in sufficient quantities. The GDR was therefore forced to build up basic industries itself instead of concentrating on traditional domestic lines of production. When the GDR's foreign trade began to expand, its main trading partners were the USSR (absorbing about two-fifths of its total exports) and other East European countries. The advantages of trade with the industrially more highly developed Western countries could not be utilized to any significant extent until a much later stage. At least during the early postwar period the above-mentioned factors appear to be among those principally responsible for the differences which emerged in the standard of living between the two parts of Germany.

The aim of the first medium-term economic plan, the two-year plan for 1949–50, was not only to get the industrial production back on its feet and to ensure a sufficient supply of consumer goods, but also to provide for adequate reparation payments to the USSR. More far-reaching in its conception was the first five-year plan for 1951–5, which concentrated on achieving essential structural changes in the GDR economy and encompassed the production, distribution and use of the national income towards these goals. High on the list of priorities was the expansion of hitherto insufficient basic industries in order to increase the supply of self-produced raw materials, iron and steel, and energy. Also allowed for was the further development and expansion of both the chemical and investment goods industries. Much of this had to be achieved at the expense of the production of consumer goods.

(2)   *The Problem of Population Decline: until 1961* The difficulties

caused by wage increases and an insufficient supply of goods for private consumption was such that after the unrest of June 1953, the GDR authorities propagated a new line of policy favouring consumers. The end of reparation payments out of current production to the USSR, which the USSR–GDR Agreement of 1953 allowed for, plus increased imports and credits from the USSR, eased but did not terminate the economic problems of the GDR. In West Germany, the standard of living had risen rapidly after the currency reform of 1948. The result was that many of the young in the GDR, comprising a high percentage of skilled labour, felt attracted by the higher living standard West Germany had to offer and no doubt, too, by the greater degree of freedom.

Thus, until 1961 the GDR suffered a decline in population of just over 2 million. For the GDR economy this meant the loss of one-fifth of the skilled labour force. Generally speaking, the economic problems seemed almost insurmountable. To fill all the gaps at once was an impossible task. A higher living standard required an expansion of the productive capacity through more investment. But devoting an increased percentage of the national income to investment would have meant reverting to a reduced share of consumption, for the scarcity of factors of production was such that it would have been impossible to raise both consumption and investment simultaneously to a satisfactory level.

The GDR authorities introduced various economic plans in search of a solution. In these plans they switched from stimulating investment to favouring consumption. In general, all economic plans of the GDR basically depend on the aims set by the authorities. The plan defines the economic aims, examines the existing capacities and the changes and development required to achieve these aims.

The second five-year plan for 1956–60, which did not come into effect until December 1957, not only attempted to assist in solving the consumer and population crises, but also aimed at regional specialization within the group of European centrally planned economies, rather than far-reaching self-sufficiency. Thus, for the GDR, coal, energy and particularly chemical production were the areas on which investment was supposed to concentrate. At the same time labour productivity, which had been rather low in comparison to West Germany, was to be raised. However, instead of completing this five-year plan, a seven-year plan was introduced covering the period 1959–65. One of the principal economic aims of this plan was for the GDR to reach, or even exceed, West Germany's per capita consumption of most industrial consumer goods and food by the end of 1961 in order to bring to a halt the loss of skilled labour to West Germany. The rise in the output of consumer goods and food required was intended to be achieved mainly by an increase in labour productivity. It was decreed that investment should concentrate less on the development and expansion of basic industries and more on industries where the GDR had a comparative advantage. The plan also allowed for substantial increases in exports. This ambitious plan could not be realized, of course. During the late 1950s, real per capita consumption in the GDR was still some 30 per cent below that of West Germany. Reaching the target growth-rates for per capita consumption and fulfilling the investment plans simultaneously proved impossible. Economic growth-rates actually declined rather than improving, and difficulties were mounting in the agricultural sector, leading in turn to food shortages. Thus, the population drift to the West gained momentum in 1960 and ultimately led to a drastic stop by building the Berlin Wall virtually overnight on 13 August 1961.

(3) *The Period of Reforms: the 1960s*   The avowed task of the economic reforms of the 1960s was not only to raise the level of both consumption and investment, but also to achieve the necessary structural changes in the economy.

A genuine search for ways of decentralizing the economy and introducing incentives at all levels became evident in 1962, when the authorities decided to abolish the unsuccessful seven-year plan for 1959–65. It was in the first instance replaced by annual economic plans which not only set new guidelines for private consumption, but also helped to bridge the gap and allowed for time to scrutinize thoroughly the entire planning system. These deliberations led to the abandonment by the newly established State Planning Commission (Staatliche Plankommission – SPK) of the frequently rigid adherence to unobtainable goals and to the introduction of a more realistic seven-year plan for 1964–70 (the *Perspektivplan*). This plan attempted to attain the ultimate goals of economic policy through a higher degree of economic efficiency and a greater scope for individual and collective initiative. An improved co-ordination of economic measures was an essential part of this new approach. These developments seemed to indicate at the time that the GDR authorities had at last realized that the planning methods, the price system and the organization of the economy required drastic changes. Too high a degree of centralization had killed the initiative in individual enterprises, while quality and productivity had suffered by laying down indiscriminate production targets. This neglect of economic factors led to poor investment decisions. In addition, the price system had the sequel of a distorted price structure, which resulted in a waste of raw materials and also slowed down technical progress. For example, prices of certain raw materials often stood at less than half the actual cost of production, the difference being met by state subsidies. Thus, there was little incentive to strive for technical progress and innovation.

To remove these distortions and to improve the planning system, the GDR introduced the so-called New Economic System (NES) in January 1963. Its foremost aim was an optimal combination of long-term central planning with an indirect control of enterprises through the use of economic levers (largely in the form of monetary instruments). Within certain limits the authority of decision-making was delegated from the central economic agencies to the newly established combines of nationalized industrial concerns, the Associations of Nationalized Enterprises (Vereinigungen volkseigener Betriebe – VVBs. This meant that for the first time in the economic history of the GDR, the managers of state factories were encouraged to maximize profits and were given the power to use these profits at least partly within the enterprise itself to achieve further expansion. Furthermore, the principle of the economic accountability of state factories was introduced, and in this connection, fixed assets were revalued and depreciation rates were met at more realistic levels. All these changes were combined with a far-reaching industrial price reform. In the monetary sector the rate of interest began to play a decisive role. The planning authorities obviously hoped that the new policy would raise the efficiency of factors of production and would generally improve the structure of the economy.

The NES while in force encompassed two economic plans, covering the periods 1964–70 and 1966–70 respectively. Both plans were new in their philosophy, in that they set guidelines and provided for adjustments as required by new developments. The aim was to raise the proportion of GNP devoted to investment, particularly in growth industries such as the chemical, electrotechnical and engineering industries.

However, after a promising initial success, new problems emerged. Productivity rises were unequally distributed over the industrial sector, and the economy began to suffer from serious dislocations. Towards the end of the 1960s, the NES was suspended by the authorities and the GDR returned to centralized planning decisions.

(4) *The Period of Mounting External Economic Difficulties: the 1970s and early 1980s* After 1971 followed a policy of consolidation, marked by clear attempts to pursue policies advantageous to consumers. These tasks had been made easier by the achievement of a more rapid rate of economic growth. Thus, the supply of consumer goods increased and so did the standard of living. The 1971–5 plan which pursued these aims was followed by the five-year plan for 1976–80, the time when GDR balance-of-trade deficits reached unprecedented levels. Most worrying was that these deficits quite

obviously called for a drastic cutting back in the improvement made in the supply of consumer goods. A reduction rather than a further advance in living standards seemed to loom on the horizon.

GDR Foreign Trade and Debt Problems

To follow the import and export trends of the GDR is a time-consuming task, as its own statistical publications only give figures for the *turnover* of foreign trade and not for exports and imports separately. Neither does the GDR publish a balance of payments. Thus, some impression of the GDR's trade, current account and balance-of-payments performances can only be gained by using the statistics of the GDR's trading partners.

The official GDR foreign-trade turnover figures reveal that nearly two-thirds of its foreign trade is conducted with other centrally planned economies, while trade with the USSR alone approaches two-fifths of the total. The share of trade with developed market economies (basically OECD countries) is just under 30 per cent. The developing market economies have doubled their share in the GDR's foreign trade from just over 4 per cent in 1971–5 to 8 per cent in 1982 (see Table 3.4). These global turnover figures conceal rather dramatic developments, which have taken place in the GDR foreign-trade sector since the early 1970s.

After 1973 the GDR was particularly badly hit by the worldwide rise in raw material and energy prices. The GDR produces few raw materials itself and has virtually no energy resources of its own, except coal. The much more modest rise in the prices of GDR export goods resulted in a disquietening fall in the terms of trade. Consequently, serious balance-of-trade deficits emerged in the GDR. Particularly worrying were those arising from trade with the developed market economies, which totalled $US 11.4 billion during the decade 1971–81. Because of the GDR's chronic shortage of convertible currencies, these deficits could only be settled by borrowing in the international financial markets of the developed market economies. It is scarcely surprising, therefore, that the GDR's net external debt against the West at its peak in 1981 had reached a figure of approximately $US 12–13 billion – next to Poland the highest net debt outstanding in hard currencies. Rising interest rates in international financial markets constituted a further aggravating factor. Thus, in 1981 interest-rate payments on the GDR's external debt to the West absorbed almost one-quarter of its total exports to developed market economies. Trade with the USSR, too, showed substantial deficits following the start of the oil-price increases in 1973, but these could be financed through more favourable credits

Table 3.3   Changes in Growth of GDR National Income and Sectoral Gross Output (annual percentage change)

	National income (in Marks billion at 1980 prices)	National Income		Industry		Gross output Construction		Agriculture	
		Plan	Actual	Plan	Actual	Plan	Actual	Plan	Actual
1960	76.7	—	—	—	—	—	—	—	2.8
1970	117.4	—	5.6	—	5.9	—	4.9	2.6	1.3
1976–80	—	5.0	4.2	6.0	5.0	5.0	3.3	1.1	—
1981–5	—	5.1	—	5.1	—	3.4	—	0.5[a]	—
1980	187.1	4.8	4.4	4.7	4.7	5.3	1.4	0.8[a]	1.5
1981	196.1	5.0	4.8	5.0	4.7	2.8	4.1	2.8[a]	0.0
1982	201.1	4.8	2.5	4.6	3.2	2.5	4.2	0.2[a]	-3.6
1983	210.1	4.2	4.5	3.8	4.1	1.4	4.3	1.0[a]	-2.5
1984	—	4.4	—	3.6	—	2.1	—	0.6[a]	—

Source: Statistisches Jahrbuch der Deutschen Demokratischen Republik (annual).
[a] Expressed in terms of net output (including food processing).

Table 3.4   *GDR Foreign Trade by Groups of Countries*

	1971–5	1976–80	1981	1982	1983
(In percent)					
Total Imports	100.0	100.0	100.0	100.0	100.0
Centrally planned economies[a]	65.0	65.8	66.7	68.1	—
Of which					
Eastern Europe	62.1	62.8	63.9	65.5	—
USSR	33.9	35.0	38.5	40.9	—
Developed market economies[b]	30.9	29.1	29.5	27.3	—
Developing market economies	4.1	5.1	3.8	4.6	—
Total Exports	100.0	100.0	100.0	100.0	100.0
Centrally planned economies	72.7	72.4	65.6	63.0	—
Of which					
Eastern Europe	68.9	68.9	63.0	60.8	—
USSR	36.6	35.4	36.5	35.3	—
Developed market economies	23.2	21.9	27.4	29.0	—
Developing market economies	4.1	5.7	7.0	8.0	—
(In VM billion)[c]					
Trade Balance	−7.00	−28.80	−1.07	+5.35	+5.44
Centrally planned economies	+6.06	−3.34	−1.41	−0.16	—
Of which					
Eastern Europe	+4.94	−3.83	−1.24	−0.04	—
USSR	+1.22	−9.06	−1.73	−2.00	—
Developed market economies	−12.84	−25.27	−1.68	+2.73	—
Developing market economies	−0.21	−0.21	+2.03	+2.79	—

Sources: Statistisches Jahrbuch der Deutschen Demokratischen Republik (annual), country data and DIW *Wochenberichte.*

[a] Soviet bloc countries plus China, Yugoslavia, North Korea and Laos.

[b] OECD countries

[c] VM = unit of account used for GDR foreign-trade purposes. VM 4.67 = 1 USSR Transfer Rouble. The rate of exchange against Western currencies fluctuates according to parity changes between the rouble and convertible currencies. For 1982: VM 1 = DM 0.713.

granted by the USSR.

To cope with, and reduce, the external debt burden, the five-year plan for 1981–5 emphasized the need for a reduced use of energy and raw materials and allowed for only small rises in private consumption and investment. Instead, absolute priority was given to a drastic increase in exports (particularly to developed market economies). This policy was to be assisted through higher rates of economic growth to be attained by means of the increased use of modern technology. However, the latter would have required a far sharper rise in investment and imports of essential high-technology investment goods

Table 3.5   *Estimated GDR Balance of Payments on Current Account with Market Economies (in $US billion)*

	1980	1981	1982	1983[a]
Trade balances with market economies[b]				
Total	−1.7	—	+1.5	+1.2
Of which				
Developed market economies[c]	−1.7	−0.5	+0.7	+0.4
Net services plus transfers				
Total	−0.1	−0.4	—	+0.4
Investment income	−1.2	−1.6	−1.3	−0.9
Current Account	−1.8	−0.4	+1.5	+1.7

Source: UN Economic Commission for Europe, *Economic Survey of Europe in 1983*(Geneva: UN, 1984).
    [a] Extrapolated, assuming a continuation of January–September trends in exports and imports.
    [b] Trade balance f.o.b.
    [c] The term 'developed market economies' comprises Western Europe (including Turkey and Yugoslavia), North America and Japan.

than the plan envisaged. Nevertheless, the authorities did manage to reduce drastically the trade deficits and the external debt through a drop in imports and a rise in exports, although the growth-rates achieved fell short of the target figures. A greatly reduced trade deficit and sizable surpluses in 1981 could be registered in 1982 and 1983 (see Tables 3.4 and 3.5). These developments resulted in a marked fall in the GDR's net external debt *vis-à-vis* developed market economies (see Table 3.6). Thus, the GDR appears to be well on the way to achieving its external economic goals, though at the cost of slowing down in the improvement of domestic living standards.

Nearly 50 per cent of GDR exports consist of investment goods, while almost three-fifths of its own imports are made up of energy and raw materials. The GDR is therefore greatly dependent on world market conditions. Its trade with the developed market economies (just under 30 per cent of its total foreign-trade turnover) plays an essential role in the economy and will almost certainly have to be expanded if higher growth rates are to be achieved through the application of more modern technology, for much of the latter will have to be purchased from the West.

Economic Links between the GDR and West Germany

The economic relationship between the GDR and West Germany

Table 3.6   *External Debt of the GDR in Convertible Currencies (in $US billion)*

	1977	1978	1979	1980	1981	1982
External GDR Debts						
Assests of reporting banks (BIS data)	4.87	6.19	7.72	9.46	10.09	8.52
Liabilities of reporting banks (BIS data)	−0.88	−1.20	−1.90	−2.04	−2.15	−1.88
Balance	3.99	4.99	5.82	7.42	7.94	6.65
Inter-German capital movements	1.29	1.85	2.13	2.15	1.64	1.52
Total net debt	5.28	6.84	7.95	9.57	9.61	8.17
Interest payments	0.22	0.40	0.64	1.02	1.29	0.90
GDR exports	2.51	2.86	3.57	4.35	5.46	6.59
Net debt						
per capita in $US	315	408	475	572	574	487
in % of exports	210	239	223	210	176	124
Interest payments as % of exports	9	14	18	22	24	14

Source: DIW *Wochenberichte.*

dates back to the Berlin Agreement concluded just over thirty years ago on 20 September 1951. This agreement is the oldest agreement between the two German states. In its version of 16 August 1960 it still forms the legal basis for trade between the two parts of Germany.

The interesting question which emerges is: why have both partners to the agreement been so anxious to maintain the status quo for more than three decades? What are the advantages both sides derive from the Berlin Agreement? The answer to these questions is partly political and partly economic. For West Germany the Berlin Agreement is taken as confirmation by the GDR that West Berlin forms an integral part of West Germany, at least in the economic sense. It must be remembered that the economic break between the two parts of the former German Reich only occurred three years after the end of the Second World War, when in 1948 a new currency, the Deutschmark (DM), was introduced in West Germany to replace the old Reichsmark. Thus the GDR authorities were forced to do the same by introducing their own new currency, the DM East. The Berlin Agreement is basically an agreement not so much between the two German states, but rather between the two currency areas of the DM – the DM West and the DM East. As the DM West is the currency in circulation in both West Germany and West Berlin, the Berlin Agreement is taken as specifically recognizing the fact that West

Berlin is part of West Germany. For example, one paragraph of the Berlin Agreement specifies that an 'adequate part' of trade between the two German states should benefit West Berlin.

If a new and more normal trade agreement between the two German states were now negotiated, it might be difficult to get the GDR to agree to similar concessions, as far as the status of West Berlin is concerned. This is, no doubt, one of the major reasons why West Germany would rather not renegotiate its trade agreement with the GDR.

How then does the GDR view the situation? Why does it appear to be equally keen to maintain the status quo? The reason in the GDR's case is perhaps less political and more economic. The Berlin Agreement provides the GDR with trade concessions, which under EEC rules West Germany is not really entitled to grant to non-EEC countries. For example, trade between the two German states is not subject to any trade barriers, such as EEC external tariffs applicable to third countries. In other words, in its trade with West Germany, the GDR is treated as if it was, in fact, a member of the EEC.

Of further importance for the GDR is the fact that any trade deficit with West Germany does not have to be settled in convertible currencies. Instead, each side grants the other automatic credits in case of trade deficits. This arrangement is obviously of vital significance for the GDR but not for West Germany which does not depend on them. To retain these various trade advantages, the GDR has been prepared to make important concessions. For example, in 1972 it agreed to the addition of an *Unberührtheitsklausel* in the basic agreement on which the relationship between West Germany and the GDR depends. But there are also some other, more general political and economic reasons why the GDR is anxious to maintain its trade links with West Germany. Two of these include the following. First, any trade restrictions the USA and its allies may use against the USSR and other countries belonging to the Soviet bloc would not affect trade between the two German states. This would ensure the supply of at least some of the goods the GDR urgently needs from the West. Secondly, the GDR is also adversely affected by domestic economic difficulties among its East European trading partners. Supplies of important raw materials from the USSR and lately from Poland have tended to decline. The resulting gaps had to be filled by importing more of these goods from the West and from the developing market economies, as is evident from Table 3.4.

What is important for the GDR is that the most pressing bottlenecks can easily be overcome thanks to trade with West Germany. The efficiency of the West German economy and its geographical closeness ensure almost immediate deliveries without the obligation of settlement in convertible Western currencies. Prices may be higher at times than in the case of supplies from the East European countries, but at least some of the bottlenecks causing delays in the GDR's own production may be overcome.

As far as the trend of trade between the GDR and West Germany is concerned, the share in GDR total foreign trade has been in the region of 6–6.5 per cent since the early 1970s, while that of West Berlin has fluctuated around 2 per cent. Thus, West Germany and West Berlin between them have a share of around 8.5 per cent in the GDR's total foreign trade, which is just over 30 per cent of its total trade with all developed market economies (see Table 3.7).

Table 3.7   *Share of Industrialized Countries including West Germany in the Foreign Trade Turnover of the GDR at Current Prices*

Year	Industrialized countries[a]	Of which West Germany	West Germany as % of trade with all industrialized countries
1960	21.1	10.3	48.8
1970	24.4	10.2	41.8
1975	25.9	8.7	33.6
1976	28.3	8.6	30.4
1977	23.7	8.5	35.9
1978	22.7	8.2	36.1
1979	26.0	8.0	30.8
1980	27.4	8.4	30.6
1981	28.5	8.3	29.2
1982	28.1	8.6	30.7
1983	29.4	8.5	28.8

Source: Statistisches Jahrbuch der Deutschen Demokratischen Republik.
[a] All West European Industrialized Countries (including West Germany) plus the USA, Canada, Japan, Australia and New Zealand.

Inter-German trade, that is, trade between the two German states, has risen rapidly in nominal terms throughout the postwar period, although the nominal annual rates of growth have been rather erratic (see Table 3.8). However, inter-German trade has for some time been in a state of stagnation, with an overall real growth rate of only 6 per cent for the entire period 1972–81 (an annual rate of growth of only 0.7 per cent). In fact, an advance in real terms worth mentioning occurred only in 1976 and then from 1980 onwards. The normally negative trade balance of the GDR with West Germany has turned positive since 1980. This reflects the GDR's desire to reduce its considerable cumulative deficit with West Germany arising from previous deficits. On invisible or services account, which includes services such as shipping, the use of foreign ports, interest payments on outstanding loans, travel, and so on, the GDR still runs heavy, though reduced, deficits with West Germany. The relatively high level of interest rates in West Germany and the need at times to make extensive use of the Hamburg docks in view of the inability to expand GDR dock facilities rapidly enough (Polish docks being often not fully available), have all contributed to the GDR's balance-of-payments deficits on invisible account with West Germany.

The limits and possibilities for a further, perhaps more dynamic, expansion of inter-German trade will remain to be determined not only by the basic political and economic conditions in East-West relations, but also by the extent to which, on the one hand, West Germany is willing to expand credits to the GDR and, on the other, the latter's willingness to get further indebted to West Germany. However, equally as important, or maybe more so, the ability of the GDR to expand exports to West Germany and the latter's willingness to absorb more GDR-produced goods. On all these fronts, the prospects for an expansion of inter-German trade do not look too promising. First, East–West political and economic relations in the 1980s look, unfortunately, far less promising than in the 1970s. Secondly, financial institutions in the West are today rather unwilling to further expand credits to Soviet bloc countries on terms acceptable to them (although the GDR is no doubt regarded as one of the most creditworthy Eastern bloc countries). Neither do these countries wish to allow their indebtedness to extend beyond what is unavoidable in view of the still high burden of servicing their already existing external debts at currently high interest-rate levels. Thirdly, an expansion of GDR exports to West Germany (or for that matter to any other Western country) requires not only a sufficient degree of price competitiveness, but also the provision of a wider range of acceptable products with an improvement in servicing facilities, the supply of spare parts and design. Dampening, too, has been the imposition of quantitative controls by West Germany for specific groups of products in its trade with the GDR. A more liberal West German trade policy towards the GDR would indeed go a long way towards the achievement of rising real growth in inter-German trade. Failing such a development, GDR foreign trade is bound to be increasingly diverted to other Western industrial countries and to the USSR and other East European trading partners.

Conclusions

The economic progress of the GDR during the postwar period and especially in recent years has been astounding. However, many vital problems remain unresolved, as indeed they do in many Western

Table 3.8 Development of Inter-German Trade

Year	In DM billion West German deliveries of goods to GDR	West German receipts of goods from GDR	Total Turnover	West German trade balance with GDR	Increase in % over previous year West German deliveries	West German receipts	Turnover
1950	0.33	0.42	0.75	−0.09	—	—	—
1960	0.96	1.12	2.08	−0.16	−11.0	25.9	5.5
1970	2.42	2.00	4.41	+0.42	6.3	20.5	12.3
1975	3.92	3.34	7.26	+0.58	6.8	2.8	4.9
1976	4.27	3.88	8.15	+0.39	8.9	16.2	12.3
1977	4.41	3.96	8.37	+0.45	3.3	2.1	2.7
1978	4.58	3.90	8.48	+0.68	3.9	−1.5	1.2
1979	4.72	4.59	9.31	+0.13	3.0	17.7	9.8
1980	5.29	5.58	10.87	−0.29	12.1	21.6	16.8
1981	5.58	6.05	11.63	−0.47	5.5	8.4	7.0
1982	6.38	6.64	13.02	−0.26	14.5	9.7	12.0
1983	6.95	6.88	13.83	+0.07	8.9	3.6	6.2

Source: West German Statistical Office, Series 6, no. 6 and *Statistisches Jahrbuch für die Bundesrepublik Deutschland* (Stuttgart: Kohlhammer, annual publication).

industrial countries. One of the foremost problems is the standard of living. Although the GDR has been able to improve the consumption structure and to maintain consumption levels, substantial further improvements in the efficiency of overall economic performance will be required to raise real private consumption to a level approaching that of West Germany. However, there is also a need to further increase exports and investment. However, the negligible increase in investment has been outweighed by a high rise in productivity, so that the incremental capital-output ratio has actually improved and by 1983 had fallen to its lowest point since the mid-1970s. This indicates a remarkable success in raising the productivity. The main task of the planning authorities will have to be to find the right balance when allocating the national product and to attempt the achievement of higher growth rates also through further increases in productivity. But higher growth rates will also require more imports of high-technology investment goods from the West and this will require stepping up exports. It is likely to take some time before the GDR can hope to raise the standard of living of its population to anything like the level achieved by West European industrial countries, although the progress made in that direction so far is certainly remarkable.

4

Education under the Honeckers

JOHN PAGE

Since all the major pieces of legislation and reforms which have shaped the course of East German education from kindergarten to university stem from the Ulbricht era and since the SED claims that its *Bildungspolitik* represents a continuum, it would be appropriate to review the three Education Acts and the salient changes in vocational training and at the tertiary level before taking a closer look at developments since Erich Honecker assumed office in 1971. In the period immediately following the establishment of the Soviet zone in 1945, the area in which the Kommunistische Partei Deutschlands (KPD) and Sozialdemokratische Partei Deutschlands (SPD) had shared the most common ground had been education. When the two parties were amalgamated to form the SED the following year their first substantial act of legislation was the 'Law relating to the Democratization of German Schools' which swept away the system of *Volksschulen,* intermediate and grammar schools inherited from the Third Reich. These were replaced by coeducational, comprehensive *Grundschulen* for all 6–14-year-olds with provision for the majority of school-leavers to undertake vocational training. The academically gifted were transferred to *Oberschulen*, high schools, on completion of their eight years of general schooling, theoretically allowing access to higher education to all suitable pupils irrespective of their parental background. Teaching staffs were rigorously purged to exclude all who did not meet with the SED's approval and new, centrally controlled syllabuses together with the appropriate textbooks came into force.

In effect, the 1946 Act consisted of a ready-made package of reforms which owed their origins to the thinking of KPD members exiled in the USSR during the Second World War, and its implementation was considerably eased by the zealous support of Red Army education officers. As distinct from later Education Acts the local population was barely consulted. Nevertheless, in the early days at least, the innovations received wide support, both from educational theorists and the general public. The changes were welcomed as a return to German educational thinking before Hitler's accession to power, in particular to the progressive ideas of the *Reformpädagogik* movement. Radical though the clauses of the Act were, they did in reality contain elements of compromise. The provision of special courses of study, for example, which prepared able pupils for the high schools was clearly a selective measure unlikely to remain acceptable for very long to those in favour of a strictly egalitarian approach to the aims of education.

By 1948, however, the spirit of accommodation had all but disappeared as, increasingly, the more orthodox Marxist–Leninist stance of the 'new-type' SED coincided with a diminution of the influence of the SPD faction within the party. The shift away from a German path to socialism towards a more internationalist course under the aegis of the USSR was to bring with it the choice of Soviet experience and theory as a source of guidance in all matters educational. In effect, the SED would henceforth be free to determine all aspects of educational theory taught in the universities and colleges. The founding of the German Democratic Republic in October, 1949, roughly coinciding with the end of the era of 'anti-fascist democratic reform', ushered in a four-year period of what has been called the 'Stalinization of the GDR'[1] which included the wholesale importation of Soviet features throughout East German education.

Support for the SED's economic policy and the ideology of Marxist–Leninism were already being demanded from the schools to an extent quite unforeseen at the time of the 1946 Education Act. Furthermore, the party's social-engineering aspirations were now receiving greater prominence. At the Third Parliament of the Free German Youth in 1949, its chairman Erich Honecker had expressed dissatisfaction at the low percentage of working-class children entering the high schools,[2] thereby frustrating the party's hopes of intakes in higher education which mirrored the class structure as a whole. The SED responded by seeking to create a rival institution to the high schools in the form of ten-year intermediate schools which would directly promote working-class interests. The attempt failed, allegedly due to the resistance of a 'group hostile to the party' within the Ministry of Education itself.[3] The *Arbeiter- und Bauernfakultäten* introduced in 1949 were more successful; these institutions offered three-year courses which prepared working-class students for entry to the universities and colleges. Further higher education reforms in 1951 remodelled the academic year on Soviet lines and introduced compulsory studies in Marxist–Leninism and the Russian language. At the same time attempts were made to make research more relevant to state economic planning.

In later years the SED would use educational reforms to signal stages of progress towards the ultimate goal of communism. Thus the historic decision taken by the Politburo in July 1952 to begin the task of building socialism might have provided an appropriate opportunity to update the 1946 Education Act. This was not the case, instead the overall aims of general education were redefined. There was to be greater emphasis on *Erziehung,* that is, the affective component of the curriculum. Teachers were urged to train 'all-round developed personalities capable of building socialism and defending its achievements', pupils with a 'socialist morality' and a 'socialist consciousness', pupils distinguished by their strength of will, stamina, determination, courage, singlemindedness and firmness of principles.[4] Conformity was likewise demanded of the teachers themselves; reactionary attitudes and a lack of ideological clarity would no longer be tolerated.

The early 1950s saw an exodus of teachers and educationists to the West as hostility grew to what was regarded as SED interference in the schools and colleges. Amongst those who stayed, opposition to *Sowjetpädagogik* remained fierce as allegiance to the German tradition of *Reformpädagogik* continued to serve as a rallying-point for all intent on fending off Soviet influence in matters educational. The official record of the period concedes that the SED faced an uphill struggle at this time: 'In the didactic and methodological sphere the debate was especially harsh and arduous.'[5] *Reformpädagogik* was labelled a manifestation of imperialism and a whole catalogue of heretical attitudes were identified amongst teaching staffs, including opportunism, pacifism, formalism, cosmopolitanism and social democratism.[6] More serious resistance continued to be offered by the Ministry of Education. During the period leading up to the events of June 1953 leading functionaries had gone as far as to issue a directive advocating the setting up of eleven-year schools, apparently without consulting the SED. A direct link was established between the way-ward officials involved and the Zaisser–Herrnstadt plot against the party. When Wilhelm Zaisser, Minister of State Security, was removed from office, his wife Else, Minister of Education, was replaced by Fritz Lange.[7] A further example of the turmoil prevailing at this time concerned the introduction of a polytechnical element into the general curriculum. Stalin's new-found interest in this area (it had, after all, been specifically prescribed by Marx and had formed an essential part of Lenin's educational programme) had caused a res-olution to be passed at the CPSU's Nineteenth Party Congress held in October 1952 calling for a polytechnical component in education as part of the USSR's transition from socialism to communism.[8]

The SED promptly convened a special conference the following May to debate the implementation of the same innovation in GDR schools. Addressing the conference, Werner Dorst, head of the German Central Institute of Education, took a different line from that of the Politburo, though one which was entirely consistent with Stalin's. He argued that polytechnical education as a concomitant of a truly communist society was best left to some future date when the GDR had consolidated the foundations of socialism. Dorst's view prevailed, postponing the introduction of polytechnical education for several years. When N. S. Khrushchev returned to the theme at the CPSU's Twentieth Party Congress in February 1956, his justification had little to do with periodization; instead he emphasized the role that a combination of school and work experience would play in overcoming the rift which had developed between the classroom and real life. Again Ulbricht reacted swiftly, promising a changeover to polytechnical education at the SED's Third Party Conference held weeks later. Teaching staffs continued to regard the proposed innovation as yet one more Soviet imposition, however, and remained unenthusiastic. In an attempt to make the subject more palatable, Minister of Education Fritz Lange at the Fifth Education Congress held the following May stressed the fact that practical work combined with formal schooling had been part of German educational tradition and went as far as to call for a 'more subtly differentiated view of *Reformpädagogik*'.[9] Lange was summarily dismissed for expressing revisionist opinions and his activities were linked with the breakaway group within the SED of Schirdewan, Wollweber and Ziller.[10] In effect, Lange was the third Minister of Education in a row to be removed from office. The party's score with Werner Dorst was likewise finally settled as he, too, was expelled from his post as member of the editorial board of the important periodical *Pädagogik*, again for revisionism.

Nevertheless, the SED survived the many forms of dissent and went over to the counter-offensive towards the end of the 1950s, stating its intentions in the field of education with a second Act in December 1959, the 'Law relating to the socialist development of education in the German Democratic Republic'. The eight-year *Grundschule* was replaced by a *Zehnklassige allgemeine polytechnische Oberschule*. The vast majority of pupils would thus henceforth complete an extra two years of schooling at an *Oberschule,* a high school, a choice of title which was meant to emphasize that the old division between working-class children in *Volksschulen* and privileged middle-class children attending *Oberschulen* had at long last disappeared. The inclusion of the term 'polytechnic' in the new designation was intended to leave no doubt in the mind as to the SED's determination to introduce a blend of academic and industrial or agricultural experience. The best-qualified school-leavers would transfer to a two-year *Erweiterte Oberschule,* an extended high school not unlike the English sixth form college, by way of preparation for entry into higher education. This arrangement has survived intact until the present day. Whereas the 1946 Act, radical though it was, had clearly contained elements of accommodation, its successor was a reflection of the SED's confidence in its ability to force through an uncompromisingly socialist educational programme and of the party's conviction that internal opposition, though not entirely vanquished, had lost momentum. Changes in the content of education were to match the structural innovations. In addition to the *Unterrichtstag in der Produktion* (UTP), one day a week for all pupils over the age of 13 to be spent in an industrial or agricultural enterprise, all subjects taught were to take on a polytechnical orientation. Pupils were to develop into 'socialist personalities' distinguished by their ethics of morality, emotions, powers of reasoning, convictions, attitudes, aesthetic tastes, their concept of reality and their understanding of the past, present and future.

The SED had now achieved the structure of education and the control of content that it had sought. The results in the early 1960s, however, were not encouraging. The polytechnical approach, far from influencing the rest of the curriculum, remained on the periphery, the day in industry or agriculture either providing inappropriate work experience or no real contact with production.[11]. The academic subjects which had been added to support the UTP, introduction to socialist production and technical drawing, were having an overly academic effect on what was intended to be practical experience. To make matters worse, there was considerable confusion over the very aims and objectives of polytechnical education, which had after all been an essential part of the 1959 Act. Minister of Education Alfred Lemmnitz expressed the view that it should be geared to manpower needs and that the final two years should be 'professionalized', that is, provide a form of specific vocational training.[12] This 'monotechnical' approach was, of course, entirely out of keeping with Marx's advocacy of polytechnical training aimed at the *Disponibilität* of the individual, rendering him fit for a variety of labours and ready to face every change in production.[13] A further question mark was raised over the social aspirations of the 1959 Act when related to the real needs of the economy. Hitherto the existence of individual gifts and talents had been played down for ideological reasons. In future they would be harnessed for their contribution to economic success. Thus the strictly egalitarian approach of the 1959 Act was to be modified to allow the introduction of Soviet-style *Spezialschulen* which would cater for exceptionally able pupils in a variety of fields. Another Soviet import, *Spezialklassen* in the high schools, which prepared above-average pupils for entry into the extended high schools, further increased the element of differentiation in the early 1960s.

These changes were codified in the third Education Act, the 'Law relating to the Unified System of Socialist Education' of February, 1965, which brought all the disparate elements of education and training together into one coherent scheme. The various ways of attaining the ultimate goal, higher education, included the extended high schools, numerous institutions providing vocational training, a range of extra-mural facilities, 'village academies', and so on. The periodization argument was further adduced to justify this second Act within six years. In 1963, the SED's revised party programme had proclaimed the victory of socialist conditions of production in the GDR;[14] the 1965 Act reinforced the claim that a new stage in the development of East German society, later termed 'developed socialism', had indeed been reached.

The 1963 party programme had also announced the SED's intention of achieving 'a well-educated nation'.[15] The stress on *Bildung*, the cognitive elements of the curriculum, during the early 1960s might be taken to indicate that formal schooling in the traditional sense was gaining ground, an impression reinforced by the increased prominence accorded to the subjects history and civics towards the end of the decade. Likewise, the inclusion of the *Leistungsprinzip*, that is, the principle of using assessed individual performance and other achievements as criteria for advancement, in Article 26 (1) of the 1968 constitution which listed the entry requirements for higher education, might be taken to imply that academic results were receiving more weight. The slump in the number of children from working-class homes successfully applying for places in the universities and colleges (declining from 52.7 per cent of the 1958 intake to 38.2 per cent in 1967) would also suggest a harder-headed preference for academic talent irrespective of class origins.[16] All these trends were in line with the bowing to economic necessity noted earlier. Nevertheless, there is no evidence that *Erziehung* in its narrower sense – socialist character-building through the medium of the curriculum – was being downgraded at this time. Successive ministerial directives specifically related to civics, which had now joined history and the chief source of Marxist–Leninist theory, stressed that this subject should, above all, stimulate the young to make their own individual contribution to the development of socialist society in the GDR, a willing and spontaneous contribution. This emphasis on unprompted activity – Margot Honecker described the role of civics as 'teaching Marxism in action' – [17] was intended to correct the overacademic tendencies in the generally wide curriculum. Teachers were further urged by the minister to be on their guard lest their pupils became *verintellektualisiert*, spoilt by excessive attention to the intellect.[18] At the same time, a balanced development of the emotions of the young alongside their powers of reasoning, the appeal to feelings of love for the socialist fatherland coupled with hatred of its opponents, for example, were included amongst the objectives of civics and history teaching which would curb sterile, abstract thinking and rouse the young to involve themselves in social action.[19] Greater use of the arts as a means of shaping socialist personalities was also recommended as a means of boosting the effective areas of the curriculum.[20]

With the introduction of the fully integrated system under the terms of the 1965 Act, the SED was able to determine more closely than ever before what went on in higher education, an area which had managed to maintain a degree of autonomy. A radical overhaul of the work of the universities and colleges was launched at the Fourth Higher Education Congress in 1967. Greater relevance to the real needs of society was demanded, research results were to be more speedily applied to production, and academic staff were expected to exert a more vigorous ideological influence over their students. In the ensuing Third Higher Education Reform, faculties were replaced by sections whose heads were acceptable to the SED, a *numerus clausus* system was introduced to control student intakes to all disciplines, and academic staff were made responsible for the implementation of party policy. The central principle shaping all courses was to be the unity of education and professional training. Students would follow a broad two-year foundation course, comprising an introduction to two chosen specialist subjects, Russian, science, social science, and an element of military training, followed by a further two-year period of vocationally orientated specialist subject studies. 'Profiling' of institutions would ensure that each would concentrate upon regionally relevant research areas and would teach a limited number of disciplines. Knowledge was to become a major factor in production, tightening the bonds between higher education and the working class and guaranteeing that teaching staffs would not be led astray into the potentially more academically satisfying pastures of pure research.[21]

The Seventh Education Congress held in 1970, over which Margot Honecker presided, provided a marked contrast with its turbulent predecessors. On this occasion, the minister took stock of a number of satisfying achievements. Within twenty years of assuming power, the SED had gained the structure of education it sought at all levels and could now exert increasing control over its content. In the more stable atmosphere which had followed the building of the Berlin Wall opposition from within the ranks of the teachers had virtually disappeared. The course of the SED's *Bildungspolitik* was set for a period of consolidation which would stretch well into the 1980s.[22]

When Erich Honecker replaced Ulbricht at the Seventh Party Congress in June 1971, the references to education in the new first

secretary's report echoed his wife's confident review of the fruits of the
1965 Act. The qualities of the new man – 'one of the noblest
aspirations and finest achievements of socialist society' – were
becoming increasingly felt in the everyday life of the GDR.[23] The main
difficulties lay in higher education, where the social and economic
justification for existing intake levels could not be found. Cuts here
would make way for improved standards of vocational training and an
increase in the numbers of specialists produced. This point was taken
up by Margot Honecker in her contribution to the congress. In the late
Ulbricht era, the false impression had been created that the high
schools and extended high schools were primarily concerned with the
preparation of young people for entry into higher education. Not only
had there been unwarranted numbers of university and college
entrants, but the representation of children from working-class homes
had declined markedly throughout the previous decade, a trend which
the minister was determined to reverse.[24]

In the meantime, the main task of the high schools was to shape
socialist personalities. The revised syllabuses for all subjects which
were being introduced at this time had been designed with this in mind,
and the process would be supplemented by an ever-growing number of
extra-curricular activities which would ensure that the work of the
classrooms continued in after-school hours.[25] This *inhaltliche Aus-
gestaltung* of the curriculum as a whole would make greater demands
than ever on teaching staffs. The necessary additional professional guidance was to be furnished by the newly formed Akademie der
Pädagogischen Wissenschaften (APW). This body's first major
publication in the field was the manual *Allgemeinbildung –
Lehrplanwerk – Unterricht,* which set out to become the *Oberschule*
teacher's vade-mecum, interpreting the new syllabuses, defining aims
and objectives and offering suggestions for methodology and
assessment in all subjects. The curriculum which had consisted of
'relatively isolated areas of knowledge' was now to be treated as a
whole.[26] Ideological awareness was to provide an all-pervasive
integrative force.[27] Subjects taught in unison were to be used to convey
the truths of Marxist–Leninism with all the conviction carried by the
exact sciences. Thus, a combination of history, civics and the German
language could amply demonstrate 'the wolf's law of capitalism' and,
with the addition of geography and German literature, could deepen
the conviction that the USSR would play the decisive role in the clash
with imperialism.[28] Each instance sought to enable pupils to perceive
the *Gesetzmässigkeiten* of the course of history, the truths of human
society which are as unshakable as the laws of the natural sciences.[29] A
second leading publication in the early 1970s was Gerhart Neuner's
Zur Theorie der sozialistischen Allgemeinbildung.[30] This work by the
president of the APW is of particular interest for its description of the

part played by *Erziehung* in bringing about communism. The character-building function of the schools can best be achieved by inculcating the attitudes of the working class and holding up its conduct for imitation:

> The attributes and attitudes of progressive workers are to be adopted by all children and young people. This means that certain features of communist morality which already inform the behaviour and thoughts of the most advanced members of the working class must serve as a model in the education and upbringing of all the young.[31]

The reference here to 'communist' behaviour in contexts where 'socialist' might normally appear is in keeping with a growing tendency during the early years of the Honecker era. Neuner himself declared that the transition from socialism to communism was becoming a 'tangible prospect for society',[32] presenting teachers with their most complex challenge so far. The 'upbringing of communist personalities' would require a qualitative change in the work and aspirations of the schools which would dominate educational debate in the years to come. Addressing a plenary session of the APW in 1974, Margot Honecker echoed Neuner's view, except that she preferred to insert a period of *reifer Sozialismus* between developed socialist society and the changeover to communism: 'We start from the belief that to-day's schoolchildren will live and work in a mature socialist society and will help shape the gradual transition to communist society'.[33] It is worthy of note that the important 'Youth Law of the GDR' *(Jugendgesetz)* which came into force at the time (28 January 1974), the articles of which dealt in considerable detail with the rights and duties of young people, made no reference to any epoch beyond developed socialism. Nevertheless, at the SED's Ninth Party Congress in 1976, the generally sanguine view of the GDR's progress towards communism was endorsed, both in addresses to the congress and in the new party programme launched on that occasion.[34] Whereas at the 1971 congress Erich Honecker had called for 'a high degree of effectiveness in socialist education';[35] he now proclaimed that the course the GDR was taking necessitated 'the perfecting of communist education' and went on to define what this would involve:

> Communist education means that the young must be made aware of the fundamental changes taking place in the world and the far-reaching social processes, must be enabled to judge correctly from the standpoint of the working class all the issues of our time and to make their own contribution to the progress of our society.[36]

The schools must concentrate on imparting 'communist morality', a 'truly communist attitude to work' and typical communist virtues such as 'discipline, organization, collectiveness, awareness of responsibilities and duties, conscientiousness, social activity and creativity'.[37] After the broader sweep of the first secretary's remarks, Margot Honecker's contribution to the congress was markedly down-to-earth. Socialist society was 'not yet complete', the greater material prosperity had not always been matched by a corresponding moral advance. Signs of opposition to the party's cause were still to be found in a society where indifference, egotistical behaviour and petty-bourgeois conformism had not been eliminated. Against this background, it was up to the schools and the home to combat the various forms of resistance:

> The signs of indolence, disinterest, reluctance to help and self-centred thinking which still exist do not arise naturally out of the way our society is developing, nor are they typical. These manifestations of a backward mentality, remnants of a society which is becoming obsolete, must be resolutely opposed in our education system.[38]

From the preceding it is clear that one searches in vain for essentially new characteristics which reveal the communist personality to be something distinct from its socialist predecessor. In one form or another the communist hallmarks which have been quoted have been associated on other occasions with socialist personalities, and they still are. The greater degree of intellectual and emotional commitment, the greater extent of the individual's affirmation of the SED's vision of a future society and the greater readiness to take part in its construction are perhaps at this stage the most we can hope to find when we look for distinguishing features. Communist personalities in the SED's image may already exist, but it is equally clear from Margot Honecker's earlier remarks that East German society still contains elements apparently unmoved by the party's ideals. This discrepancy between the aspirations of the SED and the reality of day-to-day life in East German schools may clearly be seen in Margot Honecker's address at the Eighth Education Congress held in the autumn of 1978. Some twenty years after its inception polytechnical education, which involved almost a million 13–16-year-olds, both boys and girls, in over 5,000 enterprises, continued to pose serious problems. The sites chosen for the UTP all too frequently were unable to combine practical experience with genuine production. The academic subjects supposed to link UTP experience with the work of the school, introduction to socialist production and technical drawing were failing in their purpose. When pupils were approaching their day in industry or agriculture enthusiastically and were developing positive attitudes to productive work, teaching staffs frequently failed to capitalize on the experience. The Minister of Education declared: 'It often happens that young people who are regarded as competent, creative, disciplined and comradely in their places of work receive poor marks for conduct in school'.[39] Other areas of the curriculum the minister criticized included civics, history, German and Russian language studies, all of which were unsuccessful in their attempts to relate the work of the classroom with everyday reality. The minister's severest criticism, however, was reserved for physical education where the less able pupils, a million or so of whom were not members of organized sports clubs, were being neglected.[40] All these shortcomings were mentioned again some three years later, when shortly after the SED's Tenth Party Congress in 1981, the Ministry of Education, the Teachers' Trade Union and the central council of the Freie Deutsche Jugend (FDJ) published an open letter in the weekly *Deutsche Lehrerzeitung*. The letter was particularly hard-hitting on the subject of staff commitment: 'No teacher may be content with mediocrity, intensive learning must be a feature of all lessons and discipline and order must prevail in every school'.[41]

Yet another area in which the party's intentions do not tally with actual developments in the GDR concerns the crucial area of the access of working-class children to higher education, which we have seen has been a central issue of SED *Bildungspolitik* from the very beginning. At the Ninth Party Congress in 1976, Erich Honecker announced that the intake trends of the late Ulbricht era had been reversed, that 55–60 per cent of university and college entrants and 60–65 per cent of technical students now came from working-class backgrounds.[42] In a critique of the GDR vision of 'real socialism', published in the West in the following year, however, Rudolf Bahro (see p. 83), now in exile but still a Marxist, asserted that individual opportunity in the GDR was just as 'unequally distributed as in late capitalist society'.[43] On the assumption that success in education largely depends on parental hopes and ambitions, Bahro also detected a low 'horizon of expectations' in East German working-class homes, a background against which children 'know they will remain workers'. In consequence: 'The existing division of labour is programmed into the educational system more rigidly in our society than under capitalism'.[44] If Bahro is right, and one suspects that he is, the home and family are continuing to exert much the same kind of influence upon children's careers as happens in Britain. The 'smallest cell' of socialist society may thus act as the last refuge and last remaining source of influence upon the young which runs counter to the incessant work of the two other major factors in upbringing, the school and the FDJ.

Every attempt is made to persuade parents that within the trio, school, youth movement and home, it is the first which bears the main responsibility in the field of upbringing, and it is the school which must

must guide and co-ordinate the work of the other two.[45] The marked increase in attention to *Familienerziehung* in recent years, however, reflects the party's awareness that the home continues to act as a powerful influence upon the young and a potential source of lasting opposition. The fact that the various parent-teacher associations at individual class and school level are dominated by members of the SED has not helped. Parents' evenings are not well supported, and attendance at special educational seminars aimed at parents remains sporadic.[46] A further disincentive to parental co-operation may well have come about with the introduction in 1978 and 1979 of *Wehrunterricht,* paramilitary training for all boys and girls in classes 9 and 10, the only major addition to the timetable of the high schools since 1965. Despite considerable opposition from the churches and known parental misgivings, this innovation was not widely publicized or debated beforehand.

Over 85 per cent of high-school leavers go on to undertake vocational training, generally lasting two years.[47] Regional variations and the effects of manpower planning mean that a choice of career is normally limited to substantially fewer than the two hundred or so specified occupational groups. Increasingly, trades are being brought together under one heading in a development similar to the trend towards multi-skilling in the West. These *Grundberufe* provide a broad basis of training in a general area, for example, the building trade, followed by a specialist skill which allows the trainee to become a bricklayer, electrician, carpenter, and so on. Ninety per cent of trainees complete the theoretical and practical final examinations. The standards reached are high, enabling vocational training as a whole in the GDR to be compared more than favourably with results in Britain or West Germany, for example. Nevertheless, here too the relatively slow responses of a system which proceeds by means of five-year plans have had their effect. Since the jobs for which young people have been trained do not always exist, they are increasingly being employed in areas for which they are untrained or which require no training.[48] Work, as such, has an almost mystic significance for the SED, but the task of providing creative labour for an entire population of the liberating and fulfilling kind that Marx envisaged, and which the party needs if it is to bring the new man into being, is proving more difficult than the programmatic statements of party congresses would have us believe.

With the exception of the 1974 *Jugendgesetz* there have been no major pieces of legislation or changes of direction during the Honecker era to equal the three Education Acts and three Higher Education Reforms which characterized the Ulbricht period. The pressures upon high-school teachers which were reflected in Margot Honecker's initiatives in the late 1970s were matched by similar efforts to exert greater control over the work of university and college staffs. The directive 'tasks of Universities and Colleges in the Developed Socialist Society',[49] which had its origins in a Politburo debate held in March 1980, demanded that higher-education research and teaching concentrate more closely than ever on supporting the economy and that research findings be translated into productive action 'without delay'. Increased efficiency of lecturers was to be achieved by the use of 'moral and material stimuli' and the SED's party organizations in the various sections of the institutions of higher education were exhorted to take more effective control of individual academic performance.[50] Minister of Higher Education H.–J. Böhme, at a university rectors' conference in 1981, followed this with a call for 'an even closer relationship between unequivocal ideological acceptance of the policies of the party and participation in their practical implementation in every activity in academic life'. University authorities were directed to confront staff who were unprepared or unable 'to meet fully their obligations to service, or who merely pay lip-service to the principles behind socialist higher education policy, whilst making little effort to put them into practice and succumb to the ideological positions of mediocrity'.[51] Higher cost-effectiveness in the performance of the universities and colleges and the avoidance of a surplus of trained students, as we saw earlier, has been sought by the SED since its Eighth Party Congress in 1971. The decision to reduce intakes has been carried out, both by lowering the numbers entering the extended high schools, the main route into higher education, and by raising standards in the university and college entrance examinations. Throughout the 1970s university numbers sank from the peak figure of nearly 161,000 in 1972 to around 127,000 by the end of the decade, with a slight upturn in 1981.[52] At the same time, the fostering of academic excellence, *Bestenförderung,* through a range of additional grants and other financial rewards, has ensured that the tradition of privileged treatment of gifted young people in earlier age-groups is maintained in higher education.

A brief comparison of developments in education in the Ulbricht and Honecker eras reveals striking contrasts. The resistance to the USSR's wholesale imposition of features of its system of education, the existence of a rival German tradition and its head-on clash with *Sowjetpädagogik,* the opposition to the SED at all levels from the Ministry of Education down, the regular dismissals of ministers of education and the purging of leading functionaries were all part of what has been called in an official history of GDR education 'die stürmische Entwicklung unseres Volksbildungswesens' during the Ulbricht period.[53] There is no longer any question of the GDR's failure to accept Soviet theoretical leadership in matters educational, and there are even signs of a growing respect for East German achievements in this field amongst other Eastern European states, particularly for its approach to polytechnical education. The USSR itself has, furthermore, recently taken the decision to go over to the ten-year period for general education which has existed in the GDR since 1959. Under Honecker, outright hostility from the teaching profession has gone; lack of co-operation is now the worst the party has to contend with. By contrast with her predecessors, Margot Honecker has retained the post she assumed in 1965 and thus has joined the ranks of the longer-serving ministers in the Eastern bloc. The SED's party organizations within the schools and colleges, together with its allies, the trade unions to which all professional academics belong, and the FDJ, of which the vast majority of pupils and students are members, have likewise become greater forces of stability as they extend their influence over the affairs of the various institutions.

The very tempestuousness of the Ulbricht years, however, largely disguised the fact that the real issue at stake, the education and upbringing of a new kind of human being whose efforts would make socialist society function and who would genuinely prepare the ground for communism, had yet to be faced. In the relatively calmer waters of East German society since 1971, the solution to the problem of turning the vision into reality, in spite of massive financial investment, ceaseless propaganda in the media and wide support from the arts, does not seem at this point to be within the SED's grasp. The legacy from the Ulbricht era was a homogeneous structure of education and an alignment of its content with Marxist–Leninist theory. Nearly forty years on from the SED's assumption of power, the results of the efforts within this framework to breathe life into the new man, together with the disappointing performance of an economy whose problems the revolution in education and the transformed attitude to work were meant to solve, suggest that a credible transition to communism in the GDR is not in prospect during the present century.

Notes: Chapter 4

1 Hermann, Weber, *Kleine Geschichte der DDR*, (Cologne, 1980), p. 47.
2 *Die neue schule*, no. 13 (1949), p. 419.
3 Gottfried Uhlig *et al.*, *Zur Entwicklung des Volksbildungswesens in der Deutschen Demokratischen Republik in den Jahren 1949–1956*, Monumenta Paedagogica series, Vol. 14, (Berlin, 1974), pp. 174, 238.
4 *Dokumente der Sozialistischen Einheitspartei Deutschlands*, Vol. 4 (Berlin, 1954), pp. 116 f.
5 Uhlig *et al.*, *Zur Entwicklung*, p. 75.
6 For a full definition of these terms see Georg Klaus, and Manfred Buhr, *Philosophisches Wörterbuch*, 2 vols (Leipzig, 1975).

7   See Martin McCauley, *Marxism–Leninism in the German Democratic Republic. The Socialist Unity Party (SED)* (London, 1979), pp. 78 f. See also Uhlig *et al.*, *Zur Entwicklung*, p. 176.
8   See John Dunstan, *Paths to Excellence and the Soviet School* (Windsor, Bucks, 1978), p. 28.
9   Siegfried Baske and Martha Engelbert, *Zwei Jahrzehnte Bildungspolitik in der Sowjetzone Deutschlands*, Vol. 2 (Berlin and Heidelberg, 1966), p. 305.
10   S. Doernberg, *Kurze Geschichte der DDR* (Berlin, 1964), pp. 295 f.
11   Gerhart Neuner, 'Einige Probleme der sozialistischen Pädagogik der DDR nach dem XXII. Parteitag der KPdSU und der 14. Tagung des ZK der SED', *Pädagogik*, no. 4 (April 1962), p. 312.
12   Baske and Engelbert, *Zwei Jahrzehnte*, p. 216.
13   Karl Marx, *Capital*, Vol. 1, trans. Ben Fowkes (Harmondsworth, Middx, 1976), p. 618.
14   *Programm der Sozialistischen Einheitspartei Deutschlands* (Berlin, 1963), p. 69.
15   ibid., p. 128.
16   See Arthur Hearnden, *Education in the Two Germanies* (Oxford, 1974), app. 6.
17   Margot Honecker, 'Mehr Konkretheit in der Leitungsarbeit', *Deutsche Lehrerzeitung*, no. 20 (1969), *DLZ-Information* [supplement], p. 9.
18   'Verstand und Gerfühl harmonisch entwickeln', *Deutsche Lehrerzeitung*, no. 21 1971, *DLZ-Information* [supplement], p. 4.
19   ibid.
20   'Die weitere Entwicklung der marxistisch–leninistischen Gesellschaftswissenschaften in der DDR. Beschluss des ZK der SED vom 22. Oktober 1968', *Einheit*, no. 12 (December 1968), p. 1458.
21   Karl-Heinz Günther and Christine Lost, *Dokumente zur Geschichte des Schulwesens in der Deutschen Demokratischen Republik. Teil 3: 1968–1972/3*, Monumenta Paedagogica series, vol. 16/1, (Berlin, 1974), p. 131.
22   ibid., p. 313.
23   *VIII. Parteitag der Sozialistischen Einheitspartei Deutschlands, Berlin, 15. bis 19. Juni 1971. Bericht des Zentralkomitees an den VIII. Parteitag der Sozialistischen Einheitspartei Deutschlands. Berichterstatter Erich Honecker* (Berlin, 1971), p. 70.
24   See note 16 above.
25   Günther and Lost, *Dokumente*, p. 31.
26   Gerhart Neuner, *et al.*, *Allgemeinbildung – Lehrplanwerk – Unterricht* (Berlin 1973), p. 41.
27   ibid., p. 42.
28   ibid., pp. 52, 80.
29   ibid., p. 80.
30   Gerhart Neuner, *Zur Theorie der sozialistischen Allgemeinbildung*, 3rd edn (Berlin 1975).
31   ibid., p. 64.
32   Siegfried Baske, *Bildungspolitik in der DDR 1963–1976* (Berlin and Wiesbaden, 1979), p. 371.
33   ibid., p. 398.
34   *Programm der Sozialistischen Einheitspartei Deutschlands* (Berlin, 1976), p. 9.
35   op. cit. at n. 23, p. 72.
36   *IX. Parteitag der Sozialistischen Einheitspartei Deutschlands, Berlin, 18. bis 22. Mai 1976. Bericht des Zentralkomitees an den IX. Parteitag der SED. Berichterstatter Erich Honecker* (Berlin, 1976), p. 98.
37   ibid.
38   'Unsere Jugend zu guten Kommunisten erziehen', *Neues Deutschland*, 21 May 1976, p. 3.
39   'Der gesellschaftliche Auftrag unserer Schule. Referat von Margot Honecker, Minister für Volksbildung auf dem VIII. Pädagogischen Kongress' *Deutsche*

Lehrerzeitung, no. 43 (1978), *DLZ-Information* [supplement], p. 16.
40 ibid., p. 22.
41 'Offener Brief an alle Pädagogen der Deutschen Demokratischen Republik', *Deutsche Lehrerzeitung,* no. 21 (1981), p. 6.
42 op. cit at n. 36, p. 38.
43 Rudolf Bahro, *Die Alternative. Zur Kritik des real existierenden Sozialismus* (Cologne, 1977), pp. 178 f.
44 ibid., p. 284.
45 Eberhard Mannschatz, *Einführung in die sozialistische Familienerziehung* (Berlin, 1971), p. 22.
46 See *Deutsche Lehrerzeitung,* no. 46 (1979), p. 4.
47 *Neues Deutschland,* 17/18 January 1981, p. 5.
48 See Jan Kuhnert, 'Überqualifikation oder Bildungsvorlauf?', *Deutschlandarchiv,* no. 5 (1983), p. 505.
49 'Beschluss des Politbüros des ZK der SED vom 18. März 1980. Aufgaben der Universitäten und Hochschulen in der entwickelten sozialistischen Gesellschaft', *Neues Deutschland,* 20 March 1980, pp. 3 f.
50 ibid., p. 4.
51 Bundesministerium für inner-deutsche Beziehungen, Informationen, no. 21 (1981), p. 10.
52 *Statistisches Jahrbuch der DDR 1982* (East Berlin, 1983), p. 51.
53 Karl-Heinz Günther and Gottfried Uhlig, *Geschichte der Schule in der Deutschen Demokratischen Republik 1945 bis 1971* (Berlin, 1974), p. 127.

5

The Church in the German Democratic Republic

ROLAND SMITH

Introduction

Marxism and Religion

In a famous passage in his *Critique of Hegel's Philosophy of Right* Marx wrote:

> Religion is both the expression of real distress and the protest against real distress. Religion is the sigh of the oppressed creature, the heart of a heartless world and the spirit of a spiritless situation. It is the opium of the people. The abolition of religion as the illusory happiness of the people is required for their real happiness.[1]

He remained scornfully dismissive of organized religion to the end of his days but, as this quotation indicates, ever mindful of the very real human need which had brought it about in the first place. He was against attacking religion directly, which he felt would be a waste of effort; instead, attention should be directed to bringing to an end the exploitation of man which had brought about his alienation and of which religion was but one manifestation.

The very word 'alienation', with its metaphysical and indeed religious overtones, reminds us, however, that we are dealing with a much more complex relationship than might at first sight appear. Marx was himself the grandson of a rabbi and there is more than a touch of Old Testament fervour in his writing. This can be found, too, among many of his followers and it has long been a paradox that, while utterly rejecting any kind of belief in God or the supernatural, Marxism has itself taken over many of the attributes of religion, specifically its moral dynamism, its crusading zeal and its total claim to absolute truth and personal allegiance.

The Church in the USSR

Lenin, who had the job of adapting Marxism to a society very different from that which Marx had envisaged, took a still more caustic view of religion: 'Autocracy cannot do without its twin agents, a hangman and a priest; the first to suppress popular resistance by force, the second to sweeten and embellish the lot of the oppressed by empty promises of a heavenly kingdom'.[2]

His most venomous remarks were reserved for the clergy of the orthodox Church, whom he called 'gendarmes in cassocks', though he, too, was against mounting a full-scale onslaught on the church lest this should create martyrs and bring about a coalition of opponents. Fully convinced as he was that religion deserved to die out and thoroughly willing to help the process along, Lenin thus followed a basically pragmatic policy. Nevertheless, the power of the church was drastically reduced by a measure introduced in January 1918 which, among other things, deprived the clergy of the right to vote, along with capitalists, criminals and imbeciles, and which in effect meant they had no claim to food rations nor their children to education. They also suffered severely in the often desperate conditions of the Civil War and its aftermath; in the years between 1917 and 1923 some 1,200 priests and 28 bishops met their deaths.[3]

On another, more intellectual front scientific atheism was put forward as the only possible view worthy of man, and religious faith was decried as something primitive and irrational, not in keeping with human dignity or pretensions. On Easter Day 1925, the League of Militant Godless had its first congress, one of its assignments being to devise secular substitutes for traditional religious rites.

Under Stalin the church suffered, as did other institutions, being specifically affected by a new Law on Religious Association which was passed in 1929 and which considerably reduced the already limited area of activity allowed. It might have been the prelude to a total ban on all religious practice but the German assault on the USSR in 1941 changed all this at a stroke. Almost overnight the church became the cherished, if subordinate, ally of the state, a situation which did not materially change until after Stalin's death in 1953.

The Church in Eastern Europe since 1945

When the USSR extended its sphere of influence to cover the whole of Eastern Europe in 1945 there came under its control a wide variety of societies and religious faiths, including some 60 million Roman Catholics, 30 million Orthodox, over 20 million Protestants and some Muslims. The Jews, who had been very strongly represented here, particularly in Poland, had of course all but vanished from the scene.

While the particular situation varied from country to country it would seem that, broadly speaking, policy followed generally similar lines. There was an initial honeymoon period in which all anti-fascist, democratic factions were embraced and in which the church, too, was welcome, particularly if, as in Poland, it had been active in the resistance to the Germans. Then, when the various communist parties had managed to consolidate their hold on power, there was a sharp deterioration in relations with the harassment or persecution of believers, the detention of some church leaders and the attempt by the state to set up splinter or front organizations which would work in harmony with the authorities. Things eased in this, as in every respect, with Stalin's death and following deStalinization in 1956 the churches were able to win back a good deal of power and influence. At the end of the 1950s there was a flurry of anti-religious activity, initiated by the ebullient Nikita Khrushchev but since then things have settled down to a situation of trench warfare, with no great offensives being undertaken by either side.

Having made such a sweeping generalization it is important to add immediately that in detail the situation is infinitely more complicated, the variations, as between one country and another, being enormous. Thus in 1967 there was an official proclamation in Albania that this was henceforth to be the first atheist state in the world, all buildings used for public worship were closed, all religious practices forbidden and in 1973 a priest was sentenced to death for baptizing a fellow prisoner's child. He was said to have been found guilty of 'subversive activities designed to overthrow the State'.[4] Coming a little nearer home, we find a quite vicious campaign being conducted against the Roman Catholic Church in Czechoslovakia in the name of 'normalization',[5] whereas the church in Poland goes from strength to strength and is indeed much stronger than it has ever been.

The Church and State in the GDR 1945–78

The Situation in 1945

A key difference between the occupation of Germany and that of all the other Central and East European countries, with the single exception of Austria, was that the former was undertaken by armies from both East and West and only slowly did institutions emerge which corresponded to the new division of the country. The part taken over by the Red Army, as it happened, was precisely the region of Germany which was most staunchly Protestant of all, some 15 million of the 16.5 million population being members of the Evangelical Churches,[6] 1.2 million Roman Catholics and the rest 'Free Churches' and 'sects'.[7] As yet there was no central authority for the various Protestant Churches anywhere in Germany but simply the regional churches (*Landes-kirchen*), eight of which were located in the Soviet Zone. Not until 1948 was the Evangelical Church of Germany (Evangelische Kirche Deutschland – EKD), created as an umbrella organization for the whole country and it was to take another twenty-one years for a specific GDR Protestant organization to develop.

The Need for the Church

What was indisputable was human need. The humorous writer, Tucholsky, says somewhere that man has two basic attitudes, one when things go well and the other when they go badly; the second one he calls 'religion'. By this criterion there was plenty of demand for the ministrations of the church in the GDR in 1945 for, as well as the large numbers of dead and missing, the devastation of the towns and the constantly growing numbers of refugees that were common to both parts of the country, the Soviet Zone had special horrors that were all its own. The fierce initial onslaught of the Red Army had been followed by a brief but traumatic orgy of looting and raping – it was estimated by doctors in the summer of 1945 that half the female population of Berlin between the ages of 16 and 60 had been raped at least once – while confiscation of property on a large scale and mass arrests continued until well into 1946. The consequence was a deep-rooted sense of insecurity and depression which led immediately to a wave of suicides, which was a prime factor in inducing many to go over to the West and which, it is claimed by some observers, can still be detected in the GDR today.

In all this the church was of key importance since it was the only place people could turn to in their distress and where they could find the fellowship of others who had been through the same experiences. There is a graphic description in Kempowski's *Uns geht's ja noch gold* of the scene in church on the first Sunday after the cessation of hostilities, in this case the badly damaged Marienkirche in Rostock, when the packed congregation sing and sing their last Lutheran hymn, hoping it will never end, but then when the service does finish, coming together to hear who has been raped, who has been killed and who has been fetched by the occupation forces, before stumbling out to face an unbearable world outside.[9]

Such a situation must have been common all over the GDR and initially the activities of the church seemed to be viewed with favour in official quarters. The Communist Party Manifesto, published in June 1945, seemed concerned to protect the German way of life, the CDU, which was founded on the 26 June, had as one of its objects the representation of Christians in public affairs and the church was specifically exempted from the land reform which was carried out in 1945 and 1946 and which broke up all large holdings and split them up among small farmers. The church was also invited to join in the all-party talks which were being held with a view to establishing a single, non-partisan youth movement.

The Screw Tightens 1946–53

This is not to say that life was easy for the church. Added to the material hardship and deprivation which were the lot of all in the Soviet Zone save only for the party select, there were the problems of finding buildings for worship and of getting hold of enough paper even to communicate the most basic items of information, let alone the publication of books or journals – problems which were to prove perennial in the GDR.

In addition there were the restrictions imposed by the authorities, the obligation to report all gatherings of people not coming together exclusively for the purpose of worship and the harassment of those travelling to and from the Western Zones, which affected particularly clergy and lay people wishing to attend the great national congresses (*Kirchentage*) which are so much a feature of German church life. Another group involved were the many delegates to the various conferences and working parties for the establishment of the EKD which was proclaimed in 1948 and which brought all the main Protestant Churches together in one organization.

More serious than this was the conflict over education. After the experience with the Nazis there were many in the church who wished to found their own schools and revert to an earlier German tradition. This was rendered impossible by the Law for the Democratization of German Schools, passed in 1946, which forbade the setting-up of any kind of educational institution apart from that provided by the state. Within the schools themselves Christian teaching became more and more difficult as both pupils and teachers were discriminated against. In 1951 the study of Marxism–Leninism under the title of 'social science' (*Gesellschaftswissenschaft*) was first introduced in all schools and then made compulsory, and by the end of 1952 virtually all religious instruction at school had ceased.

Still more dramatic than this was the treatment meted out to the Junge Gemeinde, the church's group for the young, which was treated as a separate organization and hence as a rival to the official youth movement, the FDJ. As time wore on it came increasingly under attack, its members accused of being the agents or dupes of Anglo-American imperialism and liable to expulsion from school or university, its meetings disrupted by the FDJ and some of its leaders given prison sentences – a fate shared also by the various Christian groups at the universities.

So bad did things get in the early 1950s indeed, with the blitz on young people's organizations, the confiscation of some church property, interference with pastoral work in homes and hospitals and the increasing harassment of church meetings that it seemed as if a full-scale onslaught was in course of preparation. The point has to be made, however, that in this as in other respects things were never so bad as they were in some of the other socialist countries, notably Hungary and Czechoslovakia. Thus there were no full-scale show trials such as occurred in those two states, presumably because of the 'open frontier' in Berlin and the disastrous impact that would have had on a situation where thousands were already fleeing to the West every year. Stalin's death in 1953 eventually brought about a general relaxation of tension all round.

The Later 1950s

The later 1950s, with their promise of a new orientation for Eastern Europe as a whole, especially after Khrushchev's deStalinization programme of 1956, brought two issues to a head in the GDR: *Jugendweihe* and the Military Chaplains' Treaty.

Jugendweihe (literally 'youth dedication') is, as its name suggests, an initiation rite, a secular equivalent to confirmation for 14-year-olds in which the participant makes an affirmation to the state, to socialism, to friendship with the USSR, and pledges himself to give of his best both at school and at work. It was launched in 1954, together with an appeal by two senior members of the cultural establishment, J. R. Becher and Anna Seghers. The church objected, not so much to the actual *Jugendweihe* itself as to the markedly atheistic nature of the ten hours of preparation for the ceremony with such chapter headings in the textbook as 'There is no room for God in the Universe' or, after the first manned orbits in the 1960s, 'We were in space but we could not find God anywhere'.

The church decided to make a stand on principle and declared that no one who went to these classes would be admitted for confirmation, whereupon the state countered with the charge that *Jugendweihe* was simply a private arrangement and that the church was in fact infringing the provisions of the constitution. This was a particularly brazen allegation in view of the fact that, at the same time, more and more pressure was being put on young people to undergo *Jugendweihe,* such that from 1958 on it was virtually obligatory for everyone and has remained so ever since. The church maintained its stand as long as it could, but the number of confirmations began to drop sharply and it became clear that if it persisted it would simply be hastening its own decline by denying itself new members. The embargo on *Jugendweihe* was therefore dropped and since the early 1970s this is now undertaken by some 97 per cent of young people.

Perhaps more than any other single episode the *Jugendweihe* affair showed clearly the limits of the church's power. It was, after all, a battle fought on ground of the church's own choosing but when it came to the crunch most of its troops deserted because they were not willing to risk their careers and prospects, not to mention those of their children, for a matter of principle.

The second great issue of the later 1950s was the Military Chaplains' Treaty. This was the agreement signed in West Germany in 1957 between, on the one hand, Adenauer and Strauss representing the Federal Government and, on the other, Otto Dibelius representing the EKD, to provide military padrés for the West German armed forces. Since the Evangelical Churches in the GDR were themselves constituent members of the EKD this provoked a great outcry in leading government circles in the GDR and the insistence that the Protestant Church in the GDR should formally and collectively disassociate from the 'NATO Church' in West Germany. Pressure was put on individual pastors to sign declarations and an attempt was made to encourage breakaway groups, but the church managed to preserve a fairly united front and even dared to make a counter-proposal to Walter Ulbricht, the first secretary of the party, that it was quite willing to ensure absolute fairness by supplying chaplains also to the Nationale Volksarmee (NVA), the East German Army. Needless to say, the offer was never taken up.

A Separate Church for the GDR

When the final break between the Protestant Churches of the GDR and West Germany did come it was at a time of the church's own choosing and satisfied at least the Marxist criterion of freedom, that of the recognition of necessity.

The background was that the EKD, as an all-German body, was finding itself having increasingly to deal with two quite separate and ever more diverging situations in the form of the two German states. The problem was made even more acute with the building of the Berlin Wall in 1961 since it was now physically impossible for the church ever to meet as one body, so the Synod was split into two parts, one East and one West, each having equal authority but meeting separately. This was an inherently unsatisfactory state of affairs and as the 1960s progressed and it grew increasingly apparent that reunification would not take place in the foreseeable future, the decision was taken to form the League of Evangelical Churches in the GDR (Bund der evangelischen Kirchen der DDR – BEK) in 1969.

It must be emphasized that this was neither the result of a disagreement between the two wings of the church nor the immediate consequence of pressure by the state but a decision from within, even though very reluctantly arrived at, since it meant that the last institutional tie between the two Germanies was now broken. Curiously enough, for all the emphasis on *Abgrenzung* that was now beginning to appear, the GDR authorities did not particularly welcome the move and it was to take some two years before the BEK was officially recognized by the State.

Undoubtedly this new development marked something that was also happening within the Church itself. By the time the BEK split off, it was some twenty-five years after the end of the war, and inevitably the former type of Protestant clergyman, firmly rooted in the past and basically defensive, if not actively hostile to much of what was going on around him, was beginning to be replaced by a new generation, no less committed as Christians but who had grown up in very different circumstances. Many of them had never known a united Germany and they saw their prime duty as being towards their own local community and the wider society of the GDR. Unencumbered with the ideological baggage of the past they were often no less fiercely critical of the state than their predecessors had been; the difference was that they shared many of the state's assumptions, not least that the state itself was here to stay. Their attitude is best summed up in the phrase 'The church in socialism' (*Die Kirche im Sozialismus*), the implication being that the church is willing to play a role within the overall political framework but that it expects to be taken seriously as a partner, and it must have been the evidence of this difference of approach that induced the state to accept the new situation.

The Meeting of 6 March 1978

On 6 March 1978 there took place an event which, it was hoped, would usher in a new era in relations between church and state. This was a meeting between the first secretary of the party and head of state, Erich Honecker, and the executive committee of the BEK under the chairmanship of Bishop Albrecht Schönherr.

Honecker began by emphasizing the common ground between church and state in respect of charitable work within the GDR, the humanitarian mission to the Third World and the search for peace. The church leaders, for their part, emphasized the importance of equal respect and of equal treatment for all denominations. Fine words were all very well but what really mattered was the experience of the individual Christian in the street. Honecker replied by putting forward a list of some ten concessions the state was willing to make:

(1)   The church would be allowed to put up buildings in new towns and new estates.
(2)   The church would be allowed access to TV for certain special occasions.
(3)   There would be help for the restoration of certain church memorials.
(4)   Access would be allowed to prisons for part-time chaplains.
(5)   Clergy and church workers would be eligible for state pensions.
(6)   Permission would be given for the import of some church literature from the West.
(7)   Support would be given for the church to run its own kindergartens.
(8)   The church to receive rent for the use of some 100,000 acres of its agricultural land by the state.
(9)   Church cemeteries to receive financial support from the state.
(10) The clergy to be allowed to visit old people's homes outside visiting hours.

Obviously some of these concessions are more important than others but they still add up to quite a sizeable package and, at the time, it was hailed as a breakthrough and as providing a model of what relations should be between church and state in a socialist country. It was undeniably the first meeting between the head of state and the leaders of a national church that had taken place anywhere in Eastern Europe since 1945 and it came so unexpectedly that the observer feels impelled to ask why the state should have taken such an initiative at this juncture.

To answer this we have to look at the overall situation in the GDR in 1978. In 1976 there had been the Biermann Affair which had unleashed an unparalleled storm of protest among literary people and shaken the cultural establishment to its foundations. In 1977 the dissident, Rudolf Bahro (see p. 83), had been arrested for publishing a book in the West with whose analysis many intellectuals in the GDR were in agreement. There was also considerable dissatisfaction among the public at large with the introduction of the Intershops and the virtual adoption of a second currency, the D-Mark, which favoured those who had connections with the West. Finally, there was the memory of Pastor Brüsewitz who, in 1976, had poured petrol over himself in Zeitz in Saxony and had then set light to it in protest against the state's treatment of the church, an example followed in 1978 by another Protestant pastor, Rolf Gunther. It may well have been the general air of uncertainty which prompted Honecker to seek stability on at least one front by coming to an agreement with the church.

The Catholic Church and the State

The territory now making up the GDR was, before the war, one where Roman Catholics were less well represented among the population at large than in any area of comparable size in the German-speaking world, no more than 1.2 million out of a total indigenous count of 16.5 million. In 1945 there was a sudden influx of Catholic refugees from Silesia and the Sudetenland to bring the numbers up to the 2 million mark.

The initial difficulty was thus one of accommodation, given the condition of buildings generally and the total lack of new construction work. Thus all that could be done was the patching up of the existing churches and their intensive use, though there was often some hospitality provided by local Protestant churches. A further problem was the shortage of priests, as there were no Catholic colleges or seminaries anywhere in the Soviet Zone and aspiring candidates had to be sent for training to Fulda, Paderborn, or other places in West Germany. After 1951 the situation became impossible as the GDR government refused to allow them back in, but after strong representations permission was finally given for the church to set up a seminary in Erfurt, which has remained the main source of new recruits ever since.

Apart from such episodes and a number of relatively minor incidents, the new regime showed itself wary of tangling with the Catholic Church. The closed religious orders for women continued much as before, there was no attempt to set up bogus front organizations such as happened in Czechoslovakia, and the lines of communication from East Berlin church headquarters to the Vatican remained undisturbed regardless of what happened to those to West Berlin. For its part, the church seemed willing to keep out of public affairs, limiting itself to the pastoral care of its own flock, viewing the willingness of the Protestant Churches to rush into dialogue with the state with some scepticism and remaining suspicious of the whole notion of the 'church in socialism'.

The one major area of dispute between state and church had to do with the ecclesiastical boundaries of the latter which, it was alleged, took no account of the political frontiers of the new state and thus offended diplomatic susceptibilities. It was a somewhat abstract argument because it concerned essentially matters of law and, in practice, the Roman Catholic Church, which has always displayed an admirable sense of the pragmatic, worked within the new political framework. It led to the charge, however, that the church was in league with the 'revanchists' and was unable to adjust to the new situation in Europe. Attempts by the bishops and clergy of Germany and Poland to seek reconciliation with each other were also viewed by the party with deep suspicion, as being attempts to undermine its prerogative of determining the guidelines of foreign policy. Once the Federal German–Polish Treaty of 1970 and the East–West German Basic Treaty of 1973 had been signed, the church proved willing enough to give virtually full acceptance to the existing boundaries.

It might thus seem that in the mid-1970s an era of complete harmony had dawned in the relations between state and church, but in recent years there have been signs of a certain restlessness among the Catholic community in the GDR. It may well be that an awareness of the events in Poland has played a part in this, as has also the new mood of self-confidence which Pope John Paul II has engendered in the Catholic Church worldwide. Whatever the reason, there can be no doubt that Catholic voices have begun to be heard in public debate to an extent previously unknown in the GDR and nowhere is this more true than in respect of the peace issue.[10]

The Situation of the Churches Today

Yaroslavsky, the first chairman of the Soviet League of Militant Godless, is reported to have said once, 'religion is like a nail, the harder you hit it the deeper it goes', and certainly the situation of the church today after nearly forty years of communist rule cannot but strike us as being surprisingly favourable. First, there has not been a dramatic change in the climate of opinion to bring about a new, secular way of life and thought. Whereas in the late 1940s some bold spirits were advocating the abolition of Christmas and its replacement by a new feast combining the winter solstice with the celebration of Stalin's birthday on 22 December,[11] today Christmas in the GDR is observed with just as much relish as in West Germany. The decay of Marxism–Leninism as a system of thought (what Havemann refers to as the 'sclerosis of Marxism') has meant that the discipline of scientific atheism is nowhere taken seriously and, most encouraging of all, the leading spirits among the young regard religion as something fresh and stimulating, an exciting challenge.

The church is the one and only organization allowed to exist independently of the party and state machine. It has a legal status and it is the only body outside the official ones which has the right of free assembly. It also receives a considerable amount of state aid in the form of upkeep for its buildings and pension funds for its clergy and church workers. It is allowed to collect its own tax (*Kirchensteuer*), it is a considerable landowner, to the tune of some 500,000 acres, the buildings it uses are its own property and it is allowed to put up new ones. The Evangelical Churches also benefit from having six theological faculties at the universities paid for entirely by the state[12] and have access to both radio and television.

The BEK continues to enjoy excellent relations with its sister organization, the Evangelical Church in West Germany (Evangelische Kirche Deutschlands – EKD) and receives a considerable amount of financial assistance from that body. The BEK is also represented on the World Council of Churches and it commands a wide measure of respect in international circles where it is regarded as a spokesman for the socialist countries but as being much less subservient to its political masters than is its Russian Orthodox counterpart.

Last but not least, the Catholic and Evangelical Churches receive a good deal of support from the public for the work they do at home, both the BEK and the Catholics providing and staffing a number of homes and hospitals. Indeed, in certain areas, notably the care of the old and decrepit, the physically and mentally handicapped, the psychologically disturbed, alcoholics and social outcasts it plays such a major part that the state services would be very hard-pressed without them, an interesting point being that much of the finance for this work comes from the contact with churches in West Germany.

This is not, however, to say that all is rosy. The apparently irreversible tide of secularism has affected the church in the GDR no less than that in the West. It is notoriously difficult to quantify churchgoing and belief, and there is the special problem in the GDR that the last census was taken in 1964. At that time some 10 million people pronounced themselves Protestant and 1.2 million as Catholic but the pace of secularization has not yet perceptibly slowed and a number of observers would put the Protestant figure now at around 5 million and Catholics at no more than 600,000.[13]

Whatever the exact figures may be, it seems clear that in this old home of Protestantism, the Lutheran heartland, the Christian faith is now professed by a minority, of which the greater part is not active. The fact is that the Protestant Church has never been able to keep its hold on the working class in the way the Catholic Church can, most notably of course in Poland. This has been exacerbated in recent years with the increase in materialism as consumer values have largely taken over and, combined with the general disinclination to stir abroad once the front door has been shut, has militated against activity on the church's behalf.

A further disappointment has been the relative lack of progress on the ecumenical front at home. In a society where all denominations have been beleaguered there has not, in general, been the coming together of Catholic and Protestant one might have expected. Even the discussions between the Lutheran and Reformed wings of the BEK, in which the regional churches or *Landeskirchen* have full autonomy, have not yet achieved full intercommunion.

When all is said and done, however, the greatest problem for the church remains the state and the relentless pressure to conform it generates. This both discourages the individual from playing a full part in church life, since he knows it may have disadvantages for him, and also has the effect of constantly pushing the church into a predetermined spiritual cum pastoral role, with no say in public life other than that of providing the odd token minister for some state function. This would effectively make the church into a ghetto, where well-meaning but ineffectual souls huddle together for warmth, a criticism which has, on occasion in the past, been levelled at the Roman Catholics in the GDR.

The Peace Movement and the Church

What has effectively prevented this from happening has been the eruption on the scene of the Peace Movement with which the church has become involved and which has not only stirred up the political situation but has embroiled church and state in a way which could hardly have been foreseen a few years ago.

The term 'Peace Movement' itself needs breaking down into different elements of which the first might be termed the protest against the militarization of GDR society. This has come about because, at the same time as the state has steadily propagated peace as an aim over the last twenty-five years, there has been an ever-increasing emphasis on military preparedness in every walk of life with the slogan 'Peace must be defended, peace must be armed' (Der Friede muss verteidigt werden, der Friede muss bewaffnet sein).

This process starts at the pre-school stage with the provision of a large number of military toys, ranging from uniforms for dolls to quite sophisticated gadgets such as remote-controlled tanks. It continues at school with explicitly military exercises, such as the throwing of dummy hand grenades as a normal part of the P. E. curriculum, the Hans Beimler competitions, which are manoeuvres conducted jointly by the FDJ and the para-military Society for Sport and Technology (Gesellschaft für Sport und Technik – GST), weekly parades in FDJ uniform for the whole school and frequent visits by professional recruiting agents to induce the brightest pupils to sign on as professional officers and NCOs in the armed services. More insidious than this, perhaps, is the use of military examples in subjects that have ostensibly nothing to do with war, such as the following example from a geometry book:

> In an NVA exercise an observer sees two enemy machine-gun posts A and B at an angle of 130^0. He hears a burst of fire from A eight seconds after the flash and from B after seven seconds. How far are the two machine-gun posts from each other?[14]

What upset the church even more than all this, however, was the introduction in 1978 of compulsory defence studies (*Wehrkundeunterricht*) as a standard school subject for classes nine and ten at school, that is, for all 15- and 16-year-olds. The subject is split into two parts, a theoretical one covering such topics as 'Why and how imperialists start wars', done at school, and a practical one, done at camp, which is taken separately by boys and girls, the latter receiving instruction in first aid and civil defence and the boys undertaking small arms training with live weapons.

It was this latter point which particularly upset the church, especially as the subject was introduced in September 1978, the same year in which such accord seemed to have been reached with Erich Honecker in March. Representations were made immediately, stating that it was not possible to accept as an integral and compulsory part of school studies a subject which accustomed pupils to divide people and countries up into friend or foe categories and which taught 15-year-old boys to kill as part of their normal education, a practice which was to be found nowhere else in the world and which could not but undermine the credibility of the GDR as a peace-loving country.

Needless to say, such protests have so far had no effect and defence studies have remained on the school syllabus. The official reasons for this are that, while the subject is compulsory, no boy is ever actually forced to use weapons, he can always opt to do civil defence with the girls instead, but this presupposes of course, first, that 15-year-old boys are able to resist the pressure to conform and, secondly, that there will be no serious consequences for them if they do, something on which past experience with the FDJ and the *Jugendweihe* is less than encouraging.

The second major issue on which church and state have been at loggerheads is that of an alternative to military service entitled 'social peace service' (*sozialer Friedensdienst*). The background to this is that military conscription for males was introduced in 1962. It was estimated then that some 3,300 young men refused to serve and in 1964 the institution of the construction units (*Bausoldaten*) was introduced. These are unarmed auxiliary units used mainly on building work and other support services but still subject to military discipline and military law.

Very little publicity was given to them; the average conscript probably remained unaware of their existence and their numbers at first remained quite small, at around 350 a year. Nevertheless, the concentration of these dissenters had its inevitable effect and such units tended to become centres for the dissemination of information. The consequence was that not only did the number of such *Bausoldaten* double in the 1970s, but the demand for their use on non-military projects grew stronger and by the end of the decade had become a programme for a completely unmilitarized peace corps (*sozialer Friedensdienst*), modelled on the West German 'alternative service' (*Ersatzdienst*) and like the latter to be used exclusively on civilian undertakings.

The church gave this movement its blessing (about half the *Bausoldaten* claim religious motivation) and took the matter up with Klaus Gysi, State Secretary for Religious Affairs, in 1981, only to be informed that he could not seriously entertain the proposal on the grounds that it would, first, undermine the principle of universal military service, which is a duty of all citizens; secondly, that it would render the GDR unable to meet its commitment to its (Warsaw Pact) allies, their military strength being the best guarantee of peace; and, thirdly, imply that service in the army was either 'unsocial' or 'non-peaceful', either notion being quite unacceptable.

The church has thus had to realize that it will not be easy to make the state budge on this issue, but has nevertheless accepted the principle of *sozialer Friedensdienst* and wishes to continue the dialogue on this. It has also considered the situation of those who totally reject any idea of compulsory service at all (*totale Kriegsdienstverweigerer*), who at the moment go straight to prison, and promised to do what it can for them.

It was partly as a result of these two campaigns that the unofficial peace movement in the GDR began to gain momentum, but what provided the greatest stimulus was the sight of the massive peace marches and demonstrations in West Germany in 1982 and 1983 which were given great prominence on the television screens of the GDR and which, above all, caught the imagination of the young there. The official intention was to provide maximum coverage to the protests against the installation of the Cruise and Pershing II missiles in Western Europe, but what was perceived by many of the public was the special German dimension of the operation, the awareness that any war would involve Germans killing Germans and that both German states had a common interest in trying to prevent such a situation arising. Thus Germans who demonstrate in Bonn are also demonstrating on behalf of their cousins in the GDR.

All this led to an upsurge of energy and enthusiasm, which found expression in meetings and conferences (particularly in Berlin and Dresden), in direct protest (as in Jena), and in the wearing of the 'swords into ploughshares' badge everywhere.[15] This unofficial peace movement has come to be concentrated in the church because, with no right of assembly or of demonstration in the GDR, the church is the only place for it to go and, of course, many of the clergy and laity were already caught up in it. Some, on the other hand, have had reservations because they see the movement as one not just of protest against war but against the regime as a whole, which could involve the church in a potentially damaging conflict.

Certainly the government has reacted negatively, finding especially objectionable the fact that the very words which had been officially sanctioned for decades were now being uttered with a conviction and enthusiasm which made them profoundly suspect. Eventually, in the autumn of 1982, the same badges which had originally been officially approved were removed from the jackets and anoraks of the young by those twin symbols of GDR authority, teachers and policemen. When challenged by the usual church delegation on this, all Klaus Gysi could say was that it had been done on orders, because of abuse.[16]

The Future of the Church

Undoubtedly the unofficial peace movement in the GDR is of great significance; for the first time people from all walks of life and of all ages, but especially the young, have been actively involved in discussing their situation and what their future ought to be. Like Czechoslovakia in 1968 the country has suddenly come alive and can be seen to be peopled not by grey-faced automata but by real human beings; the objects have become subjects.

Having established this, however, it is important to realize that the church and the peace movement in the GDR cannot merge into one, even though they will remain close allies: to think otherwise would be both to overestimate the freedom of action of the church and to misunderstand its role. The church can never take over the role of an opposition pure and simple; if it did so, it would have abandoned its claim to operate in any other than a purely political dimension.

This is not to say it does not have a very important part to play. In a society where officially everything follows fixed, immutable laws it provides a message of personal warmth and comfort and an insistence on the absolute value of the individual. This is particularly important in the GDR, which has the highest divorce rate in the world, one of the highest suicide rates and a tremendous alcohol problem.

Finally, the church provides an alternative. In a country where nothing can be said to exist unless it be given an official stamp of approval and where no opinions may be ventured unless they are received truth, so that in practice everybody talks with one voice in public and another in private, the church provides a sanctuary where people can be honest with themselves and with each other. Such a function may not hit the headlines but it surely fulfils a basic human need.

Notes: Chapter 5

1   Quoted in T. Beeston, *Discretion and Valour* (London, 1974), p. 19.
2   ibid., p. 35.
3   ibid., p. 40.
4   ibid., p. 285.
5   *The Times*, 19 January 1983.
6   'Evangelical' is used here as synonymous with 'Protestant'.
7   There are officially eleven *Freikirchen* and eleven 'sects'; R. Henkys (ed.), *Die evangelischen Kirchen in der DDR* (Munich, 1982), p. 197.
8   Wolfgang Leonhard, *Die Revolution entlässt ihre Kinder* (Cologne and Berlin), pp. 308–9.
9   Kempowski, *Uns geht's ja noch gold*, pp. 48–52.
10 John Sandford, *The Sword and the Ploughshare* (London, 1983), p. 103.
11 W. Kauft, *Katholische Kirche in der DDR* (Mainz, 1980), p. 31.
12 The Church, however, has no say in the appointment of staff to the theological faculties.
13 Henkys (ed.), *Die evangelischen Kirchen*, p. 196.
14 Wolfgang Büscher *et al.*, *Friedensbewegung in der DDR* (Hattingen, 1982).
15 The quotation comes from the Old Testament Book of Micah and the original figure was presented by the Soviet sculptor Evgeny Vuchetich to the UN in 1961 and now stands outside the UN building in New York.
16 Sandford, *The Sword and the Ploughshare*, pp. 72–4.

6

The Significance of East German Intellectuals in Opposition

ROGER WOODS

Anyone reading the GDR's home-grown critics must sooner or later ask what value can be attached to their insights and criticisms, and in what ways their ideas are significant. In attempting to answer these questions I shall concentrate on three particular intellectuals: Rudolf Bahro, Robert Havemann and Stefan Heym, partly because their views are given such prominence in the West and partly because the SED leadership clearly places them in the category of opposition.

Rudolf Bahro was a party member and economist whose attack on the SED's brand of socialism in *Die Alternative* resulted in his arrest and imprisonment. After his release in 1979 he moved to West Germany. Robert Havemann, once a professor of physical chemistry at the Humboldt University in East Berlin, was one of the SED's most tenacious critics and resisted pressure from the authorities to make him quit the GDR right up to his death in 1982. Of the three, only Stefan Heym remains in the GDR and continues to arouse controversy as an outspoken critic of the regime.

The East German View

A typical East German response to its radical critics is to dismiss them as enemies of socialism, as a 'tiny group of individuals who represent nothing and nobody'.[1] In May 1979, shortly after Heym's novel *Collin* and Rolf Schneider's *November* had appeared in West Germany, and Joachim Seyppel had protested against the authorities' treatment of Havemann, the writer Dieter Noll assured Erich Honecker that a 'few worn-out types like Heym, Seyppel or Schneider who co-operate so eagerly with the class enemy to obtain cheap recognition for themselves . . . certainly do not represent the writers of our Republic. And the party can be sure that working people throughout the country approve of the government's actions . . .' .[2]

Yet despite such denials that radical critics are in any way a representative or significant force in East German society the severity of the official reaction is a clear sign that the SED takes its critics seriously. One of the main aims of the June 1979 revision of the Penal Code was to silence East German intellectuals who had resorted to publishing their critical writings abroad. The strengthening of the cultural contingent on the Central Committee elected in 1981 also reflects a growing awareness of the potential for conflict in the cultural sphere,[3] as does the frequency of Honecker's personal interventions in the debates surrounding critical intellectuals. Honecker's interview with Stephan Hermlin, generally regarded as the instigator of the petition against Wolf Biermann being deprived of GDR citizenship in 1976, is perhaps the most dramatic proof of how seriously the party takes unrest among intellectuals.[4]

The West German View

In West Germany there is little hesitation in providing a forum for the GDR's critical intellectuals and presenting their accounts as valuable insights into what is actually going on. More importantly, their opinions about the regime are portrayed as typical of the views of the East German population as a whole. The *Spiegel* review of the film version of Heym's *Collin* was entitled 'at last the truth'.[5] This response is encountered not just in the West German press but also in some Western academic studies of the GDR. Havemann's brand of democratic communism is said to reflect a widespread feeling of opposition among the East German population,[6] and when *Spiegel* published the *Manifest der Opposition* in 1978 the debate over its authenticity on occasion gave way to the idea that, authentic or not, it could be regarded as a summary of popular feeling in the GDR.[7]

This Western assumption that the views of highly critical intellectuals are representative appears to be backed up by the findings of research into popular opinion in the GDR. There have been some ingenious attempts to find out just what the East German population does think of its political system: Gebhard Schweigler related findings of surveys conducted in the 1960s in which West Berliners returning from the GDR were questioned about the views of the East Germans they had spoken to.[8] Wolfgang Mleczkowski bases his assessment of popular opinion in the GDR on public-opinion polls undertaken in Czechoslovakia in 1968,[9] and the economist Hans Apel conducted his own small-scale polls in the GDR in the 1960s.[10] Ingenious though some of these surveys may be, however, they are all ultimately unsatisfactory, and the unscientific methods used are underlined by the radically different results each survey produced: estimated support for the system during the 1960s ranges from 7–15 per cent to over 50 per cent (Mleczkowski, Schweigler, Apel).[11]

The Intellectuals' View

The confusion is not entirely dispelled if one looks at what the critical intellectuals themselves have to say about their significance. At one point Heym can argue that writers are paid more attention in socialist society than in the West,[12] and that as far as the East German population is concerned he is the most popular East German writer of the day.[13] Yet elsewhere he expresses his fear that those who think as he does may turn against him because they do not have his freedom to travel in the West and to speak out.[14] Similarly, Havemann is at one stage not prepared to assume most East Germans think as he does,[15] yet at another claims that the 200 signatories to his open letter to Brezhnev are representative of the majority of the East German population.[16] There is also an unresolved tension running through Havemann's attitude towards what he considers to be the aspirations of East Germans: on one occasion he argues that they want more freedom, not more consumer goods,[17] yet on another he describes East German *Kleinbürger und Spiesser* and their dreams of material comfort.[18] For his part, Bahro points out that demands for greater democracy such as were heard in Czechoslovakia in 1968 are superficial, limiting any reform movement to the special interests of intellectuals,[19] and he rightly adds that the party can and does make use of popular anti-intellectualism in combating any such demands.[20]

Apart from the self-doubts of the intellectuals themselves there is some evidence to suggest that there may indeed be a mismatch between their political goals and the more tangible benefits sought by East Germans. Sociological studies, admittedly from the 1960s, have shown that young people are more interested in travel and music than in political and economic issues,[21] and a 1978 opinion poll described by East German sources as representative revealed that East Germans were particularly interested in material prosperity.[22] Bahro's doctorate also illustrates a slight mismatch of interests, with Bahro calling for fundamental reforms in the way work is organized and the cadre economists he interviewed in preparing his thesis pursuing the more modest and conformist goals of greater responsibility and less bureaucracy.[23] Bahro seems aware of this mismatch of interests when he argues that the SED cultivates materialism in order to direct the population away from social reform[24] However the divergence of interests may be explained, it qualifies the widespread assumption that intellectuals are important because they articulate the discontent of a larger sector of the population.[25]

Perhaps because there is some doubt in their own minds about their representative status, critical intellectuals can develop a fall-back position. Although their commitment to what they see as genuine socialism is obviously sincere, their insistence on applying Marxist methods in analysing East German society seems to stem, in part, from a need to provide their analyses with an alternative significance: what both Havemann and Bahro claim to offer is not merely a list of reforms East German socialism ideally needs to undergo, but an account of the forces currently at work in society which will eventually push aside the existing order and establish 'genuine' socialism.[26] The message is that their criticisms of the present and projections of a future society are significant because they are based on a Marxist analysis of how society will develop. For Bahro it is the 'intellectualizing' of the workforce which generates 'emancipatory interests',[27] and Western commentators, such as Raymond Williams, see this non-Utopianism as the most important feature of Bahro's *Alternative*.[28] For Havemann, it is the tension between the 'state and the masses' which will bring about what he calls the second phase of the socialist revolution.[29]

Yet even if one accepts the Marxist framework, this attempt to define Bahro's and Havemann's significance is also fraught with difficulties. Bahro and Havemann themselves are aware of the shortcomings of their analyses: in *Die Alternative* Bahro asserts that Marx's categorical imperative that any order must be overthrown in which man is a degraded, enslaved, abandoned, humiliated being must take precedence over any scientific proof that such a revolution is possible.[30] Bahro also reflects that his strategy for a communist alternative in *Die Alternative* is the shakiest and most incomplete part of his book, and that it runs the risk of Utopianism.[31] And it is interesting to note that after the initial enthusiasm for Bahro's theories had given way to an assessment of their validity, Western observers of the GDR found it difficult to go along with his account of precisely where the pressure for political reform would come from.[32]

The term 'Utopianism' in the sense of non-Marxist speculation on a better future also pervades Havemann's work, and on occasion Havemann can apply the term to his own suggested reforms for East German society.[33] He can go further still and argue that Bahro is indulging in idle dreams when he calls for a league of communists to be established.[34] Bahro implicitly returns the compliment, for whereas Havemann sees the call for individual freedom growing louder as the standard of living rises,[35] Bahro looks with dismay at the 'material insatiability' in the GDR which gets in the way of political progress.[36] There is then an element of morale-boosting as well as of Marxist conviction underlying Bahro's objection to what he calls defeatist social analysis[37] and Havemann's conclusion that a Prague Spring is a historical inevitability in all socialist countries.[38] Heym sums up the situation when he writes that those who want to change things need a profound conviction that things can be changed.[39]

An Alternative Approach

Although the approaches noted so far to the question of significance are often revealing about the political systems which produce them and the motives of the individuals involved, it is clear that they all pose considerable problems. An alternative approach is to ask whether the criticisms made by Havemann, Bahro and Heym reflect major concerns and debates within the GDR. To anticipate the conclusion, it is clear that these criticisms published in the West do indeed echo internal discussions. While some of these discussions are conducted by groups far removed from the decision-making process, others are conducted within the circles responsible for formulating policy and shaping East German society. To pinpoint the various discussions is to establish the existence of a continuum, of areas of overlap between permissible debate and self-criticism, on the one hand, and the radical criticisms put forward by Bahro, Havemann and Heym on the other.

The most readily accessible area in which their thoughts are echoed within official circles is the area of *Selbstkritik,* which is largely concerned with inefficiencies within the economy. Although it is generally sandwiched between thick slices of self-congratulation on the achievements of socialism this criticism can often provide unambiguous confirmation of what, for example, Bahro has to say. Anyone familiar with Politburo reports on poor morale at work, on resources being wasted, laws being ignored and unpleasant truths being concealed[40] will realize that the private speech by Erich Mielke which found its way into *Spiegel* (no. 9, 26 February and no. 17, 23 April 1979) contains much less that is new (or for that matter private) than is generally supposed. The malpractices noted by the Politburo can be dwelt upon at some length in published surveys. In one such survey directors of industrial enterprises complain about the complexity of East German labour law and state that if it were necessary they would ignore legal stipulations in order to meet their targets.[41]

When Bahro describes how workers give less than their best because the pressure to perform well is not as great as in the West[42] he is doing no more than echoing the account in the FDJ newspaper of how a visit to a Berlin building site revealed poor productivity: 'We did not pick a bad day – the practice is common. Perhaps it is because of the simple socialist truth: in this country you live in the comforting knowledge that your job is safe and that society will look after you'.[43] Elsewhere Honecker himself can publicly blame government ministers for failing to ensure uninterrupted supplies of electricity and fuel.[44] Bahro's point that the cadre economists he interviewed for his thesis showed signs of disappointment and discouragement because they were overqualified for the tasks they actually performed is directly confirmed for a wider section of the working population by East German research: a 1980 study by the Central Labour Research Institute reveals that almost 20 per cent of skilled workers are in jobs which do not make proper use of their training. East German sources estimate that approximately 1 million skilled workers do not have sufficient opportunity to utilize their training and qualifications, and conclude that this problem can result in dissatisfaction, frequent changes of job, disappointment and a resigned attitude.[45]

When Bahro questions the effectiveness of financial incentives in work and argues instead for greater responsibility to be given at the level of individual enterprises, he is able to back up his case by referring to surveys conducted not only in the USSR Union but also in the GDR.[46] East German academic sources also echo Bahro's plea for technologists to be given more say in the overall running of enterprises and his arguments against excessive centralization.[47]

In these areas, then, there is clearly an overlap between Bahro's pragmatic criticisms and public self-criticism within the GDR. And, indeed, Bahro placed his thesis within this framework of acceptable self-criticism. Although it was ultimately rejected, the positive response the thesis received from its first three assessors (two of whom were SED members) shows that his idea of what was acceptable was not that far off the mark.[48] Yet echoes of Bahro are to be heard not merely in this area of pragmatic criticism aimed at greater economic efficiency. Bahro himself points the way when he refers to economists and sociologists in the USSR homing in on the crucial issues, and Soviet artists, social scientists and journalists dismantling the official image of their country to reveal a very different reality. There are clear signs that the same process is at work in the GDR.

In his thesis, Bahro argues that the division of labour retained in the GDR is a hindrance to the development of the personality.[49] In *Die Alternative* the idea resurfaces in more aggressive form, with Bahro arguing that self-development is a worthier goal than the economic growth which the SED accords such high priority, and that material insatiability is costing the GDR its freedom to develop into a higher form.[50] That these points were also being raised within the SED close to the time when *Die Alternative* appeared is suggested by a report in which a Central Committee head of section responsible for agitation took issue with the argument that increasing material prosperity was laming the social energy and activity of East German citizens. Shortly before that, Politburo member Konrad Naumann had attacked what he called radical left-wing critics who accused the party of pursuing its consumer policies at the expense of ideology,[51] and Honecker had reaffirmed his commitment to the linking of economic and social policy in the face of critics who were reminding him that 'man cannot live by bread alone'.[52]

The debate in the late 1970s between Harry Maier, deputy director of the Central Institute of Economic Science, and Harry Nick, research director in the Academy of Social Sciences underlines the fact that Honecker's remarks are not merely directed against his critics abroad. Maier stresses that material wealth is only the means enabling members of a society to develop all aspects of their character, and that the economic goal of socialism should be to increase the amount of free time available for individual development and to pay particular attention to the quality of work. Ranged against Maier, and very much one of the majority, Nick adamantly rejects any such arguments which seem to him to call into question the goal of economic expansion.[53]

In the case of the unofficial peace movement it is clear that Havemann could, and Heym can, rightly claim to echo, indeed to be part of, a debate going on within the GDR, and to represent a growing body of public opinion. Havemann's and Heym's provocative and challenging stance has placed them nearer many young East German peace campaigners who are growing increasingly impatient with the circumspection of the Catholic and Evangelical Churches. Although the influence of the unofficial peace movement on SED policy is minimal the representative status of Havemann and Heym within it remains. Moreover, the praise for the movement expressed by Stephan Hermlin and Volker Braun makes it more difficult for the party to draw its usual distinction between its radical critics, such as Havemann and Heym, and its valued but 'difficult' intellectuals.[54]

Havemann's advocacy of some measure of political pluralism and his rejection of Soviet domination of Eastern Europe mean that he has much in common with the Eurocommunism of the communist parties of Spain, France and Italy. This Eurocommunism, in turn, has given the SED cause for concern since it appears to have raised its head within the party itself. The Conference of Communist and Workers' Parties in 1976 and the Karl Marx Conference in East Berlin in 1983 must have done much to stimulate the debate on Eurocommunism in the SED, for at these conferences Western European and Japanese communists made it clear that the USSR was no longer to be accepted as the leader of world communism and that political and ideological pluralism were essential elements of socialism. Moreover, the proceedings of the conferences were published in *Neues Deutschland*.

In December 1979 the Central Committee passed a resolution to review the state of the party by interviewing all of its 2,130,671 members and candidates. Whereas the previous party review of 1970 had resulted in expulsions for simple inactivity, the 3,944 members expelled in 1980 were said to have been unwilling to observe the party statute, and the expulsions were preceded by warnings from Erich Mückenberger, head of the Central Party Control Commission, against false and damaging ideas, hostile influences, reformism, revisionism, anti-Soviet attitudes and ideas of a third way,[55] a reference, as Timmermann points out, to the path between social democracy and Soviet communism which the communist parties of Italy and Spain were advocating.[56] At a confidential meeting of party members in the Academy of Sciences, Professor Gerhard Ziegengeist spoke after the Biermann affair about the popularity Eurocommunism enjoyed among East German writers, and he concluded that 'the Berlinguer model is getting a sympathetic hearing. Among large numbers of artists an image of socialism has become entrenched consisting of left-wing, revisionist and SPD elements.'[57] Timmermann also traces Eurocommunist sympathies among the scientific and technical intelligentsia critical of what they regard as the ideological dead-end of consumer communism.[58]

It is perhaps in the area of East German literature that voices are heard which echo most clearly not only the themes but sometimes also the viewpoints of Havemann, Bahro and Heym. Thus it is not just Heym who can mock socialist realism in art, where as he puts it in *Collin*, the men all have massive hands and tiny heads, and the women all look six-months pregnant.[59] Jurij Brezan complains that a significant number of talented young writers not only do not take socialist realism as their model, they actually wish to be seen in opposition to it.[60] Similarly, Hartmut König, secretary of the FDJ Central Council with responsibility for cultural affairs, has spoken out against young East German writers who announced in a journal for literature, aesthetics and cultural theory – the reference is to *Weimarer Beiträge* – that literature is a form of opposition and resistance, initially to parents and school and then later in ideology. König is obviously dismayed that not enough young writers are praising achievements such as the completion of the building programme with songs like 'In Potsdam wird gebaut' ('They're building in Potsdam'). He objects to young East German writers suggesting that the pressures of socialism made the free development of the personality impossible and that the individual develops not through East German society but against it.[61]

The concern Bahro, Havemann and Heym show for the individual *vis-à-vis* the state is clearly shared by many writers whose work is published within the GDR. These writers can thus meet with terms of disapproval which are very similar to those applied to more extreme critics of East German society and to 'pessimistic' Western literature. Where Reiner Kunze was condemned for adopting the standpoint of a 'critical individualist' in work he published in the West, Klaus Höpcke, Deputy Minister of Cultural Affairs, has recently registered with regret the subjective views put forward by some young East German writers,[62] and a discussion in *Weimarer Beiträge* about Doris Paschiller's *Die Würde* is typical of many reviews critical of new literary developments which have little to do with the SED's exhortations to East German writers to help 'strengthen the love and loyalty of young people towards our socialist fatherland'.[63] Paschiller is said not to be greatly concerned with examining the possibilities for self-fulfilment in society, and to view with scepticism the individual's chances of helping to shape society. The heroine instead seeks self-fulfilment by withdrawing from society, regarding her environment as mysterious and threatening.[64]

The recent anthology of works by East German writers born after 1946, *Kein Duft von wilder Minze,* is criticized for its lack of appreciation of social issues, for its apparent lack of interest in the struggle between imperialism and socialism, for the excessive interest the writers show in their own individual problems and an entirely private form of self-fulfilment.[65] Other young writers are taken to task for portraying the relationship between the individual and the state as antagonistic,[66] and in the journal *Temperamente* Sylvia Kögler makes a similar attack on young authors for their individualism, their disillusionment and their lack of revolutionary commitment.[67] This tendency to withdraw from the social and political arena is in fact at odds with the highly political reaction to political problems from Bahro, Havemann and Heym, but the idea of an antagonism between the individual and the state remains as a link between them and young writers publishing in the GDR.

Weimarer Beiträge has recently attempted a defence of this rising tide of individualism, arguing that it is a trend one can afford since the figures portrayed by young writers are all in agreement about the basic social issues.[68] Yet this argument tends to underestimate the potential for conflict underlying what has been described as the growing understanding among East German intellectuals that only a literature which describes and intensifies social contradictions can help the GDR out of its problems.[69] This attitude can often be complemented by statements from those responsible for getting authors into print: at the October 1983 conference of the Kulturbund, held in Leipzig, Roland Links, the publisher and chairman of the Central

Commission for Literature, announced that publishers should be issued with fewer red pencils, and he came out in favour of more self-critical literature.

This development in literature is expressly acknowledged by Uwe Jens-Heuer, (one of Ludz's 'revisionists' from the 1960s). Heuer notes that the themes of personality and individuality loomed ever larger in East German literature of the 1970s and provided inspiration for discussions in legal circles. He detects a trend away from the idea that under socialism the interests of the state are identical to those of the individual and towards recognition of the fact that state and individual are separate, that even under socialism there should be 'subjective rights', that is, rights of the individual in his dealings with the state. On these issues Heuer is at odds with East German legal theorists such as Haney who see implicit in Heuer's view the danger of a confrontation between society and the individual and of a pluralistic fragmentation of society.[70]

In the social sphere a lively debate is gathering pace over the issues of the emancipation of women. Although Heym and Havemann have little to say on the subject, Bahro is certainly critical of the patriarchal tradition and of the subordinate role played by women in the GDR.[71] In many ways recent developments in the internal discussion of women go beyond what Bahro has to say.

Whereas work and family tasks are traditionally regarded as complementary in East German society, with the mother deriving important stimulation for motherhood from her employment and a more mature relationship developing between mother and child,[72] the literary historian Karin Hirdina has recently taken up Brigitte Martin's simple question: 'why, despite all the equality between men and women, are there more unhappy women?', thus starting a public discussion on the issue of women in the columns of *Für Dich*, the mass-circulation women's magazine. Emancipation, Hirdina concludes, seems to have become a burden, and she points to the many East German women writers portraying the demands of work as a danger to personal relationships, to the survival of the family and to the well-being of the children.[73] Similarly, Irene Dölling, a lecturer in cultural theory at Humboldt University, describes the situation of East German women with the term 'double-bind', a more subtle and critical label than the usual double-burden (*Doppelbelastung*), for it means that women are not simply weighed down with responsibilities in two areas, but that they are involved in contradictory, not complementary activities. Social norms encouraged by socialist states emphasize marriage, family and motherhood as essential to women's happiness, yet they do not draw the necessary conclusions for other female aspirations. Dölling argues that emancipation can only be a genuine liberation if women can bring their qualities and values into all spheres of productive activity and thus bring about changes in the nature and the aims of this activity. Dölling's rejection of the idea that work equals emancipation seems to be a criticism of SED policy on women which is so concerned to create the conditions for women to combine motherhood and employment.[74]

In her preface to Maxie Wander's best-selling *'Guten Morgen, du Schöne'*, Christa Wolf writes that East German society gave women the opportunity of doing what men do, and that this eventually led women to ask whether this was, in fact, what they wanted for themselves. She argues that for the first time women are now demonstrating their 'otherness', and that they may wonder why they should assume roles which have done men such harm over the centuries.[75] Just what practical effect such questions might have on public life was demonstrated recently in an open letter to Erich Honecker in which several hundred East German women objected to the March 1982 military service law which provides for female conscription if the need should arise: 'we women see military service for women not as an expression of their equal rights but as something which is at odds with being women'.[76]

Although feminism is rejected by East German critics of the current situation of women, the often-heard complaints about the dominance of male standards and male institutions[77] have been interpreted in the GDR as evidence of an 'anti-male attitude',[78] and this, in turn, is regarded by more conformist East German sociologists as an essential element of feminism.[79] There is then a growing feeling among writers and academics that the issue of emancipation, declared by Ulbricht to have been resolved in his own time,[80] is more complex and subtle than originally thought and that the time has come to throw it back into the melting-pot.

Such debates from the political, economic and social spheres suggest that it is worth approaching the question of the significance of radical critics by looking for resonances of their criticisms within the GDR.[81] These resonances vary in their strength, their acceptability to the SED leadership and their influence on SED policies, yet they do show that between SED policy and the reform programmes of Bahro, Havemann and Heym there are many intermediate positions within the GDR. Their existence tends to undermine the East German (and occasionally West German) view that these radical critics are irrelevant, and it also qualifies, however slightly, the argument – which Bahro himself advances in modified form – that the GDR is a monolithic society which, because it is incapable of discussion, is also incapable of change.[82]

Notes: Chapter 6

1   Quoted from *Militärwesen* by Hendrik Bussiek in *Notizen aus der DDR* (Frankfurt-on-Main, 1979), p. 257.
2   *Neues Deutschland*, 22 May 1979. The government actions referred to were the currency charges brought against Heym and Havemann.
3   See Hartmut Zimmermann's analysis of the composition of the Central Committee in his contribution to Klaus von Beyme and Hartmut Zimmermann (eds), *Policymaking in the German Democratic Republic* (Aldershot and New York, 1983).
4   See the account of this interview by Karl-Heinz Jakobs in *Spiegel*, no. 48, 23 November 1981, pp. 86–108.
5   *Spiegel*, no. 49, 30 November 1981, p. 247.
6   See Hermann Weber, 'Demokratischer Kommunismus', in Hartmut Jäckel (ed.), *Ein Marxist in der DDR* (Munich and Zurich, 1980), p. 172.
7   See Werner Volkmer, 'East Germany: dissenting views during the last decade', in R. Tökés (ed.), *Opposition in Eastern Europe* (London and Basingstoke, 1979), pp. 137 f. Similarly, Ilse Spittmann, quoted by Wolfgang Mleczkowski in 'Der neue Moralismus – Zur politisch-geistigen Alternative in der DDR', *Liberal*, no. 4 (1979), p. 272.
8   *Nationalbewusstsein in der BRD und der DDR*, 2nd edn (Düsseldorf, 1974), p. 94.
9   'Grenzprobleme regimekritischen Denkens', *Liberal*, no. 21 (1979), pp. 552–4.
10 Apel's findings summarized in Hermann Rudolph, *Die Gesellschaft der DDR – eine deutsche Möglichkeit?* (Munich, 1972), p. 17f.
11 Peter Ludz estimates that in 1975, 25 per cent of the East German population accepted the political system and 20 per cent rejected it. *Die DDR zwischen Ost und West* (Munich, 1977), p. 224. Ludz gives his source as Bonn, suggesting that surveys of the type Schweigler refers to are still being conducted on behalf of West Germany, but that the findings are not being made generally available.
12 Quoted by J. B. Bilke in 'Menschenrechte im SED-Staat', *aus politik und zeitgeschichte*, 15 November 1980, p. 8.
13 'Gespräch mit Stefan Heym', *GDR Monitor*, no. 8 (Winter 1982/3), p. 1.
14 *Spiegel*, no. 22, 31 May 1982, p. 97.
15 *Berliner Schriften*, ed. by A. Mytze (Munich, 1977), p. 22.
16 See the interview with Havemann in W. Büscher *et al.*, *Friedensbewegung in der DDR: Texte 1978–1982* (Hattingen, 1982), p. 186.
17 *Berliner Schriften* p. 142.
18 ibid., p. 109.
19 *Die Alternative* (Reinbek, 1980), pp. 254 f.
20 ibid., p. 271.
21 W. Jaide and B. Hille (eds), *Jugend im doppelten Deutschland* (Opladen, 1977), p. 240.
22 Reported in *Frankfurter Allgemeine Zeitung*, 11 July 1978.
23 *Plädoyer für schöpferische Initiative* (Cologne, 1980), p. 32n.
24 *Die Alternative*, p. 263.
25 See, for example, Jiři Pelikán and Manfred Wilke (eds), *Menschenrechte: Ein Jahrbuch zu Osteuropa* (Hamburg, 1977), p. 17.
26 *Berliner Schriften*, p. 17; *Die Alternative*, p. 206.
27 *Ich werde meinen Weg fortsetzen* (Cologne and Frankfurt-on-Main, 1979), pp. 28 f.
28 *Problems in Materialism and Culture* (London, 1980), p. 261.
29 *Berliner Schriften*, p. 17.
30 *Die Alternative*, p. 22.
31 ibid., p. 209.
32 See, for example, the discussion of this point in *Deutschland Archiv*, no. 11

(November 1978), pp. 1160–81, particularly the contributions by D. Waterkamp and G.-J. Glaessner.

33 *Ein deutscher Kommunist* (Reinbek, 1978), p. 102.

34 ibid., p. 98.

35 *Berliner Schriften*, p. 26.

36 *Die Alternative*, p. 335.

37 *Die Zeit*, 16 January 1981.

38 *Berliner Schriften*, p. 28.

39 *Collin* (Munich, 1979), p. 228.

40 See the Politburo resolution of 18 May 1977 in *Neues Deutschland*, 21/22 May 1977, pp. 3 f.

41 Details in Uwe Jens-Heuer, *Recht und Wirtschaftsleitung im Sozialismus* (Berlin, 1982), pp. 196 f.

42 *Die Alternative*, p. 172.

43 *Junge Welt*, 8/9 December 1979.

44 *Neues Deutschland*, 28/29 April 1979, p. 3.

45 See Jan Kuhnert, 'Überqualifikation oder Bildungsvorlauf?', *Deutschland Archiv*, no. 5 (May 1983), pp. 497–520.

46 *Plädoyer*, pp. 33, 82, 134.

47 ibid., pp. 53n, 142.

48 Heym also placed his *5 Tage imJuni* in the framework of acceptable debate by prefacing it with a quotation from the party statute on the duty to encourage criticism and self-criticism. In his statement on Poland, Heym stressed that the trade union Solidarity was a consequence of social and political defects *(Misstände)*, a typical SED expression used to acknowledge shortcomings (Büscher *Friedensbewegung in der DDR*, p. 236).

49 *Plädoyer*, p. 46.

50 *Die Alternative*, pp. 218, 335.

51 See the report in *Süddeutsche Zeitung*, 14 November 1978.

52 Reported in *Die Zeit*, 21 April 1978.

53 The debate is summarized in K. M. Gyöngyösi *et al.* (eds), *Der Bahro-Kongress*, (Berlin, 1979), pp. 233–5.

54 See the contributions by Hermlin and Braun at the December 1981 meeting of writers and scientists from East and West in East Berlin. The proceedings of the meeting appeared in *Berliner Begegnung zur Friedensförderung* (Darmstadt and Neuwied, 1982), pp. 38, 161. At the writers' meeting of April 1983 in West Berlin Hermlin again praised young East German peace campaigners whom the authorities regarded with suspicion.

55 See K. W. Fricke, 'Die SED nach der Überprüfung', *Deutschland Archiv*, no. 7 (July 1980), pp. 680–3.

56 Heinz Timmermann, *Reformkommunisten in West und Ost: Konzeptionen, Querverbindungen und Perspektiven*, Berichte des Bundesinstituts für ostwissenschaftliche und internationale Studien, no. 31, 1980), p. 25.

57 Minutes of the meeting were published in *Die Zeit*, 20 May 1977.

58 *Reformkommunisten in West und Ost.*, p. 24.

59 ibid., p. 117.

60 Quoted by Ingrid Pawlowitz, 'Kein Duft von wilder Minze', *Weimarer Beiträge*, no. 9 (September 1982), p. 137.

61 Hartmut König, 'Die Verantwortung der FDJ für Kultur und Kunst in den Kämpfen unserer Zeit', *Junge Welt*, 22 October 1982, pp. 3–10.

62 'Phantasie für das Wirkliche', *Einheit*, no. 2 (February 1982), p. 178.

63 Kurt Hager's speech to the FDJ's Conference on Culture, October 1982 reported in *Frankfurter Allgemeine Zeitung*, 23 October 1982.

64 W. Gabler, 'Doris Paschiller: Die Würde', *Weimarer Beiträge*, no. 1 (January 1983), p. 16.

65   Pawlowitz, 'Kein Duft von wilder Minze', loc. cit. at n. 60, pp. 141 f.
66   König, 'Die Verantwortung der FDJ', loc. cit. at n. 61, p. 8.
67   'Zur Diskussion junger Künstler', *Temperamente*, no. 2 (1980), pp. 140–4.
68   R. Bernhardt, 'Die Sonderlinge der Debütanten', *Weimarer Beiträge*, no. 1 (January 1983), p. 7.
69   Alexander Stephan, 'Cultural politics in the GDR under Erich Honecker', in Ian Wallace (ed.), *The GDR under Honecker 1971–1981* (Dundee, 1981), pp. 39 f.
70   See W. Biermann, *Demokratisierung in der DDR?* (Cologne, 1978), p. 27.
71   *Die Alternative*, pp. 367–9.
72   H. Kuhrig and W. Speigner, *Zur gesellschaftlichen Stellung der Frau in der DDR* (Leipzig, 1978), p. 56.
73   Karin Hirdina, 'Worüber Frauen schreiben', *Für Dich*, no. 29 (1983), pp. 9–11.
74   Irene Dölling, 'Zur kulturtheoretischen Analyse von Geschlechterbeziehungen', *Weimarer Beiträge*, no. 1 (January 1980), pp. 59–88.
75   Maxie Wander, *Guten Morgen, du Schöne*, 14th edn (Darmstadt and Neuwied, 1983), pp. 9–19.
76   Letter reproduced in *Spiegel*, no. 49, 6 December 1982, p. 117.
77   See Hirdina's criticism in 'Worüber Frauen schreiben' (loc. cit. at n. 73) of the novelist John Erpenbeck's *Der blaue Turm* and her account of female writers in the GDR seeking to mark women off from the standards of male society and Dölling, 'Zur Kulturtheoretischen Analyse', loc. cit. at n. 74, p. 72.
78   Hirdina, 'Worüber Frauen schreiben', p. 11.
79   Kuhrig and Speigner, *Zur gesellschaftlichen Stellungder Frau*, p. 14.
80   See Gisela Helwig, 'Frauen in der DDR', *Deutschland Archiv*, no. 7 (July 1979), pp. 754–8.
81   cf. Zimmermann, in Beyme and Zimmermann (eds), *Policymaking*.
82   *Plädoyer*, p. 7.

7

Woman, Myth and Magic: On Christa Wolf's *Kassandra* and Irmtraud Morgner's *Amanda*

J. H. REID

> Die Philosophen haben die Welt bischer nur männlich interpre-
> tiert. Es kommt aber darauf an, sie auch weiblich zu interpre-
> tieren, um sie menschlich verändern zu können. (*Amanda,*
> p. 361)[1]

April 1983 was the occasion of an unexpected literary constellation. For the first time, the West German Südwestfunk's literary programme placed two East German novels on its merit list of new publications, its *Bücherbestenliste*. The one, in first place, was Christa Wolf's *Kassandra,* the other, in fifth place, was Irmtraud Morgner's *Amanda*. Both continued to be highly ranked in the following months: *Kassandra* second in May, sixth in June, *Amanda* third both in May and in June. These are positions assessed by a select jury of academics, journalists and writers, not to be confused with conventional bestseller lists. *Kassandra* figured on the latter as well. According to *Der Spiegel* it was one of the ten bestsellers in West Germany from April 1983 until well into 1984. And this came at a time when it was widely claimed that in view of the number of writers who since 1976 had chosen exile in the West the GDR had lost all claims to being a major literary nation.

Amanda appeared simultaneously in the GDR and West Germany.[2] It is a long novel in itself, but only the middle section of a trilogy, the first part of which came out in 1974 under the title *Leben und Abenteuer der Trobadora Beatriz nach Zeugnissen ihrer Spielfrau Laura. Kassandra* is relatively short. However, in as much as it is described as the fifth and last part of a series of lectures on poetics which its author was invited to deliver at the University of Frankfurt-on-Main in 1982, it is comparable to *Amanda,* which, as it were, embodies its own poetics. In West Germany the four lectures and the novel were published separately; in the GDR they appeared in one volume, but not until February 1984 – the fourth Frankfurt lecture had appeared in February 1983 in *Sinn und Form*.[3]

Wholly remarkable is the similarity of themes and ideas in the two works. It is perhaps fortunate that the two authors were unaware of each other's activities[4], as they might otherwise have found themselves in some embarrassment. The congruity extends to the use of identical newspaper reports. Both quote UN figures stating that there are now three tons of TNT per head of the earth's population. Both quote reports on the defective US computer which on several occasions announced that a Soviet rocket attack had been launched. Both quote assertions that the US strategy is to impoverish the USSR by forcing it to increase its arms expenditure. Both quote US statements that a nuclear war in Europe could be won by the West. One reason for the popularity of the two books must have been their topicality in a year which witnessed continual debate in East and West on the arms build-up and the likelihood of nuclear war. But the similarities do not end there. Both authors link humanity's present predicament with the specifically patriarchal way in which European society has developed. Male concern for scientific and technological progress for its own sake, and at the expense of the wider needs of humanity, finds expression not only in the subjugation of women, but also in the overexploitation of the earth's natural resources and, ultimately, in preparations for war. Hence both novels explore varieties of feminism as responses to the current crisis. They do so, moreover, with reference to myth, both using and revising traditional myths and creating their own as Utopian models for future behaviour. This, in turn, leads to a reassessment of the role of the poet and writer. One-sided abstract thought has destroyed the 'images' which early humanity used to understand the world. Writers, not least women writers, who are concerned not merely with the logical, but also with the sensual, appropriation of reality, are alone capable of re-creating the wholeness of life.

Kassandra reproduces the situation in the middle section of Aeschylus' *Agamemnon* where Cassandra, daughter of Priam, booty of Agamemnon, waits outside the Lion Gate at Mycenae, behind which she knows Agamemnon, and eventually she herself, are to be murdered. The novel consists almost entirely of her inner monologue, bearing witness to what she has experienced, 'rebuilding' the Troy of her childhood, the Troy which has been destroyed by the Greeks but much more by its own betrayal of what it once stood for, and accusing herself of complicity in Troy's downfall, failing to protest until it was too late. The monologue is occasionally interrupted by brief passages of dialogue, but the overall impression is one of a Cassandra alone with her thoughts, isolated from the world about her, not unlike the two outsider poets Heinrich von Kleist and Karoline von Günderrode in the author's previous novel *Kein Ort. Nirgends*. This isolation contributes to the profound melancholy which diffuses the novel, a melancholy intensified by the framework narrative, an opening and concluding paragraph by an anonymous voice of today, the voice of somebody standing on that very spot before the Lion Gate, surveying the ruins of what was Mycenae. By pointing out the transience of the Mycenae that destroyed Cassandra and her Troy, this contemporary voice underlines the continuing relevance of Cassandra's message: the sky is 'unchanged', the Cyclopean walls as menacingly close today as yesterday. What then is Cassandra's message for today? Why did nobody believe her in the past? The answer is that survival will depend on humanity's adopting a new, female-oriented myth of healing, reconciliation and community, and that Cassandra's prophecies were not taken seriously because her people were blinded by male-oriented myths of heroism; the destruction of Mycenae following that of Troy implies the possibility today of an even more devastating catastrophe.

The anti-heroic stance is made explicit towards the end of the novel when Cassandra accounts for her refusal to accompany Aeneas into exile. Her words anticipate or echo that other great iconoclast, Bertolt Brecht. Aeneas was about to become a hero and she could not love a hero; an age that needs heroes cannot be helped. Brecht's Galileo, too, deplored 'the land that needs heroes'. The theme is central to the novel. Cassandra's monologue is a 'tiny stream' to counter the 'mighty torrent of heroic lays' emanating from the Greeks (p. 284). A central figure is Achilles. Traditionally viewed as 'the most handsome, swift and brave of the Greek heroes at Troy'[5] for Cassandra he is simply 'Achilles the brute' (pp. 224 and *passim*, twenty-two times in all), utterly ruthless and brutal in all that he does, whether he is slaughtering Troilus in the sanctuary temple or committing necrophilia on Penthesilea. Sexuality and brutality appear as one in Achilles, and in this respect he represents the worst features of 'maleness' in the novel – that Christa Wolf furthermore stresses his homosexuality is an unexpected stricture which contrasts with the more liberal attitude expressed in *Amanda (Amanda*, p. 343).

According to one version of the myth, Achilles met his death when Polyxena, Cassandra's sister, extracted from him the secret of his vulnerability and betrayed it to the Trojans: male valour falls victim to feminine wiles: As with Eve and Pandora – the latter figures in Irmtraud Morgner's novel – women's sexuality is the cause of the world's ills. Not so in *Kassandra*. Polyxena is the victim of male strategies, strategies which Cassandra herself refuses to sanction.[6] Helen is not the temptress beauty who launched a thousand ships, but the object of male vanity – Paris does not in fact bring her to Troy, but loses her to the King of Egypt. But the principal subject of

Christa Wolf's 'demythologizing process' is Cassandra herself. Cassandra's is the 'first female voice to have been recorded in history',[7] but male mythologists have turned her into a negative figure. Why, for example, is a gloomy prophet of doom called a 'Cassandra' rather than a 'Laocoon', when the latter was equally pessimistic? (*Kassandra*, p. 112). Christa Wolf explores her character in great depth, giving her both social reality and psychological development, turning her into one of the great humane figures of literature.

Her social function is defined in two respects: she is the daughter of Priam, King of Troy, and therefore belongs to the 'establishment'; and she is a woman in a society which is becoming increasingly male-dominated. As priestess and prophet she has the duty to tell the truth, to ask uncomfortable questions, to unmask the hypocrisy and lies of court propaganda; as princess she feels loyalty to her class and her family. *Kassandra* has many of the ingredients of classical tragedy: the inner conflict betwen family ties and moral duty, the paradoxical blindness of the seer, the guilt thus incurred, which is ultimately expunged when she allows herself to be taken prisoner and led to the death she foresees. Her guilt is threefold. In the first place there is the traditional element of hubris, the feeling of being different, which prevents her from fully communicating with the other women. This is related to the class barrier of which she becomes aware when Marpessa conducts her to the caves by the Scamander where the common people dwell. But equally significant in her tragic downfall is her desire for power. She becomes a priestess 'to gain power' (p. 252). But power leads to blindness and contradicts her vocation as seer. Clytemnestra, she knows, will die in her turn, stricken by the blindness that attaches to power (p. 242). Most seriously of all, Cassandra fails to oppose the policies of the governing party in Troy until it is too late. She knows that the expedition to bring back Hesione will be unsuccessful; she knows that Helen is in Egypt, that the war is being fought over a phantom and is therefore bound to be lost. But while she remonstrates with Priam, she does not tell the population at large. Even when the war is becoming more bitter, the methods of both sides more barbaric, she convinces herself that her own aims are the same as those of the ruling party, namely the preservation of Troy, when in fact Troy has become no longer worth preserving. She has 'inner reservations' (p. 289), but these are not enough.

Her development has three stages: from the false collective of the palace, through the emptiness of pure self, to the discovery of a true collective, one with which the 'new' Cassandra can identify and which gives her self content and meaning. Christa Wolf describes an underground community opposed to the warmongering establishment. It consists mainly, but not exclusively, of women from all social classes, Arisbe, Priam's former wife, and Marpessa, Cassandra's servant, and even female slaves from the Greek camp. Anchises, the father of Aeneas, and one of the few positive male characters in the book, plays a central role in their meetings and is somebody whom Cassandra trusts and confides in long before the final break with her family. This international community is a refuge to all who are persecuted and it is here that Cassandra at lasts finds her real identity, here that her hubris is banished. The process is a long one – the others are naturally distrustful at first. The crisis eventually occurs with Achilles' brutal killing and rape of Penthesilea, followed by the almost equally repugnant slaying of Panthoos, the Greek priest, by Penthesilea's women. With this episode, in which the two sides become mirror images, Cassandra loses consciousness, is carried by Aeneas to the caves and finds at last 'consciousness' in the other sense, identity in community. There follows her one, belated act of resistance when she learns of the stratagem to destroy Achilles. However barbaric he may be, she refuses to sanction the degrading of Polyxena into an object, a decoy to lure him to his death. Since she will not agree to keep silent on the plan she is imprisoned (in the ironically named 'Hero's Tomb') on the orders of her father, an imprisonment which anticipates her captivity under the Greeks and further emphasizes the way in which the two sides have become identical.

In this process of losing and finding oneself, Christa Wolf again makes use of myth, that of Apollo and that of the Mother Goddess. The Frankfurt lectures point out the historical primacy of matriarchy and how the original female gods were unseated by male gods. Apollo is one of the new gods, taking over the oracle at Delphi, while his son Asklepios usurped the art of medicine, hitherto the exclusive domain of women. The author imagines Troy as a place in which various religions and cults existed side by side and where Cassandra gradually breaks away from her former beliefs in order to find herself. In the novel, Apollo is the embodiment of maleness, in that it is for her refusal to sleep with him that he punishes her by stipulating that nobody will believe her prophecies; it is he whom she curses when she discovers just how true this is; it is to Apollo that Polyxena prays for deliverance from pregnancy, a wish so unnatural, as Cassandra sees it, that Polyxena could not possibly have expressed it to a female god. Similarly, it is to Poseidon that Agamemnon sacrifices Iphigeneia, rather than remembering Athene. By contrast, increasingly important for Cassandra is the moon-goddess, the mother goddess, the snake-goddess, personified now as Athene, now as Silene, most frequently as Cybele, whose cult is part of the activities of the underground community in the caves. Cassandra first hears the name Cybele when her nurse Parthena involuntarily exclaims 'Cybele, help us!' Later she encounters the cult on her first visit to the caves. In the end 'Cybele, help us!' is Cassandra's prayer too, when her twins are born and when she remembers the fall of Troy. In one of the novel's many significant dreams, Cassandra finds herself forced to decide whether sun (Apollo) or moon (Silene) shines more brightly, and sadly has to admit it is the sun. She feels guilty without knowing why. Arisbe explains that the question was wrong, the answer therefore invalid. That the sun shines more brightly than the moon does not give Apollo greater moral authority than Silene. In terms of the novel: the male is physically stronger than the female; but power leads to blindness and tyranny.

Myth thus underlines the feminist element in the novel. We have already seen examples of man's barbaric exploitation of women. Wherever possible Christa Wolf seems to emphasize the maleness of the exploiters: *male* laughter (p. 284), *male* hands (p. 331). At times Cassandra feels that the men of both camps are uniting against the women. However, the novel is less sexist than such features suggest. Anchises is a focal point of the commune; his age makes him a representative of more humane times. Aeneas is an exception to male brutality, his tenderness and considerateness are stressed throughout. Indeed the love between Cassandra and Aeneas is as central to the novel as anything, and it contrasts strikingly with the other manifestations of sexuality. In the end, however, even Aeneas deserts her, casts the snake-ring into the sea, as if turning his back on the pre-patriarchal myth. Cassandra herself becomes aware how easy it is to be prejudiced, how convenient, for example, the phrase 'Achilles the brute' may become. When her indignation at the sacrifice of Iphigeneia leads her to claim that nobody could have made Priam carry out such a sacrifice, a look from Arisbe reminds her that Priam did indeed sacrifice a child – a male child, however, as if that were less serious. And the collective identity which she attains includes the recognition that all, not only men, are capable of limitless barbarities. The Amazon Penthesilea is the militant, radical feminist in the story – for the author she represents a hopeless regression to matriarchy (p. 151). Her fight is not merely against the Greeks, but against all men. She would happily envisage universal destruction in her cause (p. 332) – a veiled allusion to the contemporary situation and one which transcends feminism. Penthesilea, like Clytemnestra, rules her state absolutely, 'like any king' (p. 321). Again power is ultimately self-destructive, violence begets violence.

In her Frankfurt lectures Christa Wolf touches on the central role of Minoan Crete in contemporary feminist thinking, a land in which women were equal with men (p. 80), an essentially peace-loving state in which labour was meaningful and the individual was part of a social and religious community without being reduced to a mere function (p. 77) – a socialist Utopia, one might say. That there was a relation between Crete and Troy, that the struggle between Greeks and

Trojans was one between the patriarchal, war-like Myceneans and the matriarchal, peaceful Minoans, is probably fanciful but not impossible. At any rate Christa Wolf describes *her* Troy as 'the model for a kind of Utopia' (p. 83). The Troy we actually encounter in the novel has few Utopian features – ritual defloration, human sacrifice are scarcely such. What we see is a rather endearingly incompetent society once founded on the old-fashioned virtues of courtesy, honesty and respect for the individual, being gradually infected with the cancer of militarism, opportunism and exploitation. The Greeks are undoubtedly the villains. They think only in alternatives: either truth or falsehood, either victory or defeat, friend or foe, life or death. For them what cannot be seen, smelt, heard, or touched does not exist. Their sharp analytical minds are incapable of detecting the mean, which is life itself. According to Anchises, rather than iron it would have been more useful if they had invented empathy (p. 310). The nuance, the emotional response, empathy, synthesis – these are the hypothetical Trojan qualities and they imply a rejection of the simple antagonism male–female. But, in the course of the war, the Trojans lose their sense of proportion and gradually accept 'Greek' values. Eumelos, the captain of the palace guard, is the key figure in this respect. He embodies the new age, he is the nihilist, he will find his niche in the opposite camp when the war is ended, the single-minded devotee of the war effort to which everything else has to be subordinated. And as his power in Troy increases, so does the hopelessness of the situation, for the Greeks are always one stage ahead in their ruthless efficiency.

The Utopian element in the novel lies rather in the commune surrounding Arisbe and Anchises. In the last days they realize they are living a kind of experiment, 'projecting a narrow band of future into the dark present' (p. 339). This fleeting anticipation of the future is one element which might save Christa Wolf from Marxist accusations of historical pessimism. Can people change? Panthoos denies it, Arisbe leaves it open: when Cassandra asks her whether life is merely an eternal Nietzschean recurrence, she replies that she does not know, but that they are living in a kind of 'time pocket' (p. 328). This time pocket contains a possible future for humanity. In her lectures Christa Wolf asks whether it is possible to imagine rational beings which do not know our division of the personality into body, mind and soul, and describes Cassandra as one who had this division physically forced on her (p. 114). As we shall see, it is a central motif of *Amanda*. In *Kassandra* the commune reintegrates these three aspects of humanity. They tell each other their dreams; each imparts her individual knowledge to the others; they make – carvings, pottery, images; they touch each other; they learn 'how to dream with both feet on the ground' (p. 339). The Utopian dream then is a 'real' possibility. Will it have a future? When the Greeks finally capture the city, the women are dispersed or massacred. But they have sealed the caves in the hope that later generations will find what they have left. And in the one significant passage of dialogue which breaks Cassandra's isolation, she is able to impart to the sympathetic charioteer her message: only when the desire to triumph over others is gone will humanity be able to look forward to a future (p. 320).

The topicality of these ideas is evident. While *Kassandra* is not simply an allegory of current East-West relationships, numerous parallels and associations at once come to mind, not least through the author's occasional use of contemporary jargon in the midst of what is otherwise elevated, rhythmical prose: 'East–West trade' (p. 249), 'prewar years' (p. 220), 'increase productivity' (p. 268).

Parallels can be drawn on three levels: the social, the political and the personal. On the social level, the feminist message needs no repeating. Not all of the associations evoked by the commune are felicitous. That women's pottery classes might contain the clue to peace in our time is not especially convincing. The commune bears many of the marks of the 'alternative scene' with its concern for whole food and transactional analysis. On the political level one must resist the temptation to identify the Greeks with the capitalist West, the Trojans with the socialist East. Nevertheless, the message that a humanist socialism will destroy itself if it combats barbarism with the methods of barbarism is clear enough; the GDR's slavish imitation of the crasser aspects of capitalist materialism must similarly have been in the author's mind. That the Greeks could become 'the enemy' even before a single one of them had set sail for Troy is reminiscent enough of official Cold War language, not least but not only in the GDR. The body searches, the suspicions which those encounter who return from visiting 'the other side', are similarly close to actual practice. When Achilles is described as the Trojan war party's best ally and when we are told that Eumelos needs Achilles 'as one old shoe needs the other' (p. 308), the notion that the militarists on both sides of the world are giving each other help and encouragement with every new weapons system they deploy is clearly implied.

The personal dimension relates to the figure of Cassandra herself. As seer she is a kind of poet (cf. p. 33). It is not fanciful to see parallels in the development of Cassandra and Christa Wolf herself, who from being the author of *Der geteilte Himmel,* a work which after initial controversies proved highly acceptable to the GDR establishment, has in *Nachdenken über Christa T., Selbstversuch* and *Kein Ort. Nirgends* questioned some of the premises on which this establishment works. The war party in Troy, just like the SED, has its own court poets (p. 297) – Cassandra and Christa Wolf will not join them. Cassandra's refusal to join Aeneas in exile thus has renewed significance. In the lectures Cassandra's captivity is described as giving the author a foretaste of the horrors of exile (p. 33); elsewhere she refers to the growing list of those who are departing from the GDR and the paralysing effect it has on her (p. 124). On the evidence of the novel Christa Wolf does not intend to join Günter Kunert, Jurek Becker and the many others who have emigrated in the past decade.

If *Kassandra* has the ingredients of classical German tragedy, *Amanda* is akin to the Romantic German novel. When the (fictitious) narrator criticizes the (real) author, we are reminded of similar ironies in Clemens Brentano's *Godwi*. When men turn into ravens and fly off to the Brocken mountain from the Arnimplatz in Berlin, or witches meet in the Huguenot Museum, we remember a similar mixture of the empirically real and the fantastic in the works of E. T. A. Hoffmann. Hoffmann indeed is mentioned on several occasions in the novel and his story *Der goldne Topf* must have influenced the 'Brocken Mythology' of the book and possibly also the author's choice of profession for Konrad Tenner, archivist like Lindhorst in Hoffmann's story. *Kassandra* is set in the Mycenean past, *Amanda* in the present-day GDR; its message is correspondingly more direct.

Amanda is premised explicitly on two sets of myth, the one Greek, the other Germanic and outlined in separate chapters entitled 'Parnassus Mythology' and 'Brocken Mythology' respectively. The former tells one of the Greek creation myths, surrounding the figure of Prometheus. Prometheus created only men; the fire he stole from Olympus was used to make weapons. Gaia, Mother Earth, unhappy with this turn of events, realizes that he lacks love and gives him Pandora. Zeus, however, afraid that if Prometheus' children learn solidarity and friendship they will unite to overthrow him, spreads the rumour that Pandora's dowry contains nothing but evils and has Prometheus chained to a rock for all eternity. Epimetheus, Prometheus' brother, marries Pandora, opens her box and discovers that Zeus has lied: it contains not evils, but 'images of the future'. These images are of two kinds: 'figures of air', which embody finite, practical qualities, 'always knowing better, a sense of justice and utility, unwillingness to compromise, patriotism, conquests, victories and wealth'; and 'winged values', which denote infinite qualities, 'love of earth, for example, a sense of harmony and cherishing, capacity for compromise, peace' (pp. 82–3). The sons of Prometheus are interested only in the former, the 'male' virtues in terms of the novel, not unlike the Greek preoccupations in *Kassandra*; Pandora tries to prevent the others, qualities similar to those which Cassandra's cave commune cultivates, from escaping, but it is too late and only Hope remains in the box. Pandora flees, taking her box with her. Accordingly, one strand in the novel relates to the return of Pandora, not the bringer of evil as anti-feminist Hesiod[8] would have it, but as the only hope for humanity's survival. Promethean man has produced admirable works in the past; science and technology have brought progress, but they are now leading to catastrophe; man must be convinced of the one-sided, fragmentary nature of his activity, must persuade Pandora to return and with her create a fourth race of human beings, ones who will prefer compromise to victory and will outlaw wars (p. 159). In all this Irmtraud Morgner is largely following Goethe's festival play *Pandora* as interpreted by Peter Hacks, whose postscript to his adaptation of Goethe's work she extensively quotes (p. 301);[9] *Amanda* does not portray the return of Pandora; whether the final part of the trilogy will do so remains to be seen.

The alternative creation myth appears to be largely Irmtraud Morgner's own, although it embodies elements familiar to readers of the Romantic *Märchen* of Novalis, Hoffmann and even Goethe. It is much more satirically humorous than the first. Two main topics are involved: male domination of women and the notion that women today are only half-beings. In the beginning was Mother Earth; all creation proceeded from her union with Air, hence the division of being into the visible (earthly) and the invisible (airy, not to say airy-fairy) world. By trickery Air imprisoned Mother Earth and asserted not only the primacy of fatherhood but also that of the invisible over the visible. Bored with himself, he then divided himself into two, the principles of assertion and contradiction, later to become good and evil, God and Devil, each with his chief representative, Zacharias and Kolbuk respectively. Humanity, the visible creations of Earth, believed Air's dogmas fearing the torments of Hell, looking forward to rewards in Heaven, and accepting the divinely ordained order of the sexes – apart from certain heretics, dissidents, rebels. These were initially women, since the latter had least to lose, 'witches' who visit 'magic mountains' all the world over, in Germany the Brocken, to hold assemblies there, gather herbs and minerals, brew medicines and resist the ruling order, after the manner of the cave community in *Kassandra*. However, the male heretics who followed them promptly re-established male hegemony, reducing the witches to passive spectators. The men were tricked by Kolbuk into making him visible, whereupon he imprisoned them all. He explained that remnants of Earth's magic vase, a red stone and a white stone, had the properties of, on the one hand, turning everything into gold and enabling one to dominate the world, and, on the other, making silver, liberating from bondage and making indivisible. As a special favour he freed the men, who promised the women to make the white stone in order to liberate them too; instead, however, they were easily distracted into searching for the red stone, which duly led them through alchemy to chemistry, mathematics and all the other sciences, but left their female counterparts in bondage. As soon as the witches became too rebellious, Kolbuk bisected them all: the one half returned to live a conformist life in society as most women do in any case, the other half, the inquiring, non-conformist half, was sent to staff Kolbuk's bordello – itself patronized by the men, whom Kolbuk allowed to take the form of ravens.

Shortly before the novel begins a revolution has taken place on the Blocksberg (an alternative name for the Brocken mountain); Zacharias and Kolbuk have been overthrown. How this came about we are not told. We do learn that there are three female factions competing to overthrow the regime, and there are parallels with *Kassandra*. The most radical faction is led by Isebel, calling itself the 'Witches' Underworld Underworld Organization'. Like Penthesilea, they totally reject men and use violence in furthering their aims. The second group is the 'Green Skirts' or 'Daughters of Mother Holle'; their aims are 'obscure', they wish merely 'not to be like men'. Finally, there is the 'Owls' Party', led by Amanda, 'androgynous' and apparently the most dangerously subversive group. It may perhaps be equated with the Anchises–Arisbe group in *Kassandra:* the owl, we remember, is associated with Athene. In the three factions we can recognize varieties of contemporary feminism, as familiar, it seems, in the East as in the West. Conversely, among the 'ravens' Irmtraud Morgner distinguishes three types of male chauvinism. There are the 'gysoticians', who indulge in intellectual activities purely for sport without any concern for the practical consequences. They regard women as sex objects, as do the 'neoconstructivists', who are engaged in genetic engineering, aiming at the biological perfection of mankind. The third group is the least intolerable, the 'conservative avant-garde', conservative in that they would admit women their historical possibility of achieving status, as the hetaerae of antiquity, the mistresses of the eighteenth-century salons.

The two mythologies are obviously related. Promethean man is preoccupied with the search for the Philosopher's Stone. To the return of Pandora corresponds the quest for liquid silver – here, too, the resolution must await the final volume of the trilogy. Into these myths, the Greek and Germanic dimensions of the novel, the author has embedded two separate plots, both of which add a third dimension that of the contemporary GDR. *Amanda* touches on three topics which are of particular relevance to the GDR. First, it undermines the GDR's boast of having achieved complete equality among the sexes, of which more will be said later. Secondly, it takes issue with one of the pillars of the GDR's industrial policies, the stress laid on the scientific-technical revolution in progress towards socialism. Irmtraud Morgner is implying that a socialist revolution which is exclusively concerned with 'Promethean' activities is not sufficient and requires to be complemented by the 'Pandoran' revolution, a humane understanding of the need for ecological balance. Thirdly, her theme of the Brocken is not only based on its traditional associations with witchcraft, but also on the fact that it is on the very frontier between the GDR and West Germany. In view of the subject of international tensions in the novel, this is a cleverly chosen location. However, it is a highly sensitive military area, restricted to very few visitors, and she found it necessary to complicate her myth still further by having the Brocken 'evacuated from the Brocken' and transferred to what appears to be the Kyffhäuser some sixty kilometres to the south-east, with the help of the National People's Army, until international relations will have improved sufficiently to allow it to return to its rightful place! In other words, even when international tensions have ceased, official institutions will still be conniving at patriarchal structures of thought.

The Cassandra voice in *Amanda,* the voice of the poet, is that of Beatriz de Dia, the medieval trobadora who was reincarnated in 1968 in the first part of the trilogy and had fallen to her death in 1973 while cleaning the windows of her flat in East Berlin. She is reborn in Delphi in 1980 as a 'siren'. Again myth is being revised. There is a curious discrepancy between the two meanings of 'siren': the female beings who lure men to their destruction in the anti-feminist *Odyssey* and the device which *warns* mariners of dangers. In *Amanda* sirens are the reincarnation of 'wise women'; they sing only in times of peace. As such times are becoming less and less frequent it is imperative that they use their voices even in times of war in order to try to preserve both the world and humanity. Beatriz's designated area of operations is Berlin, GDR – other sirens include Yetunde of Benin, Catharine the Great of Russia and the poet Sappho. Her guide and mentor is the winged serpent Arke, daughter of Earth Mother Gaia and sister to Kolbuk, from whose guardianship she has escaped, and an important link between the Greek and Germanic mythologies. Arke, too, has her sisters, who inhabit various parts of the globe – including the Bermuda Triangle and Loch Ness. As in *Kassandra,* where the snake-goddess is an important motif, the author is exploiting age-old associations of the serpent with matriarchy – Christa Wolf points out the ritual significance of the snake in pre-patriarchal Minoan times (*Kassandra,* p. 127).

In Berlin, Beatriz is the victim of an attack by persons unknown who cut out her tongue. Arke's Asian sisters surmise that this was to sabotage the peace message and was perpetrated by those circles which have chosen Europe as the battlefield for a limited nuclear war between the USA and the USSR. At the end of the novel, on New Year's Eve 1980, her tongue is restored to her by witches from the Blocksberg. Meanwhile, however, tongueless, she has been forced to write her message, using a claw as her pen, and the subject of her message is Laura Salman, her former assistant or *Spielfrau*. On arrival in Berlin, Beatriz had been given a copy of Irmtraud Morgner's novel *Leben und Abenteuer der Trobadora Beatriz;* she at once resolved to tell the true story of her old friend, rectifying some of Frau Morgner's mistakes and bringing it up to date.

The biography of Laura Salman, therefore, is paradigmatic for the perilous state of the world. She is also paradigmatic for the status of woman. Both Isebel, the radical feminist leader in the Blocksberg, and one of the 'daughters of Mother Holle', the feminine feminists, take an active interest in her early development, and she soon shows signs of an independent, questioning nature. Her first ideals are her engine-driver father, Mozart's Don Giovanni and Goethe's Faust – all male stereotypes. But even after the founding of the GDR she encounters patriarchal attitudes which lead her to take up alchemy in private, 'the one science not exclusively male' (p. 139), and a university course in history – Heraclitus had called war the 'father of all things', Laura wishes to know the 'mother of all things' (p. 141). Already we see the connection between war and man, between Beatriz's peace-singing and the biography of Laura. Her career as a non-conformist comes to an abrupt end when she is one day visited by Kolbuk himself, who splits her down the middle with his sword. The one half flies off to the Brocken to become a witch under the name Amanda (leader of the third feminist faction), the other remains in Berlin as a quieter, more conformist Laura, who at once abandons her revolutionary study of history in favour of German literature, gets married, divorced, earns her living as a tram-driver, marries again and has a son Wesselin, all of which is described 'more or less correctly' in the first part of the trilogy, but which is, literally, only half the truth.

The sudden death of Laura's second husband ends the idyll. An extraordinary series of pressures converge on her. There is the psychological pressure caused by the death of a loved one. Material pressures on the single-parent family force her to go on night shifts, which are exhausting and expose her to attacks from drunken men. In despair she returns to alchemy in order to poison herself and Wesselin painlessly. But the greater the pressure, the harder the material. Instead of poison she discovers an elixir which summons up witches – and her other half Amanda appears. Laura has gained consciousness and self-consciousness, she has realized the social deficiencies around women and her own lack of 'wholeness'. But further pressures arise. She is now exhorted by Amanda to help her overthrow the regime in the Blocksberg; but Isebel likewise demands her support. Worse is to follow. Both Kolbuk and Zacharias are alarmed at the rumblings of revolutionary discontent among the witches. Konrad Tenner, Laura's one-time lover, now Kolbuk's court jester, is instructed to forge a radical feminist pamphlet entitled *A Woman without a Man Is like a Fish without a Bicycle,* whose author is given out to be none other than Laura Salman and which is promptly hailed by the West German media as a new 'Bible of Feminism'.[10] Laura is visited by Kolbuk himself, then by a Jesuit emissary of Zacharias, who try to blackmail her into marriage (in the latter case to Zacharias). If she accepts, it will undermine the feminist movement, if she refuses she will be betrayed to the GDR authorities, accused of entertaining contacts with Western journalists and engaging in subversive activities. Woman's emancipation is, it seems, being hindered by a coalition of interests ranging from the West German press through the Roman Catholic Church to the rulers of the GDR!

By the end of the novel Laura's problems have not been solved. Her consciousness remains incomplete, unlike Cassandra she does not find community. Basically she is concerned only for herself, seeking a private haven of security which, after Eduard Mörike's nineteenth-century myth, she calls her 'Orplid'. Moreover, no doubt again because of her 'halfness', she is unable to see the wider issues. She accuses Amanda of kicking at open doors, pointing out that in her local clinic there are more women doctors than men, to which Amanda retorts, 'But at the Palace all openings are still barred to us' (p. 296). It would be an oversimplification to identify 'Blocksberg Palace' with, say, the Council of Ministers, the regime of Kolbuk/Zacharias with actual political structures of authority in the GDR, although the absence of women in the Council of Ministers is indeed pointed out in a later argument. Irmtraud Morgner is concerned more with attitudes than with institutions. The constitutional position is ideal, the GDR remains in that respect the 'Promised Land' as which it appeared to Beatriz when she was first introduced to it by hearsay. And official study groups can proclaim 'In the GDR the problem of equal rights for both sexes has been solved', and find women enough to agree (p. 539). Discrimination against female applicants for higher education as they would otherwise swamp the universities (p. 561), may be untypical, although Rolf Schneider's novel *Die Reise nach Jaroslaw* made a similar point.[11] More serious is the mentality of a Kurt Fakal, who with an unblemished record as miner, communist and concentration-camp survivor, declares 'Woman is the soldier's hinterland' (p. 139), tyrannizes his wife and on her death expects his daughter, rather than one of his sons, to look after him. His son Heinrich had a secretary who announced at a trade union meeting that the GDR did not need foreign workers, since the job of the Turks was done by women working a second and third shift (p. 568), and was sacked at the first opportunity. Konrad Tenner is the major example of male chauvinism. His name links him to the Don Juan myth (Tenner = Tenorio), the most obvious instance of a myth of male domination of woman – as we have seen,

Laura's early wish to play Don Giovanni was thwarted, and later in the novel we encounter the ironically named Don Juan of Meissen. Konrad can tolerate no woman who does not regard him as the focus of her life, while the focus of *his* life is science. The kitchen is the one place where his wife Vilma and Laura are safe to carry on their experiments, as he never enters it, preferring to watch five television programmes simultaneously.

It *is* possible for a woman to hold a leading position in the GDR, as the story of Hilde Felber illustrates, but superhuman qualities and exertions are required and the end-product is a caricature. More realistic are the portraits of Ingrid and Peter Zirbel and Inge Petri, all of them with comparable qualifications and in comparable professions, but of whom only the man is ruthlessly ambitious, the woman being content to play the subordinate role. For the aware woman a number of stratagems are available to help her to cope with the stresses of the sixteen-hour day. There is Vilma's *Leibrede*, the art of swallowing one's words, so that she can make subversive remarks without causing offence. Laura and Vilma are 'jesters' rather than 'witches'. Just as the court jesters of medieval times had the right to tell the monarch unpleasant truths without fear of punishment but also with no guarantee of effectivity, so Laura and Vilma play a series of practical jokes on Berlin society, designed to show up its weaknesses and faults; for example, Laura stands in for Anita, whose husband Sven is sexually overdemanding. At best these activities are evolutionary; at worst they are merely a safety-valve, like the *Walpurgisnacht* celebrations on the Brocken in which the witches give vent to their frustrations once a year without Kolbuk having to fear for his position.

Alternatively there is 'magic'. Another important myth which Irmtraud Morgner adapts is that of Faust. In his drama *Faust* Goethe created the myth of restless, egocentric man seeking to dominate the universe by means of science and technology, in terms of the play, alchemy and magic. The conventional East German interpretation of the work regards Faust as a 'positive hero', one who would have felt at home in the socialist state.[12] Irmtraud Morgner stresses Goethe's own 'vision of the questionable, even destructive consistency of the Faust character' (p. 299). The Faustian myth, like the Promethean one, has led the world to the brink of nuclear war and ecological disaster. The allusions to Goethe's play are numerous, ranging from direct quotation to parody of individual scenes – the Brocken is an important location in *Faust* too. Both the principal male antagonists, Konrad Tenner and Heinrich Fakal, are scientists, both Faustian in their way. But at the end of the novel, when Heinrich's stratagem to steal the liquid silver has failed, it is to him that the words 'is condemned' refer (p. 651), not to Laura–Gretchen as in Goethe's play – whether he, like

Goethe's Gretchen, will also be 'redeemed' must await the final part of the trilogy. On the other hand, Laura is not merely the conventional, domestic Gretchen of the novel, not even after Kolbuk has sent her Amanda half to the Blocksberg. She is a female Faust as well, dabbling in alchemy, invoking witches. Christa Wolf points out that magic was originally the exclusive domain of women, one from which they were later excluded by priests wearing women's garments (*Kassandra,* p. 172), just as in the 'Brocken Mythology' the witches' role is usurped by men. She, too, discusses *Faust* and in this context reports the horror with which a group of scientists received her suggestion that they should swear a kind of Hippocratic oath forbidding them to engage in military research (p. 173). For Laura, however, magic is primarily a quest for self-preservation. Her experiments in alchemy are directed at discovering a potion which will make sleep superfluous – only then will she be able to cope with the demands of her son and her job. After a nocturnal seance she can return home in time only with the help of a broomstick; and when she throws herself out of her window in despair she is saved by the sudden ability to fly – something which causes much debate among passers-by and *Neues Deutschland* to replace its editorial matter with the text of Goethe's *Faust* (presumably an attempt by the patriarchal establishment to reassert the patriarchal myth). 'Magic' is severely practical; it also underlines the message – if women must depend on flying broomsticks, their plight is desperate indeed.

Like Christa Wolf, Irmtraud Morgner makes it clear that her novel is not anti-male. She does not support the party of Isebel, who invariably appears with a comic paper crown. Men, too, are 'divided', one-sided creatures through social convention – Heinrich Fakal keeps his other half, Henri, in a cupboard. The most obviously Marxist element in the book is its insistence that the division of labour, specialization, is original sin. Only when man *and* woman are permitted to become integrated wholes will war and the reckless exploitation of the environment and the opposite sex come to an end. Wesselin is the key to the novel's conclusion. It is for him that Beatriz is writing, hoping that the story will have for him the significance that Goethe's *Faust* had for earlier generations. He is the citizen of the future. He has no father, no male figure with whom to identify. His mother is worried that he is not self-assertive enough, even that he may become a homosexual. We may assume these fears are groundless. Amanda's faction is 'androgynous'. Wesselin will display both 'male' and 'female' characteristics; he, with the aid of Beatriz's book, will achieve 'wholeness'. A long line of myths seems to have inspired the author here. There is Plato's myth put into the mouth of Aristophanes in the *Symposium,* according to which 'love' is man's attempt to regain the hermaphroditic wholeness of which Zeus deprived him. There are the 'two souls' which threaten to tear Goethe's Faust apart. But Irmtraud Morgner is especially influenced by her reading of Jakob Böhme. In 1978 she extolled him as one who as cobbler-philosopher transcended the traditional division into thinkers and doers, and whose ability to combine abstraction with sensuality made him peculiarly relevant to the needs of today.[13] He is mentioned by name in *Amanda* (pp. 190, 501). The red and white stones of the Brocken Mythology are taken from his *Aurora*; but most significantly, there wisdom is symbolized by a hermaphrodite.[14] There is also a parallel with ideas expressed by Christa Wolf almost ten years earlier. Her *Selbstversuch* urged both sexes 'to recognize that they have different needs and that it is not the male who is the model for humanity but *man and woman*'.[15]

Kassandra and *Amanda* are thus two further important contributions to the debate on the position of women in GDR society. They use quite different styles, both related also to feminism. In the fourth lecture Christa Wolf attempts a definition of feminine aesthetics. Traditional aesthetics from Aristotle onwards have been male-oriented. Epic poetry not only arose in the struggle for patriarchy, its very structure, its insistence on the hero as model, was an instrument to maintain patriarchy (p. 188). The selection of one story-line, one hero exactly reflects the analytical process which has dominated Western thought, by definition *male* thought, to this day (p. 177). Against male analysis, she sets female synthesis, a 'narrative network' which corresponds more accurately to the network of the brain (p. 160). At every turn, one is reminded of her (almost) namesake Virginia Woolf, whose essay 'Modern Fiction' (1919) likewise rejected plot and hero conventions in the name of the way the consciousness actually works, and whose *Three Guineas* (1938) made similar links between male exploitation of women and preparations for war. Christa Wolf herself feels that *Kassandra's* 'closed form' contradicts her own aesthetic (p. 153). Cassandra is undoubtedly the figure with whom we identify, although it is harder to view her as a 'model'. By delineating her in terms not of what she does but of what she remembers, the author is dissolving the conventional conception of personality. *Kassandra* is certainly not a plot-novel, but a work held together through associations and memories, the latter not so much of facts as of feelings. Moreover, the juxtaposition of the story with the lectures, mingling narrative, discourse, diary and epistolar form, tends to relativize the impression of classical form still more. In this respect the East German version in one volume is preferable to the West German one, something which those reviewers who contrasted the novel unfavourably with the lectures ignore.[16]

Irmtraud Morgner approaches the question from an opposite angle. *Amanda* has a plot, indeed several; and Laura, like most of the other characters, is as clearly delineated as any figure in a traditional 'male' novel. If Christa Wolf's approach is psychological, Irmtraud Morgner's is sociological. *Amanda* consists of a multitude of short chapters (135 in all). Besides the two main narrative strands, a host of disparate semi-independent elements can be distinguished: extracts from historical texts, folk tales, scenes in dramatic form, stories told by subsidiary characters, journalism. In *Trobadora Beatriz* this *montage*-form was justified with reference to the circumstances under which it was produced. The male author can expect to remain free from distractions throughout his working day; not so the woman who has a household to run and a child to look after. For the latter the episodic form is essential.[17]

In terms of its effectiveness, one might feel it is also the appropriate form to be *read* by the female worker with her sixteen-hour day. *Kassandra* is all of a piece, an extremely dense work of literature which requires inordinate mental concentration on the part of the reader. *Amanda* may be picked up and put down again at quite short intervals. The *Kassandra* novel *can* be read in isolation from its essayistic concomitants; it then appears, as Baumgart suggests,[18] monumental, rather obviously 'literature' in the grand style, and therefore assimilable. *Amanda* has more 'rough edges', is therefore perhaps more of an irritant, more likely to raise the reader's consciousness.

This may be an unexpected conclusion. After all, it was Christa Wolf, not Irmtraud Morgner, who signed the Biermann petition in 1976, Christa Wolf, not Irmtraud Morgner, who attended the Berlin meeting of writers in December 1981 to discuss international tensions. Irmtraud Morgner has been the less prominently 'witch-like' of the two, although she has also had her difficulties. Her novel *Rumba auf einen Herbst* (1964) was suppressed; parts of it appeared in *Trobadora Beatriz* ten years later. And *Amanda,* too, it seems, had to be revised – it was originally advertised for publication in 1982.[19] Nevertheless, the official reception of *Amanda* in the GDR indicates that the authorities have been attempting to give it the seal of official approval and by implication contrast it with Christa Wolf's work.

What created difficulties for Christa Wolf and caused the publication of *Kassandra* to be delayed so long, was not, it can safely be assumed, the novel itself. Since the early 1970s literature *qua* literature has not been regarded as subversive; only direct statements explicitly differing from the party's line have been censored.[20] What caused offence was the Frankfurt lectures, where the author does not disguise her message in allegory and parable. Even the relatively harmless extract published in the February 1983 issue of *Sinn und Form* provoked a fierce controversy. In the following number Wilhelm Girnus launched a virulent attack on Christa Wolf:[21] she had used trivial translations of Sappho and Aristotle, she had misinterpreted the myths, her criticism of the classics was Germanic chauvinism of the worst kind, and, most seriously of all, in substituting the sex war for the class war she was being unmarxist (by contrast, Jürgen Engler merely noted a similar phenomenon in *Amanda*)[22] and giving comfort to the 'enemies of peace' in the West. The novelist defended herself two issues later, and Girnus returned to the attack in October, albeit in more measured tones.[23] But the October issue also contained three indignant contributions from supporters of Christa Wolf, accusing Girnus of being tasteless and intolerant; his article was reminiscent of the worst polemics of the 1950s.[24] Heinz Berg was especially puzzled by Girnus's linking the peace issue with Christa Wolf's lecture – indeed there is only one brief allusion to armaments in it. Girnus's attack was, of course, motivated by the lectures as a whole, something of which only the initiated could be aware.

When *Kassandra* eventually did appear in the GDR the scandal was complete. Ellipsis points draw attention to the omission of eight passages from the third lecture, which is clearly labelled 'abridged version'. In three of these Christa Wolf implies that both sides are to blame in the arms race (Luchterhand edn, pp. 84, 97, 108) – Irmtraud Morgner is silent on this point; elsewhere she appeals to the East to disarm unilaterally (p. 88), refers to censorship and self-censorship on East German writers (p. 108), to the rulers who cultivate hatred and self-hatred for their own ends (p. 106) and who are so shielded from reality that they are ignorant of what ordinary people feel (p. 112).

One can only regard this piece of censorship as an own goal. RIAS in West Berlin immediately broadcast the offending passages for East Germans to record for themselves. The ellipsis points merely draw attention to the very passages to be suppressed. Clearly there is a high degree of uncertainty in the GDR at the moment (March 1984) over policies relating to writers and the peace movement. Two conclusions, however, stand out. On the question of East–West armaments negotiations genuine disagreements are being openly voiced. To Wilhelm Girnus's uncompromising refusal to have any truck with the West, Heinz Berg retorted that in that case he could not understand why the East was talking of peaceful co-existence at all.[25] And there evidently exists an articulate section of East German society which is not content with official pieties about women's equality and which can see through attempts by those, like Girnus, to obscure the issue with philological finesse and references to imperialist aggression. Christa Wolf, or rather Friedrich Engels, whom she quotes in her defence, may have the last word:

> The first class conflict to appear in history coincides with the development of the antagonism between man and woman in marriage, and the first oppression based on class coincides with that of the female sex by the male.[26]

Notes: Chapter 7

1   'Hitherto philosophers have merely interpreted the world in a male way. But it is our task to interpret it also in a female way, in order to change it in a human way.' The words parody the eleventh of Marx's *Theses on Feuerbach*. All quotations in text are from the East German edition of *Amanda* (see note 2 below).

2   Irmtraud Morgner, *Amanda. Ein Hexenroman* (East Berlin: Aufbau, 1983; Darmstadt: Luchterhand, 1983).

3   Christa Wolf, *Kassandra. Erzählung* (Darmstadt: Luchterhand, 1983); *Voraussetzungen einer Erzählung: Kassandra. Frankfurter Poetik-Vorlesungen* (Darmstadt: Luchterhand, 1983); *Kassandra. Vier Vorlesungen. Eine Erzählung* (East Berlin: Aufbau, 1983) (not distributed until 1984). All quotations in text from *Kassandra* and the Frankfurt lectures are from the East German edition.

4   Sigrid Löffler, 'Eine anmutige Spinnerin. Die Frauen müssen die Welt instandbesetzen', *Die Zeit*, 10 June 1983, p. 59.

5   So *Brockhaus Enzyklopädie*, 17th edn, Vol. 1 (Wiesbaden, 1966), article on 'Achill'. On the other hand, Robert Graves, one of Christa Wolf's sources, asserts that in view of the way in which it portrays Greek barbarities, the *Iliad* can be regarded only as satire written by one who sympathized with the Trojans (Graves, *The Greek Myths* (Harmondsworth, Middx, 1955), Vol. 2, pp. 311–12).

6   cf. the story of Christine Torstensen, which so disturbed Christa Wolf and her alter ego Nelly Jordan (Wolf, *Lesen und Schreiben. Neue Sammlung* [Darmstadt, 1980], p. 21; *Kindheitsmuster. Roman* [Darmstadt, 1977], p. 262). Even the words 'not that' with which they react to the story recur in *Kassandra* with regard to the fate of the other female victim Briseis (p. 283).

7   Christa Wolf, 'Documentation: Christa Wolf', *German Quarterly*, Vol. 57 (1984), p. 100.

8   Graves, *The Greek Myths*, Vol. 1, p. 148.

9   Peter Hacks, *Pandora. Drama nach J. W. von Goethe. Mit einem Essay* (East Berlin, 1981); See also J. P. Stern, 'On Goethe's *Pandora*', *London German Studies*, vol. 2 (1983), pp. 31–49.

10   This is a private joke on Irmtraud Morgner's part. The West German reviewer of *Trobadora Beatriz* in the *Frankfurter Rundschau*, 16 August 1975, described it as 'a kind of Bible of women's emancipation today'.

11   Rolf Schneider, *Die Reise nach Jaroslaw* (Rostock, 1974), p. 26.

12   Paul Michael Lützeler, 'Goethes *Faust* und der Sozialismus. Zur Rezeption des klassischen Erbes in der DDR', *Basis*, vol. 5 (1975), pp. 31–54.

13   Irmtraud Morgner, Address to the Eighth Writers' Congress of the GDR, in *Die Verantwortung des Schriftstellers in den Kämpfen unserer Zeit. Materialien zum VIII. Schriftstellerkongress der DDR* (Munich, 1978), pp. 48–53.

14   See Ronald D. Gray, *Goethe the Alchemist. A Study of Alchemical Symbolism in Goethe's Literary and Scientific Works* (Cambridge, 1952), pp. 44–5.

15   Christa Wolf, *Lesen und Schreiben. Neue Sammlung* (Darmstadt, 1980), p. 94.

16   See Elsbeth Pulver, 'Der Zorn gegen Achill. Zu Christa Wolfs "Kassandra" und den Frankfurter Vorlesungen "Voraussetzungen einer Erzählung" ', *Schweizer Monatshefte*, vol. 63 (1983), pp. 750–5, and Reinhard Baumgart, 'Ein Marmorengel ohne Schmerz', *Der Spiegel*, 4 April 1983, pp. 208–10.

17   Irmtraud Morgner, *Leben und Abenteuer der Trobadora Beatriz nach Zeugnissen ihrer Spielfrau Laura* (1974) (Darmstadt: Luchterhand, 1977), p. 170.

18   Baumgart, 'Ein Marmorengel ohne Schmerz', loc. cit. at n. 16.

19   See *Sinn und Form*, vol. 34 (1982), p. 470.

20   Hamish Reid, 'Literature without taboos. Writers in East Germany since 1971', in Graham Bartram and Tony Waine (eds), *Culture and Society in the GDR* (Dundee, 1984).

21 Wilhelm Girnus, 'Wer baute das siebentorige Theben? Kritische Bemerkungen zu Christa Wolfs Beitrag in Sinn und Form, 1/83, - S. 38ff.', *Sinn und Form*, vol. 35 (1983), pp. 439–47.

22 Jürgen Engler, 'Die wahre Lüge der Kunst', *Neue deutsche Literatur*, vol. 31, no. 7 (1983), pp. 135–44.

23 Christa Wolf, 'Zur Information', *Sinn und Form*, vol. 35 (1983), pp. 863–6; Wilhelm Girnus, '. . . kein "Wenn und Aber" und das poetische Licht Saphhos. Noch einmal zu Christa Wolf', ibid., pp. 1096–1105.

24 'Zuschriften an Wihelm Girnus, *Sinn und Form*, vol. 35 (1983), pp. 1087–96.

25 ibid., p. 1095.

26 *The Origin of the Family, Private Property and the State*, quoted in *Kassandra*, p. 114, and in *Sinn und Form*, vol. 35 (1983), p. 863.

8

Youth – Not So Very Different

DAVID CHILDS

It need not be unduly emphasized that youth – however that group of young people is defined – has always been of particular concern to the leaders of Marxist–Leninist political systems. The reasons for this particular concern are no mystery. Communism is an optimistic world outlook concerned more with the future than with the past, youth represents the future. Secondly, Marxist–Leninist regimes have never come into existence by securing a majority in competitive elections, and the revolutionary leaders have assumed that their limited support among the more mature sections of the electorate could be made up for by the mass indoctrination of youth. In the case of the GDR, the SED (and the Soviet military authorities) had an even greater concern for youth based on the belief that the Hitler Youth (Hitler Jugend – HJ) had been diabolically effective in brainwashing Germany's young people. This widespread belief made it easier for the SED to justify its early control of the activities of youth and of education. By the time the GDR was established in 1949 the SED seemed to be in an impregnable position in regard to youth in that it controlled the education system, the only authorized youth movement, Free German Youth (Freie Deutsche Jugend – FDJ), the media, the forces of coercion, the offices determining the careers of young people in the already largely state-run economy and most of the places of entertainment and recreation frequented by young people. But despite the apparent strength of the SED among the young, the public manifestations of which were the massive rallies of the early 1950s, such as the first *Deutschlandtreffen* of the FDJ in Berlin in May 1950, it was by no means in total control of the situation. It suffered from the penetration of the Western media into the GDR (then especially the radio), from the Western contacts of young people, from the influence of the churches, from the influence of parents and grandparents and, not least, from its own political mistakes and weaknesses. Throughout its existence the SED has waged a constant and unremitting struggle against these, from its own viewpoint, negative influences on young people. It has as yet largely failed to counter them.

Education, the FDJ and the NVA

In formal terms the SED would seem to have its best chance of convincing the rising generation through the education system. Articles 17(2) and 25(1) of the constitution of 1974 refer to the education system as being 'socialist' while article 1 ensures the leading role of the Marxist–Leninist party. Under article 38(4) parents are obliged to educate their children to beome 'patriotic citizens'. As John Page's contribution to this book makes clear (see Chapter 4), the entire education system of the GDR is devoted to implementing what the leaders of the SED regard as the correct educational policy at any given time. Obviously, the SED is interested in seeing to it that as many future citizens of the GDR as possible enter into formal education as early as possible. For this reason, as well as because of the needs of working mothers, the GDR has a well-developed system of preschool institutions. Young babies and children up to the age of 3 can be looked after at a crèche. Probably as many as two-thirds of the relevant age-groups are now catered for. The next stage is the Kindergarten for the 3- to 6-year-olds. By 1981 over 91 per cent attended. Compulsory schooling proper continues from 6 to 16. The young person in the GDR is then legally obliged to undergo further (vocational) education and training which usually lasts two years and leads to a qualification as a skilled worker. These are sandwich courses. Roughly a quarter of the apprentices live away from home in hostels. Throughout these years boys and girls are subject to ideological training both directly in the sense of periods set aside for Marxism–Leninism, and indirectly through the party's influence on all school subjects. There is also the influence of the FDJ.

Set up in March 1946, the FDJ is open to those between 15 and 25. Its chairman until May 1955 was Erich Honecker. It is modelled on the Soviet Komsomols. The Young Pioneers (the 6- to 8-year-olds) and the Thälmann Pioneers (which recruit those aged 9–14) are also based on similar organizations in the USSR. Constitutionally, the pioneer organizations accept the leadership of the FDJ and the FDJ accepts the leadership of the SED. Margot Honecker, who has been Minister for Education since 1963, was for several years in charge of the pioneer organizations, after which she was responsible for teacher training. This gives some indication of the close ties between education system, youth movement and the Marxist–Leninist party. Every school, vocational institution, factory, apprentice hostel and university has its

FDJ organization which is responsible for a wide variety of activities which are designed, essentially, to raise the level of political awareness (in the sense of the SED) of the pupils/students. *Einheit* claimed in October 1982 that 86.6 per cent of the relevant age-group were members of the Pioneers and 77.2 per cent were members of the FDJ. The last figure given disguises the fact that the majority of those aged between 18 and 25 are *not* members of the FDJ. Not only is there a genuine change of interest but this age-group is no longer quite as vulnerable to pressure as the younger age-groups.

Fear of desertions prevented the leaders of the GDR from introducing compulsory military serivce before they built the Berlin Wall in 1961. Such service has been a reality since 1962. Young men must expect to face eighteen months in the armed forces (Nationale Volksarmee – NVA). They will already have, to some extent, familiarized themselves with small arms during the periods of compulsory (since 1978) military training which is given to the older children in all the schools of the GDR. Ideological training is seen as an essential part of military training and once again the FDJ organization within the services is meant to help in this work. One other organizational/ideological influence on the young person is the trade union, membership of which is compulsory. The trade unions are led by SED members and are seen as transmission belts which explain party policy to the broad working masses.

On its side in the battle for hearts and minds, the SED also has a ban on Western reading material and a ban on Western travel for virtually all of its young citizens. It has to live with Western television and radio.

Western Media

Speaking at the Fourth Parliament of the FDJ held in East Berlin in 1952 Erich Honecker claimed:

> The youth of West Germany is being ideologically prepared for the American war by the pornographic trash and filth being published in millions of copies . . . In the name of the young generation we protest vigorously and angrily against the criminal attempts of the American monopolists to distort the moral countenance of German youth through trash and pornography, brothels and crime films. We vigorously oppose the [West German] government's recent attempts to impair the moral fibre of youth in the GDR by smuggling in trash and pornography.

This claim of Honecker's exposes the fear of the SED leadership of the influence of the Western media and Western culture. By 1952 the West German and US and British radio stations operating on German soil had established a tremendous influence in the GDR. And although Western books, magazines and newspapers were banned in the GDR many magazines and books circulated, especially in East Berlin. Shops, just within the Western sectors of Berlin, did a good trade selling secondhand copies of a wide variety of West German magazines and books to East German customers. Naturally, Western relatives also provided such reading material as well. East Berliners went in large numbers to West Berlin cinemas where they gained admission at reduced prices. The reason was that the GDR's own media were dull as entertainment and unreliable as channels of information. The average East German cinema goer preferred 'slap and tickle' comedies set in Bavaria to iron and steel epics made in Moscow. Western radio stations won young East German listeners with their light or 'pop' music and scored heavily during the crises of that period, such as the Berlin airlift (1948–9), the death of Stalin (1953) or the revolt of 17 June 1953. Habits of listening thus formed were not broken. They became normal and were passed on to the next generation. The building of the Berlin Wall in 1961 made the 1 million East Berliners even more desperate to get reliable sources of news. None of this is to deny that there was a sordid side to the Western media. There were, and are, publications which could be regarded either as politically or sexually pornographic, but the great majority never belonged to these categories.

The spread of television from the end of the 1950s onwards merely intensified the competition between the two media systems. I have written about this in Chapter 9 of *The GDR: Moscow's German Ally* and in the last chapter of this book.

Writing in the GDR literary journal *Weimarer Beiträge* (February 1981), Lothar Bisky reported that the 14–16 age-group of a middle-sized East German town devoted 40 per cent of their free time to the media. He was quoting a survey carried out in 1977 and by 'media' the researchers meant books, magazines and newspapers as well as television, radio and the cinema. Television used up 505 minutes per week, radio 218, reading of all kinds 210 and the cinema only 24. It was calculated that another 12 hours per week should be added if using the media as a secondary or background activity was included. Of these 12 hours, 10 involved listening to music. Among Bisky's other findings were the importance of the transistor radio and the cassette recorder. Already in 1978 even the majority of 12-year-olds claimed to have their own radio. And in the same year 58 per cent of 16-year-olds claimed to own a cassette recorder. Bisky also noted the importance of feature films and *Unterhaltungssendungen* (light programmes such as quizzes, music, and so on) for the majority of 14- to 17-year-olds. He felt there was a slight connection between intelligence and viewing habits with the less intelligent watching such programmes more frequently. But he found that other factors such as the absence of parents – over 90 per cent of women go out to work in the GDR – and living amenities also influenced the demand for television and the radio. In the GDR, as elsewhere in Europe, the majority of film-goers are the older teenagers and those in their early twenties. Bisky found that the decision to go to see a particular film was made largely as a result of recommendations by friends rather than by newspaper commentaries, film experts, teachers, or those in authority. The country of origin was also relatively important.

Herr Bisky did not discuss the extent to which young people in the GDR watch Western television, listen to Western radio broadcasts or prefer films from Western states. He certainly knows that interest in Western media products is widespread. It is difficult to be sure just what influence these products have. Juvenile delinquency in the GDR is often blamed on Western programmes. But rather than presenting a glossy picture of the West, West German news and current affairs programmes often expose the seamy side of life in Western states and some of the feature films broadcast are socially critical. However, their usually accurate reporting of events in the GDR and the other Warsaw Pact states help to produce a healthy scepticism which is widespread among young people in the GDR.

Western contacts

It should be pointed out that there have always been West German visitors to the GDR. In the period before the Basic Treaty between the GDR and West Germany (signed 21 December 1972) such visits were much more difficult. For one thing, millions of former residents of the GDR who had left illegally (according to the laws of the GDR) risked arrest if they returned. For another, it was not quite so respectable for West Germans to visit the GDR. It was not unknown for perfectly innocent West Germans to attract the unfavourable attention of their state's security authorities because they had visited the GDR. West Berliners could not get through the Berlin wall on a normal regular basis. The agreements of the early 1970s altered all of this. In 1970 there were 1.2 million visits by West Germans into the GDR, eight years later the figure was 3.1 million. Even though the figure remained high, there was some decline in the 1980s because the GDR authorities increased the admission charge – the money West Germans were forced to spend in the GDR. In addition there were millions of visits by West Berliners, an increasing number of visits by GDR pensioners to the West and by those on 'urgent family business'.[1] Altogether these were enormous numbers of people coming together when one remembers that the GDR's population is only about 16.9 million. Most of the West Germans making the trip did so in order to see relatives. West Germans without relatives in the GDR are much less enthusiastic about going there. There have also been increasing numbers of business and political visitors, and school groups and other educational groups. For instance, Heinrich Windelen, Federal Minister for Inter-German Relations, reported on 13 September 1983 that in 1982, 196 school classes with 5,019 participants had, with public money, visited the GDR. This compared with only 37 classes and 834 participants in 1979. Clearly, however, both in numbers and in psychological impact, the private family visits are the most important ones for East–West understanding. It would be naïve to suppose that the East German hosts always hit it off completely with their West German relatives. They are at a disadvantage. They cannot make the return trip. The West Germans are usually more affluent and nobody likes to be patronized too often. But, on the whole, 'blood is thicker than water' and the visits continue, ideas and experiences of life and of the two German systems are exchanged.

One other type of exchange relevant to youth which has developed has been in the field of sport. There was a significant expansion of sport exchanges in the 1970s. According to the *Jahresbericht* for 1982 of the Bundesminister für innerdeutsche Beziehungen, there were in 1982, 41 East–West German sports meetings in the GDR and 37 in the Federal Republic. This compared with 7 and 10 respectively in 1972. Unfortunately these events rarely lead to many individual encounters and West Germans have been angered by their hosts' methods of distributing tickets to such features. When the football team Werder-Bremen played against Lokomotive Leipzig in Leipzig in 1983, it was claimed that only 600 of the 24,500 tickets were available for public sale. Nevertheless, many young East German fans of the Bremen team managed to seek out their heroes in their hotel. The Bremen captain told *Die Frankfurter Allgemeine Zeitung* (20 October 1983), 'the enthusiasm was inconceivable'. My personal experience confirms this impression of youthful enthusiasm for Western football stars.

The Churches

We do not know exactly how much influence the churches have in the GDR. Their influence was forcibly curtailed in the 1950s. In West Germany, too, the churches have lost some of their influence, caused by the social, educational and structural changes in society in the postwar period. Even without the SED, then, we could have expected the same to happen in the area which is now the GDR. However, unlike the churches in West Germany, those in the GDR are of interest to young people as the only institutions able to offer alternative values to the dominant Marxist–Leninist ideology. They have a curiosity value, they offer a discussion of the fundamental questions about existence beyond the merely political/ideological, questions so often neglected by the SED. And they offer an alternative way of looking at the problem of securing world peace. If they suffer from their historic association with intolerance, repression and reaction, they invite the young to ponder why they have survived for nearly two thousand years. Over the last twenty years or so the SED has been prepared to recognize some Christian heroes – Albert Schweitzer, Martin Luther King and, with new emphasis most recently, Martin Luther himself. These take some explaining! The churches also have a tremendous cultural presence which has also been increasingly recognized by the SED. Even their buildings often serve to relieve the shabby utilitarianism which forms much of the work of the GDR's architects.

Anyone who has visited the GDR frequently and has made a point of observing a little of the life of its religious groups will have noticed the increase of interest among young people in the Christian message. The influence of the churches among the young should be neither underestimated nor overestimated.

Life on the Estates

At its Eighth Party Congress in 1971, the conference at which Honecker took over from Ulbricht, the SED declared war on the housing problem. In that year the number of dwellings completed was well below what it had been in 1961, 87,000 as against 92,000. In the decade that followed things did indeed improve, and in 1982, 187,000 homes had either been built or renovated. Despite the progress housing remains a major problem. A high proportion of the GDR's housing stock is pre-1945 or even pre-1919. Most of the new homes are small flats constructed on large estates. All the well-known problems associated with such places in other countries have made their appearance in the GDR. These are noise, lack of amenities, psychological problems, boredom. Boredom is a problem particularly among teenagers and young adults. No doubt the FDJ does its best but many want diversion outside its functions. The FDJ reminds them too much of school, work, duties rather than pleasure. As elsewhere, the large estates of the GDR produce their crop of vandals, and this despite the residents' associations. Boredom is also a problem which can lead to mischief in the many neglected small towns of the GDR. Most of the building is done in Berlin and the main industrial centres.

Leisure and Hobbies

From the GDR's brilliant performances at recent Olympic Games the outsider probably imagines that the mass of GDR young people spend most of their free time involved in organized sport. This is certainly not the case. For one thing, sports facilities are not so readily available as is sometimes believed in the West. In the past much emphasis was placed on using the modest resources (modest after the prestige projects had taken their cut) to provide facilities for paramilitary sports and activities within the FDJ. The idea of individuals, groups of friends, or families simply using sport as a non-competitive leisure activity was almost completely alien. There has been some change for the better in recent years. Perhaps for this reason sport does not figure prominently in either the free time 'budgets' of young people or in their apparent interests (see below). The GDR publication *Die Freizeit der Jugend,* published in 1981, gave a picture of how the young spend their time (see Table 8.1). Even allowing for a certain amount of 'improving' of some scores to make it more acceptable to the GDR's Establishment, the survey seems roughly accurate.

Table 8.1   *Leisure Activities of GDR Youth*

Activity	Time Spent in Hours per Week		
	School pupils	Apprentices	Young workers
Television	8.9	7.6	6.3
Being with friends, colleagues, relations and acquaintances	6.5	5.1	5.6
Listening to radio and music	3.7	3.5	1.8
Participating in sport	3.0	2.2	1.0
Going for walks	2.4	0.9	2.1
Discos and dancing	2.2	3.2	1.9
Cultural, or scientific, or technical activity	2.0	3.7	2.0
Cycling, motorcycling, driving, or being driven by car	1.3	1.4	0.8
Relaxing	1.1	0.8	0.3
Playing cards or similar games	0.5	0.9	0.6
Visiting pubs or restaurants	0.5	0.8	2.9
Watching sport	0.4	0.5	0.2
Cinema	0.3	0.5	0.2
Exhibitions and similar	0.4	0.5	0.2
Other activities	3.5	4.9	4.6

The personal columns of the FDJ's daily paper *Junge Welt* also give us some guide to the interests of young East Germans. As this is an official organ (there are no unofficial ones), those who are extremely unorthodox are less likely to use this facility to find a friend of the opposite sex. Perhaps the most successful in this direction do not advertise either! Those who do use the columns of *Junge Welt* are likely to be more 'conservative', in the sense of supporting the regime, than the average young person. Finally, when evaluating these columns one must expect that the editors will reject submissions which they regard to be ideologically unacceptable. Nevertheless, an analysis of the hobbies mentioned gives us some indication of the interests of young people in the GDR today (see Table 8.2). These entries are from one particular issue of *Junge Welt* but they are typical. The term 'music' really means pop music rather than classical music. If we consider that only twenty-four men and eight women mentioned sport as a hobby we see how unreal is the normal Western view of East German people. Westerners can, of course, be forgiven for their view of East German youth because the official image projected is largely one of mass parades, Olympic victories and military preparations. I shall not rush to conclude that my analysis shows that FDJ members totally reject the SED regime which governs them, I shall merely cautiously conclude that even FDJ members are far less enthusiastic about the preoccupations of their leaders and far closer to Western youth in their interests than we often believe. My own on-the-spot observations and contacts with former residents of the GDR lead me to the conclusion that lack of interest in politics, apathy and indifference to many of the causes pushed by their leaders are normal. Most people probably never ask themselves, 'Am I for or against the GDR, for or against West Germany?' They fear the military build-up on both sides of the frontier, regard it as unnecessary and want more personal freedom than they are allowed. Many would grudgingly admit that life is not so bad in the GDR. The best of them, whether supporters of the SED or supporters of the churches (not mutually exclusive groups), harbour feelings of guilt about Third World poverty, but there are far less of them in this category than all the official manifestations of solidarity would lead one to believe. Most do not hate the Russians, but most do not find the USSR so very attractive. Even those who are strongly loyal often admit to, or show, embarrassment about the USSR.

Olympic boycott

The decision to pull out of the 1984 Olympic Games must have damaged Honecker and the SED leadership. Let it be said that in the past there were many in the GDR who felt that the attempt to build up the world's best Olympic medal-producing machinery was a waste of resources. But once it had been done they could not suppress a certain amount of pride at the GDR's successes in this field. The young were

Table 8.2   *Hobbies of* Junge Welt *Readers*

Hobbies of 77 Young Men as Given by Them in Junge Welt *(1 March 1983)*

music	dancing/disco	sport	travel	reading	camping	'everything beautiful'
57	22	24	40	18	13	11

motor sport	the arts	cinema	nature	'everything that gives joy'	other
9	1	3	4	10	5

Hobbies of 72 Young Women as Given in Junge Welt *(1 March 1983)*

music	dancing/disco	sport	travel	reading	camping	'everything beautiful'
52	34	8	26	18	4	20

motor sport	the arts	cinema	nature	'everything that gives joy'	other
3	2	2	4	10	13

'everything that's mad'	theatre
5	2

taught that these successes showed the superiority of socialism over capitalism. Young and old were enjoined to take pride in the GDR's separate national identity within the socialist camp. The Olympic boycott will have, at a stroke, and as has happened on other occasions in the past, destroyed billions of marks' worth of propaganda. I have no doubt that even young people accepting official explanations, which most do not, would argue that it would have been better to take the risks involved in going to Los Angeles – the exploitation of the games by anti-socialist groups, the lack of guarantees for the safety of the participants from the socialist states, the lack of guarantees for appropriate accommodation, training facilities, and so on for these participants (text *Der Morgen* 11 May 1984) – than to leave the field open for their opponents. They would argue that GDR victories would have furthered the cause of world socialism. The decision must have been a shock to those interested in either sports, or politics, or both. For months the media had been attempting to arouse interest in the games. Suddenly they did not matter any more. Little space was given over to the ritual interviews with members of the sport's community and general public saying how they agreed with the decision. Discussions with the older generation will lead to the conclusion that the GDR remains a vassal of the USSR rather than an esteemed partner. The attempts to convince young people of the correctness of the decision at the Seventh Gymnastics and Sports Conference of the Deutsche Turn- und Sportbund (DTSB), the official sports organiza- tion of the GDR, in May 1984 did not seem very convincing. The same is true of the National Youth Festival (June) of the FDJ which climaxed with a *Kampfdemonstration* of 750,000 blue-shirted mem- bers in Berlin.

Skinheads and Punks

At these official youth ceremonies there were no 'Bikers and hippies, skinheads and punks, mohicans and new romantics' of the kind found by Ian Walker (*Observer,* 28 August 1983) on a visit to East Berlin last year. He found that youth culture is flourishing and heard that in East Berlin there were a 'hundred-odd unofficial rock groups' called cellar bands which occasionally have gigs in churchyards. According to his informant, these are more or less tolerated: 'There'll be a load of security cops keeping an eye on things, just watching, maybe taking photographs. But they never break up the gigs. The church is off-limits'. Walker experienced such an event. East Berlin is probably more free than most of the middle-sized and small provincial towns.

Personally I have seen manifestations of youth culture in Potsdam and Magdeburg in the 1960s and Jena in the 1980s. Dresden and Leipzig, too, have their punk scenes. In East Berlin itself the old working-class district of Prenzlauer Berg has become known as a place where those young people seeking an alternative life-style congregate. Unlike those they are imitating in the West, East German 'drop outs' are required to work by law. Corrective labour can be the lot of those without regular employment. Some do, however, get by with a series of temporary jobs. But even in the GDR jobs do not seem quite so easy to come by as they once were and employers appear to be tightening up on labour discipline with the backing of the law. As Dr Hans Neumann, a judge in the GDR's supreme court, pointed out in *Der Morgen* (14 July 1984), 'Those who violate their work responsibilities must take the consequences'. He quoted paragraphs 54 and 56 of the labour code. In these circumstances employers may well be in a position to demand greater conformity of dress as well from young people. But at the present time punks and other outsiders can still walk the streets. If they want to do much more than that they had better do it in private. Private music sessions, poetry readings, discussion circles and art exhibitions have been a feature of teenage life in the GDR for a long time. Once the authorities get wind of these they are usually subject to surveillance and eventually to closer inspection by the police. Those taking part are then questioned, sometimes arrested and even held in custody. The West German paper *Deutsches Allgemeines Sonntagsblatt* (8 May 1983) has painted a very depressing picture of the lives of these young people, even though it recognized that the authorities had made some concessions.

It is difficult to be sure just how political the GDR's manifestations of alternative culture are. Many of those involved in such groups in the West deny any interest in politics. In the GDR, however, the SED's past lack of understanding for such groups has probably pushed more of them into a political position than would otherwise have been the

case. Whether the SED will take the advice of some of its own experts –
such as Professor Wolfgang Kessel of Leipzig University who,
according to *Der Tagesspiegel* (18 January 1983), urged more
understanding of young people's desire to be independent – is open to
doubt. Most SED leaders will see manifestations of youth culture as a
failure of their own educators rather than as a result of the SED's
attempt to turn all young people into the idealized FDJ heroes of the
early 1950s, who never really existed.

Juvenile Delinquency

Statistics on crime are notoriously difficult to interpret and compare
and are easily open to manipulation. The SED, for its part, is not
interested in giving information of use to the 'class enemy', in other
words, to the West. Statistics are published but they are rather
sketchy. Crime is partly a matter of definition and since 1968 whole
categories of minor offences such as petty theft, breach of the peace,
and so on, were no longer counted as crimes but counted as lesser
misdeeds which were excluded from the statistics. Thus, at a stroke,
the amount of crime was greatly reduced. If we look at the
development of the GDR since the mid-1960s we see a number of key
factors which in other societies have led to the increase in crime. These
are the development of supermarkets, the increase in the numbers of
private cars, the increase in alcohol consumption, the increase in free
time, the improvement of transport, the weakening of parental
authority, and children and young people spending less time with their
parents. The supermarket, with its open shelves and larger variety of
goods on display, is a greater temptation to would-be shoplifters than
was the traditional shop. Over the years I have seen more police in
East German stores than in British ones. More private cars means
greater temptation for youngsters to take them away without the
owner's permission for joy-riding. The shortage of spares in the GDR
has led to widespread thefts of parts from cars as they stand parked.
With increased prosperity in the GDR, alcohol consumption has risen.
The population of the GDR consumes just slightly less beer than is
consumed in West Germany, but a great deal more spirits – and West
Germany admits it is worried about alcoholism! Greater free time and
improved transport seem to be a factor in juvenile delinquency in that
they give greater opportunities for large numbers of young people to
congregate. 'Rowdyism' can develop. There is also a greater
possibility of boredom leading to crime being committed for the sake
of 'kicks'. East German children are likely to see less of their parents
than West German, British, or American children. The reason is quite
simply that far more women go out to work than in these other states.

Shift working is also widespread. Despite the after-school clubs and the FDJ, children are likely to spend considerable amounts of time unsupervised. And as Professor Donald West of Cambridge University, a noted authority on juvenile delinquency, has confirmed, 'Poor supervision could be one of the most important ways in which parents fail to protect their sons from delinquency'.[2] Lack of supervision is likely to be that much greater among broken homes and in this area the GDR has real problems (see Table 8.3). I shall make no judgement on these figures except to say that the SED finds the development unsatisfactory and that, from the point of view of juvenile delinquency, they could be of considerable significance.

Table 8.3   *Divorce in the GDR*

Year	Marriages	Divorces	Divorce rate (per cent)
1950	214,744	49,860	23.2
1960	155,410	25,736	16.2
1970	130,723	27,407	20.9
1980	134,195	44,794	33.7
1981	128,174	48,567	37.9

The discussion of juvenile delinquency on the GDR television and cases reported in the GDR press confirm my personal impressions that young offenders are, in the GDR no less than in other states, a considerable problem. In looking at individual cases from the GDR press we must be clear that crime reporting in Warsaw Pact states is not the free-for-all it is in the West. Crimes are reported only to illustrate, educate and deter. The published accounts of crimes give some idea of what the authorities regard as important at any given time.

The GDR Ministry of Interior reported in May 1984 that in the first four months of the year no less than 176 fires – mainly in homes or in the countryside – had been caused by children. In one case in Gera two boys of 7 and 8 had caused a fire which burned down three large barns. In Rostock, according to the same report, a 2-year-old set fire to his home in the absence of his mother (*Der Morgen,* 14 May 1984).

Crimes involving the abuse of alcohol are reported quite frequently. On 5 May 1983 *Der Morgen* reported the case of a 19-year-old Schweriner who was convicted of rowdyism, which in this incident meant being drunk and disorderly with another and causing grievous bodily harm. It was his fourth appearance and he received eighteen months' custodial sentence. In another case, reported 12 May 1983, an 18-year-old and a 20-year-old were sentenced to four and a half and two and a half years' detention respectively for setting fire to a livestock co-operative near Magdeburg. The same paper (10 August 1984) published a report of how a 22-year-old man killed another in a drunken brawl in a Halle-Neustadt disco. He was sentenced to ten years' imprisonment. According to *Der Morgen* (11/12 August 1984), vodka led two punks, a 20-year-old plumber and a 22-year-old mechanic, into an attack on an older person in Berlin's Friedrichstrasse. Both got prison sentences, but one was released as he had already been in prison awaiting trial for three months.

Boredom and excitement-seeking can be just as dangerous for young people in the GDR as in other countries. *Der Morgen* (2 June 1983) published an account of a 16-year-old in *Bezirk* Cottbus who was convicted of attempting to derail trains. He claimed he just wanted to see what happened! On 8 March 1983 *Junge Welt* reported the court appearance of three apprentices who were convicted of damaging socialist property at their place of work (a wood-processing plant). They claimed they were bored. The same paper (1 March 1983) reported the case of an apprentice aged 17 who, caught travelling without a ticket on a tram, beat up the volunteer ticker inspector. Luckily, his boss came forth to give him a positive character reference mentioning his active participation in the paramilitary sports organization, Gesellschaft für sport und Technik (GST). He got off with a fine and a suspended sentence. Another 'lucky' 18-year-old got off with a suspended sentence in Schwerin, after being convicted of taking out his father's hounds without permission and being unable to stop them assaulting a man and his 12-year-old daughter (*Der Morgen*, 26 May 1983). Another case involving dogs and carelessness was that of a 22-year-old shepherd who appeared in court after his dogs had savaged his flock. He had not bothered to secure them properly for the night (*Der Morgen*, 10 May 1984). Social security frauds appear to be another relatively common occurrence in the GDR. *Der Morgen* (19/20 May 1984) published the story of 'Moni', a 24-year-old postal employee who had been claiming benefit for years for children she did not have. She got a suspended sentence and was ordered to pay restitution.

More serious, and typical of crime in the GDR, was the case of the 27-year-old Gera man who by day was an ambitious, hardworking head of the shift at the factory where he worked, and by night was a car thief. In two years he stole nine Trabants, the most widely used GDR car, which he then cannibalized, selling the parts at a good profit. These activities, according to *Der Morgen* (26 July 1984), eventually earned him a sentence of seven years' imprisonment. It says a lot about the GDR motoring scene that he could find a ready market for the parts of such a very basic car. In Magdeburg a 19-year-old who, although a first offender, had a record of being difficult, was sentenced to three years and seven months' loss of liberty. He was also ordered to make full restitution for having set fire to a bookshop. He had tried to cover his tracks after breaking into the shop to steal money. He had been under the influence of alcohol. This case was reported in *Der Morgen* on 2 August 1984. In neither of these cases did anyone come forward to speak up for the accused. On, perhaps, a lighter note, under the headline, 'It wasn't Manfred's', *Der Morgen* (14 June 1984) brought to public attention a case which, it said, 'is not exactly rare' in the GDR. A 21-year-old woman in Halle claimed maintenance for her daughter from a certain Herr Manfred. She was described as 'attractive, slender and well-proportioned' by the (obviously sexist) reporter. Who could resist her? Manfred apparently had! He denied he was the father. Medical evidence confirmed this. Monika got a suspended sentence for false testimony.

As mentioned above, many minor offences are not brought before the courts but are dealt with by citizens commissions. Shoplifting, which is believed to be prevalent, is under the jurisdiction of store managers who can impose instant fines on culprits.

The cases mentioned are just a small selection of crimes reported in the GDR press over a short period. They help to make the GDR appear less of an Orwellian Utopia compared, that is, with how it often appears in both Western and Eastern literature.

The FDJ is proud of the part played by its own members as *Schöffen* (lay assessors) in the courts. In 1984, 3,200 members had been elected to these positions but these individuals are just a small part of the total number of lay assessors. I would not like to guess at their effectiveness or otherwise. Those in favour of such young assessors would claim that they are more likely to understand the problems of their peers. Against this one could argue that only the super conformists are likely to be selected for formal election and that these can be easily manipulated from above.

I do not know whether any of these young FDJ enthusiasts were on the bench the day that Karl-Heinz Bomberg, a young medical practitioner and a pacifist, was convicted in Berlin-Pankow for unlawful contacts. He had made tapes of his own songs which proclaimed his pacifist convictions, and passed these on to Western friends. In reporting his case, the *Süddeutsche Zeitung* (28/29 July 1984) brought attention to nine other young East Germans, four in Erfurt and five in Gera, sentenced to terms of imprisonment for their version of the struggle for peace. The four Erfurt Christians had produced leaflets criticizing GDR defence policy and calling for a boycott of the 1984 local elections. The Gera group had put leaflets through letterboxes making similar criticisms.

Though the GDR claims it has a progressive criminal code, unlike the situation in many Western European states including West Germany, the full rigour of the criminal code is applied to all those who have reached the age of 18. This applies to all types of crime but can be particularly harsh on young noncomformists.

The fears of the early postwar period that the SED, through the FDJ, the media, the school system and other agencies would create an indoctrinated, obedient, uncritical youth have not been realized. Today, the youth of the GDR are as likely to be critical and questioning as the youth of any other state in Europe or America.

Notes: Chapter 8

1 See David Childs, *The GDR: Moscow's German Ally* (London, 1983), pp. 88–90, for more details.
2 Donald West, *Delinquency* (London, 1982), p. 49.

9

East German Naval Build-up

DALE R. HERSPRING

Despite its importance in the overall NATO-Warsaw Pact balance, Soviet–East European naval strategy in the Baltic has received little attention in the USA. Instead, the tendency has been to view this issue as primarily a matter of concern to the West Germans and the Danes. Yet, as recent developments (for example, the presence of Pact submarines in Swedish and Norwegian waters) in the region illustrate, the Baltic naval picture is too important to ignore. This is particularly true regarding the GDR navy, which over the past thirty years has been transformed from a small inland police force outfitted with wooden ships to a modern naval force second only to the Soviet navy among Pact forces in the Baltic.

As a result, the GDR's role in Soviet Baltic strategy is growing. Furthermore, if current trends continue, the fleet of the GDR will become still more important in Soviet naval policy – especially if the Polish navy continues its slide toward obsolescence. From East Berlin's perspective, too, the navy is likely to play a bigger part in the overall political mission of the country's armed forces at home and abroad.

Role of the military in the GDR

The GDR military serves two primary functions. On the internal scene, it is important as a vehicle for socializing the country's youth. It teaches discipline, works actively to counter Western ideas and influence, and, to the degree possible, inculcates in the minds of its recruits acceptance of, if not enthusiastic loyalty to, the GDR.

The second and more important function of the military in the

GDR, for the purposes of this chapter, lies in foreign policy – particularly in that country's relations with the USSR and the Warsaw Pact. One of East Berlin's most pressing concerns has been that the Soviets might sacrifice vital GDR interests in their pursuit of improved relations with Bonn. To counter this potential threat, the East Germans have attempted to make themselves indispensable to the Soviets in a number of key areas: economic, technological, diplomatic and military. This is, for example, one of the main motives for GDR willingness to support the USSR in Africa, despite the political and financial costs, by providing security, paramilitary and cadre development assistance.

East Berlin's hope appears to be that if such support becomes important enough to Moscow, the GDR bargaining position on other questions will be enhanced. For example, the GDR might argue that closer relations between the two Germanies – Bonn's primary goal – could undercut political and social stability within the GDR, thereby making it increasingly difficult for East Berlin to carry out its commitments in other areas of importance to the USSR. East Berlin knows well that it cannot completely avoid being pushed into closer contacts with Bonn if Moscow is determined to move in that direction. Nevertheless, the GDR seeks to persuade the Soviets either not to adopt policies it feels are particularly threatening, or at least to devise counters to the more dangerous aspects of closer ties with the West.

Despite the key role that the armed forces play in the GDR's policy towards the USSR, there is no indication that the military is developing into an important interest group lobbying for increased arms expenditures. Rather, as has been argued elsewhere, most such lobbying – to the degree it occurs – takes place within the framework of the Warsaw Pact. In the GDR there appears to be a general consensus on the part of all the top leaders, civilians and military officers alike, that the National People's Army (Nationale Volksarmee – NVA) is a key vehicle for increasing the GDR's influence *vis-à-vis* the USSR.

However, according to one recent study, the GDR's ability to fulfil its preferred role as a key partner of the USSR in the economic and technical spheres is decreasing.[1] If true, and if this trend continues, it could increasingly detract from GDR ability to support Soviet foreign-policy goals. The GDR appears to recognize this, since it is making a major effort to strengthen its military capabilities. This is particularly true of the naval area, which plays a vital part in overall Soviet strategy. The increasingly important mission of the GDR navy is evident both in recent doctrinal statements and in the GDR's impressive ship-construction programme over the years.

Doctrinal Developments

Historically, East Germans writing on naval matters have avoided addressing broad strategic questions, preferring to translate important Soviet articles into German. Instead, East German authors have focused on practical questions, such as tactical operations or personnel, or on political issues. Recently, however, the East Germans took the unprecedented step of publishing a major article on strategic naval issues, by Captain G. Poschel, in the GDR's most important (and army-dominated) military-theoretical journal, *Militärwesen*.[2] The author, a senior member of the faculty at the Friedrich Engels Military Academy – the principal GDR postgraduate officer training facility – draws heavily on Soviet naval writings (for example, Admiral Sergey Gorshkov's *Sea Power and the State*). Nevertheless, in discussing Soviet naval concepts, he places them within a specifically GDR context and, in so doing, indirectly argues for an increased role for the navy within his country's military establishment.

Poschel's focus is on the concept of *Seeherrschaft*, which he equates with the Russian *gospodstvo na more*. According to Poschel, the concept has been variously translated into English as 'control of the sea, sea control, command of the sea, mastery of the sea, and sea supremacy; all 'incorporate the meaning of *Seeherrschaft*'. To be useful, however, the concept must be updated to 'accord with new conditions', a view Poschel notes is shared by leading Soviet writers like Gorshkov. The bulk of Poschel's three-part article is devoted to updating and applying the notion of *Seeherrschaft*.

First, Poschel defines his central concept as 'the result of combat operations by naval forces, which as a rule are carried out in the form of independent operations or in co-operation with other units, and as a result create a situation in all or part of the area of naval operations where the planned major task of the fleet can be carried out without being adversely influenced by an opponent' (p. 44). But the key part of the article comes in the third section, where the author discusses 'some peculiarities of the struggle for *Seeherrschaft* in enclosed [*geschlossenen*] naval areas of operations'. There are, according to Poschel, a number of special characteristics of such operations. For example:

- The degree, time, and area of *Seeherrschaft* are dependent upon the 'goal and purpose' of land forces operating in coastal areas. Indeed, *Seeherrschaft* is vital for land operations in coastal regions; without it, it would be necessary to tie down significantly larger numbers of army troops.
- Conversely, the success of land forces in coastal areas, and the overall situation on the front, will have a major impact on

the 'achievement and maintenance of *Seeherrschaft*'. For example, the loss of bases and other important ground military installations could make the attainment of *Seeherrschaft* impossible. Likewise, as long as important hostile naval bases remain intact, it is possible for an opponent to reorganize and re-emerge as a serious threat.

- Air superiority, including the use of helicopters, is vital in enclosed areas: 'it is the most important criterion'. 'Without it, *Seeherrschaft* cannot be achieved, and the tasks of the naval forces will not be carried out successfully, or only with heavy losses'.

- The goal of naval operations is continuous, all-around *Seeherrschaft*. It may be possible to achieve temporary *Seeherrschaft* in closed areas through ground operations and air superiority. This is particularly true if one's own forces are successful in blockading all entrances to the area of operations. However, given the other side's possession of missiles and aircraft, it will not be possible to attain total *Seeherrschaft* without significant sea-based operations.

- There are several ways to achieve *Seeherrschaft:* (1) by destroying an opponent's forces at sea, (2) by destroying an opponent's forces in their bases, (3) by blockading an opponent's forces in their bases, (4) by blockading the entrances to, or exits from, enclosed areas, and/or (5) by destroying key installations with land and air forces.

- Finally, the possession or loss of *Seeherrschaft* will have a significant influence on the behaviour of neutral countries bordering on enclosed areas (p. 59).

Poschel's article is notable for a number of reasons. His emphasis on the importance of operations the moment hostilities begin suggests that the Pact continues to place strong emphasis on surprise in its naval as well as in its ground and air doctrine. Still, Poschel expects the GDR navy to suffer serious casualities in a naval conflict with NATO forces. His reiteration of the impossibility of attaining absolute *Seeherrschaft*, and his stress on the need to sustain operations in the face of enemy actions, indicate that he has some doubts about his navy's ability to prevail, or at least about the number of casualties it might suffer. The importance he assigns to maintaining an 'operative regime' and to preparations for attaining *Seeherrschaft* suggests that the GDR navy will continue to place considerable stress on training operations.

The emphasis Poschel places on co-ordination between naval and ground forces is not surprising in a military establishment dominated by the army. Here Poschel appears to be taking a page from Gorshkov, who faces similar problems. An effective navy requires heavy expenditures, which the army would probably prefer to use elsewhere. Poschel's message is that funds must be allocated for the navy, too, if the army hopes to conduct operations successfully in the Baltic region. Furthermore, the army must be prepared to co-ordinate operations with the navy, in some cases (for example, amphibious operations) perhaps even subordinating itself to naval command.

The weight Poschel attaches to air power is also not surprising, given the GDR's location. Poschel does go beyond most other East German writers, however, in stressing the key role of naval air forces. In one key passage, he calls for specially trained naval aviators. Since the GDR's naval air forces are now limited to a squadron of Mi-14 helicopters, his comments could be interpreted as lobbying for the creation of specially trained pilots to man fixed-wing aircraft for naval operations, under naval command. Indeed, the GDR's need for a better-equipped naval air arm seems obvious. For even if the USSR's Backfire fighter/bombers are assigned the primary strike role in Baltic naval operations, a GDR naval air arm is required not only for antisubmarine warfare (ASW) operations, but for air defence and reconnaissance operations as well. Poschel's focus on naval air forces is probably also indicative of his navy's genuine concern over the naval air threat of the West German navy, the Bundesmarine.

Poschel's comments on the attitude of neutrals suggest that he expects the Swedes to adopt a more forthcoming stance if the Pact is winning. It is not clear, however, whether this would be the result of a voluntary act by the Swedes or of Pact pressure to support Soviet actions. While it is probably unwise to read too much into Poschel's remarks, they do suggest that the position of neutral neighbors is an important GDR concern. They may also indicate that in a NATO-Warsaw Pact confrontation, the Pact has plans for at least containing the Swedes.

The article's stress on the GDR's intention to strike the other side's military bases, while not unexpected, does indicate that the GDR considers them fair game if hostilities begin. Naval facilities on the Baltic almost certainly figure high on the Pact's target list. Finally, the importance Poschel assigns to blockading suggests that the navy expects to play a major role in this area. The Pact would probably attempt to blockade major ports such as Lübeck, while other GDR naval units, together with their Soviet and Polish allies, simultaneously move to seize the Danish straits, thereby cutting off the access of Western naval forces to the Baltic.

Poschel's article is also notable for its failure to focus on the Western submarine or surface threat in the Baltic. There are a number of possible explanations for this. First, the author may either consider the Bundesmarine's submarine or surface ships not to be a major threat, or – more likely – he may recognize that the GDR is simply not equipped to deal with the Bundesmarine's impressive submarine force. Discussion of the magnitude of the problem could reveal the extent of the threat, thereby undercutting morale. Also, Paschel probably recognizes that ASW is not the GDR's primary mission, and he may assume that this threat will be neutralized by Soviet forces.

Carrying out the tasks Poschel has assigned to the GDR navy will require a specially configured force. Yet the GDR's efforts over the years to build a maritime force capable of carrying out these increasingly ambitious missions have never before been adequately detailed in the open Western literature. In order to understand just how far the GDR navy has come, and how important it may yet become, it is desirable to fill this gap with a brief review of evolution to date.

Historical Overview

The history of the GDR navy can be divided into four rough periods: its origins as a naval police force; its emergence as the Volksmarine and incorporation into the Warsaw Pact; a subsequent sharp increase in its versatility and combat role; and its inclusion in a multinational Baltic 'combat service' since the early 1970s. Let us briefly review each of these periods.

Origins: 1950–6

The origins of the GDR navy can be traced back to the GDR Politburo's decision in February 1950 to establish a naval police (*Seepolizei*). During the first years, however, even this force was poorly equipped, and so devoted its main efforts to the 'education and training of suitable cadres'. It was only in 1952 that units of naval police were actually set up. Until that time, 'the security of the borders on the Baltic coasts' was entrusted to 'small boats on internal waters'.[3] The available ships were primitive at best. According to one authoritative source, they consisted primarily of wooden ships of Second World War vintage, with an average length of 15 metres.

East Berlin set out to improve this situation with typical Prussian thoroughness, and by the end of 1955 had made major strides towards acquiring an impressive naval inventory – most of which was built in GDR shipyards. Included were Halbicht and Schwalbe class minesweepers, coastal and harbour defence craft and a number of auxiliary craft. As Vice-Admiral Ehm put it: 'These ships contributed significantly to solving security tasks, the surveillance of coastal areas, and the protection of the GDR's sea borders.'[4] It is noteworthy that no claim was made at this time that the GDR navy possessed the ability to operate outside coastal waters.

1956–62

In 1956 the GDR naval police were transformed – at least on paper – into a navy, as the GDR joined the Warsaw Pact and took on an obligation to contribute to overall Soviet Baltic strategy. The problem, however, was that the GDR's navy was not in a position to assume a meaningful role in Pact Baltic operations. To begin with, ships were lacking – a problem that the Soviets helped solve by supplying the East Germans with a number of naval craft, including nine motor torpedo boats. At the same time, Soviet advisers were attached to the GDR navy. As a result, the 'combat capability of the naval forces increased significantly'.[5] While expanding this anti-ship capability, the GDR navy also began to build anti-mine and amphibious capabilities. Some ten Krake class minesweepers were added, as were Labo and Robbe class amphibious craft – all produced in the GDR.

Another factor inhibiting development of the GDR navy, though, was the absence of any operational infrastructure to facilitate joint Warsaw Pact naval operations. As the commander of the GDR navy later put it: 'The young generation among the members of our fleet will find it hard to believe, but up to this point there was no unified command and no unified document for the interaction and leadership of the unified fleets'.[6] But in mid-1956, tactical operations involving the Soviet, Polish and GDR fleet began, and joint manoevres with ground forces were undertaken. In addition, a staff of representatives from all three navies to oversee joint manoevres and carry out liaison work was established.

Of symbolic importance at this time was the decision to change the name of the navy (Seestreitkräfte) to Volksmarine (People's Navy). According to its commander, this not only symbolized the navy's more important role, it also demonstrated that 'the revolutionary military tradition of the struggle of the German working class had found a secure home in the GDR'.[7] Finally, on 4 November 1961, only months after the Berlin Wall was built, the GDR's border forces along the coast were tranferred to naval command.

By the end of this period, then, the GDR navy had changed significantly in comparison with its status five years before. It possessed 4 destroyers, 6 corvettes, 37 sub-chasers, 10 minesweepers, and 49 motor torpedo boats.[8] (Figures in this chapter for the size and characteristics of the Polish and GDR fleets are taken from the appropriate annual volumes of this publication.) Numerically, the Volksmarine already compared rather favourably with the Polish navy, which at that time had 4 destroyers, 6 submarines, 16 minesweepers and 40 motor torpedo boats. In Soviet eyes, however, both the GDR and the Polish contributions to Pact Baltic operations must still have been considered minimal.

1962–70

According to the commander of the Volksmarine, the introduction of missiles by the end of 1962 marked a major turning-point in the technical development of his fleet. It gave the navy a significant anti-ship capability and, together with its fast torpedo boats, expanded its role in Pact naval operations. Moreoever, with the acquisition of Labo class landing craft in that same year and the training of special army units for amphibious operations, the GDR contribution in that key area grew as well. By the middle of the decade, as Ehm later claimed, 'co-operation with motorized infantry units was perfected'.[9] Also, for the first time, a naval air arm was created, though it was limited to a squadron of Mi-4 helicopters outfitted for ASW operations.

According to GDR sources, Pact naval exercises also increased at this time. As Hesse put it, 'from 1961 on, operational exercises and strategic undertakings in which all types of forces and branches of service participated came to the forefront'.[10] In 1962 the first exercise was held involving 'all three fleets under the direction of a joint [*gemeinsame*] leadership organ'.[11] The next several years saw a number of other such exercises, including *Flut* (1963) and *Woga* (1964). Multilateral exercises reached a new high point, according to East German analysts, in 1968, with the command-staff exercise *Nord*. This time four fleets participated: the Soviet Northern Fleet, the Soviet Baltic Red Banner Fleet, the Polish navy, and the Volksmarine. Admiral Ehm of the GDR observed: 'The exercise area comprised the Baltic, the North Sea, the European Northern Sea, the Barents Sea, and the Northern Atlantic ocean. For the first time, fleets of the Warsaw Pact coalition were involved in an exercise involving such broad areas'.[12] By the end of the 1960s the Volksmarine alone possessed an impressive array of major combatants: 2 destroyers, 18 minesweepers, 12 missile boats, 62 fast torpedo boats, and 20 landing craft of moderate size. Except for submarine and naval air forces, this fleet now compared favourably with the Polish navy.

By 1970, accordingly, the Volksmarine was beginning to play an important role in the Baltic. This was particularly true of amphibious, anti-ship, and (to a lesser degree) ASW operations. The Volksmarine still had a long way to go, however, before it would be able to make the vital contribution in the Baltic called for by GDR foreign policy.

1971–83

In 1971–2, in an effort to avoid surprise attack from the sea, a 'combat service' (*Gefechtsdienst)* involving the Soviet, Polish and GDR fleets was established. The three navies began to co-ordinate their planning for combat training programmes. In addition, joint programmes in areas such as navigational training were created.

Baltic naval co-operation meanwhile continued in frequent joint exercises. For example, such exercises were held off Poland in 1972, and again in 1977. In 1979 alone, according to Hesse, '29 common discussions and consultations with the fraternal fleets were held'.[13] More recently, in July 1981, an exercise was commanded by an East German admiral; previously, all had been conducted under Soviet command. Similar exercises were held in 1982 in the North and Norwegian seas. Their purpose was officially described as antisubmarine warfare, and replenishment at sea.[14] According to a recent article by an East German naval officer, 'the exercises by the unified squadrons [*vereinte Geschwader*] as well as the common minesweeping forces, carried out in the past three years, played a special role in the 1982 training year'.[15] Such exercises are apparently conducted on at least a yearly basis, and clearly figure prominently in the Volksmarine's operational plans.

In the meantime, within the Volksmarine, increased emphasis has been placed on automation through the introduction of increasingly sophisticated electronic equipment. According to the commander of the Volksmarine, the new equipment enabled the navy to achieve 'a higher level of combat readiness'.[16] Most ships in service in 1971 have been replaced by more modern versions. In addition, the GDR fleet has expanded in size. Thus, while the Volksmarine held two outdated Riga class destroyers in 1971, by the end of the decade these had been replaced by two modern Koni class frigates. In addition, nine Parchim class corvettes have been deployed, and nine more are said to be under construction in GDR shipyards. They are probably intended as replacements for the much smaller (300 tons *v.* 1,200 tons) Hai class patrol craft.

The GDR has also devoted considerable effort to upgrading its amphibious sea-lift capability, putting it in a better position to carry out several of the tasks mentioned by Poschel. For example, the Labo and Robbe class landing craft have been replaced by the much larger Frosch class landing ships/tanks (LSTs) and there is an unconfirmed report that the Volksmarine may be adding more amphibious craft of a new 'Eidechse' class.[17] In addition, at least one East German naval officer has argued that 'naval artillery' will continue to play a key role in support of landing forces – thus corroborating the importance that Poschel assigns to naval forces in such operations.[18] Finally, Mi-14 helicopters were introduced in the mid-1970s to update the navy's air capability. The Volksmarine's major combatants are listed in Table 9.1.

Table 9.1   *GDR Major Naval Combatants*

Type (class)	Years built	Number in service	Gross displacement (tons)
Frigate (Koni)	1978–9	2	2,000
Corvette (Parchim)	1981	9[a]	1,200
Large patrol craft (Hai)	1963–9	9	370
Fast attack craft/missile (Osa 1)	1960–5	15	210
Fast attack craft/torpedo (Shershen)	1962–74	18	175
Fast attack craft/torpedo (Libelle)	1975–80	31	30
Landing ship/tanks (Frosch)	1976–80	14	4,000
Minesweeper (Kondor)	1970–83	27	280
Naval air helicopter (Mi-14)		8	

[a] Nine more are under construction.
Source: Jane's Fighting Ships, 1983–4 (London, 1984), pp. 181–7.

Contemporary Strategic Assessment

The increased importance that the Volksmarine has assumed in the Baltic is perhaps best illustrated by comparison with the Polish navy. To begin with, the GDR navy now possesses a significantly larger number of combatants (139 *v.* 114), despite its much smaller personnel structure (16,000 *v.* 22,500).[19] From a structural standpoint, the primary difference between the two navies is the possession by the Poles of four Whiskey class submarines and of fixed-wing aircraft. In so far as surface combatants are concerned, however, one is struck by the greater modernity and capabilities of GDR ships. For example, the GDR has two new frigates, compared to one outdated destroyer for the Poles. Furthermore, while the East Germans have nine corvettes and are building nine more, the Poles have nothing comparable. Likewise, in the case of amphibious craft, Warsaw's 23 Pólnocny class ships can carry 6 tanks each and have a displacement of 1,150 tons when fully loaded. The GDR ships, by contrast, can carry 12 tanks each and have a displacement of 4,000 tons; they are thus significantly more capable than those of other Baltic powers. Altogether, the Polish navy represents a rapidly aging force in urgent need of replacing its existing ships (Vego).

In strictly military terms, the Volksmarine's primary concern appears to be its ability to blockade strategic points in the Baltic. This is evident not just from doctrinal statements, but also in the strong push for an expanded amphibious capability. To further upgrade capabilities in this area, the Volksmarine needs to devote more attention to its minelaying forces. This, after all, will be one of its major tasks if it hopes to seize and hold the Danish straits.

The Volksmarine also appears to be acquiring an improved antisubmarine capability, but this, too, remains insufficient. In addition, its anti-ship forces (Osa 1 and Osa 2 class missile boats) are becoming dated. The GDR navy clearly needs to expand significantly in both these areas. Yet Poschel's failure to mention the need for submarines may mean that the GDR has no intention of acquiring any. The Volksmarine's most serious defect is its lack of a fixed-wing naval air arm. Poschel's stress on the importance of a naval air arm may indicate that this problem is being given serious consideration.

Thus, despite East Berlin's impressive build-up of naval forces, the Volksmarine still faces a number of difficulties that need to be overcome if it hopes to match the Bundesmarine. No one can say whether East Berlin will be 'permitted' by the Soviets to overcome all of those difficulties. Nevertheless, based on the experience of the past thirty-odd years, one thing appears certain: to the degree that the East Germans acquire new systems and equipment, they will continue to operate and integrate them into the fleet with a high degree of efficiency.

Altogether, as of 1983, the Volksmarine has developed into a modern navy, a force to reckon with in the Baltic. As the most important non-Soviet Pact navy there, the Volksmarine must figure large in Moscow's strategy for that theatre. Seventeen per cent of the Pact's frigates will be East German, once the new Parchim corvettes join the fleet. Furthermore, over two-thirds of the Pact's LSTs belong to the GDR. As a result, while the Volksmarine may not yet be truly indispensable for Soviet naval operations in the Baltic, it plays an ever more important role in certain areas, and certainly enhances Soviet capabilities in the region. The GDR contribution to the new Warsaw Pact Baltic order of battle is shown in Table 9.2.

Conclusion

The decision by the GDR political and military leadership to push ahead with the development of a modern, highly trained, technically advanced navy has a number of ramifications. On the internal scene, the increasingly important mission of the Volksmarine should enhance its role within senior GDR military councils. The navy's push for greater naval influence over amphibious operations, its call for a naval air arm, and its impressive building programme all suggest an expanded role for that service branch, perhaps at some cost to the air force and the army.

Within the Warsaw Pact, the increasing size, number and quality of

Table 9.2 Baltic Order of Battle (GDR, Poland, USSR): Selected Major Surface Combatants

	GDR		Poland		USSR	
		% of		*% of*		*% of*
Class	*Number*	*Class*	*Number*	*Class*	*Number*	*Class*
Destroyers[a]	0	0	1	9	8	91
Fast frigates[b]	18[c]	17	0	0	86	83
Landing ship/tanks	14[d]	70	0	0	6	30
Landing ship/ medium	0	0	23	56	18	44
Light forces	73	31	41	18	120	51
Minesweepers	27	13	49	24	125	62

[a] Includes guided-missile destroyers.
[b] Includes guided-missile fast frigates.
[c] Includes nine Parchim class corvettes under construction.
[d] Includes two Frosch 2 class LSTs outfitted as transports.
Source: Jane's Fighting Ships, 1983–4, pp. 181–7, 386–92, 486.

the ships possessed by the Volksmarine, the decline of the Polish navy, Moscow's increased tendency to supply its forces in the GDR by sea (a practice followed during periods of tension in Poland), and the more important role in Soviet Baltic strategy that the GDR navy appears to be assuming, all combine to strengthen that navy's role in Pact military councils. In this context, while the decision to build up the Volksmarine may not have been a direct result of the GDR's economic/technical decline in other areas, it probably will help to compensate for this development.

Assuming that a parallel phenomenon is also occurring in relation to the GDR's air and ground forces, East Berlin's overall influence within the Pact is likely to increase. (In that regard, it is worth noting that not only is the GDR spending a greater percentage of its GNP on defence than any other East European Pact member, it is also the only one besides Bulgaria that has regularly increased its military budget since 1971.)[20] This is not to suggest that the East German 'tail' may be 'wagging the Soviet dog'; only that the GDR's influence on military (and perhaps also political) questions will probably rise, most likely at the expense of its other East European allies.

From the standpoint of the West, the build-up of the Volksmarine is at least partially offset by the growing obsolescence of Poland's navy, and by the political instability of that country over the past three years. If, however, the Poles modernize their fleet and stabilize the political situation within their country, the overall naval threat facing NATO in the Baltic will obviously increase significantly. In the meantime, the GDR navy – notwithstanding its diverse problems – should not be taken lightly. Like the overall Baltic military balance, it deserves far more attention than it has generally been given in the USA.

Notes: Chapter 9

1   Ronald A. Francisco, 'East German foreign policy: an economic perspective', paper presented at the Wingspread Conference on the GDR, Wingspread, 14-17 April 1983.
2   G. Poschel, 'On command of the sea', *Militärwesen*, Nos 5, 6 and 8 (May 1982, June 1982, August 1982).
3   Wilhelm Ehm, 'The development of the People's Navy of the National People's Army', *Militärgeschichte*, no. 4 (1979).
4   ibid., p. 407.
5   ibid., p. 408. See also G. Hesse, 'On the development of co-operation among the Allied Baltic Fleets of the Warsaw Pact', *Militärwesen*, no. 4 (April 1980), p. 29.
6   Wilhelm Ehm, 'For a reliable protection of coastal boundaries – vigilance and combat readiness!' *Militärwesen*, no. 2 (February 1976), p. 37.
7   Ehm, 'The development of the People's Navy', cit. at n. 3 above.
8   *Jane's Fighting Ships 1962–3* (London, 1963), pp. 108–9.
9   Ehm, 'The development of the People's Navy', cit. at n. 3 above, p. 412.
10 Hesse, 'On the development of co-operation', cit. at n. 5 above, p. 31.
11 Ehm, 'The development of the People's Navy', cit. at n. 3 above, p. 412.
12 ibid., p. 414.
13 Hesse, 'On the development of co-operation', cit. at n. 5 above, p. 30.
14 Milan Vego, 'East European navies', *Proceedings of the US Naval Institute* (Annapolis, Md, March 1983), p. 44.
15 L. Heinecke, 'Joint combat training of the Allied Socialist Baltic Fleet', *Militärwesen*, no. 4 (April 1983), p. 19.
16 Ehm, 'The development of the People's Navy', cit. at n. 3 above, p. 415.
17 William P. Baxter, 'National security', in *East Germany: A Country Study* (Washington DC, 1981), p. 223.
18 H. Metzschke, 'The use of naval artillery in the support of amphibious forces', *Militärwesen*, no. 5 (May 1977).
19 *Jane's Fighting Ships 1983–4* (London, 1984), pp. 181–7 and 386–92.
20 US Arms Control and Disarmament Agency, *World Military Expenditures and Arms Transfers 1971–1980* (Washington DC, 1982), pp. 41, 45, 49, 51, 63, 64.

10

The German Democratic Republic and the Soviet Union

MARTIN McCAULEY

Introduction

Erich Honecker, in an interview on Soviet television, once informed his viewers that, as far as the GDR was concerned, friendship with the USSR was not only the 'decisive foundation of our state' but was also a 'vital necessity'.[1] This neatly underlined the patron–client relationship between the USSR and the GDR and the lack of self-confidence with which East Berlin viewed the outside world. When he made this statement, in late 1971, Honecker had only a short time before he succeeded Walter Ulbricht as leader of the SED. The new first secretary owed his advancement, in part, to Ulbricht's obstinacy in holding out for greater concessions from the West during the negotiations which eventually led to the Berlin Agreement. Hence Ulbricht, who in 1945 had been a malleable instrument in the hands of the Soviet policy-makers, as the GDR matured gradually acquired the self-confidence to defend what he held to be vital GDR interests, even though these were not regarded as such in Moscow. Ulbricht misjudged Soviet, mainly Brezhnev's, resolve to pursue *détente* which promised to bring the USSR a rich harvest. The Brezhnev of 1971 was capable of decisive leadership. Had this conflict occurred in 1981 when Brezhnev's hold on the reins of power were loosening, the outcome might have been different. The main lesson which emerged from the removal of Ulbricht was that Moscow placed its internat-ional interests ahead of those of the GDR in inter-German relations. East Berlin's foreign policy, until the Basic Treaty of 1972, was Germanocentric. Its prime concern was to oblige Bonn to recognize the fact that the GDR state was legitimate. Moscow's foreign policy, on the other hand, was global and Soviet–GDR–West German re-lations were only part of a larger Soviet–American superpower relationship. Soviet perceptions about their interests change over time as objective circumstances alter. In the light of this, the clause in the Treaty of Friendship, Co-operation and Mutual Assistance, signed by the USSR and the GDR in October 1975, which speaks of eternal friendship between the two states is only relevant to the existence of the GDR in its present form. Moscow may decide sometime in the future that the GDR can pass away and be replaced by an all-German state. Whereas the GDR could not continue to exist in its present political and economic form without the protection of the USSR, the latter could carry on as a sovereign state without the existence of the GDR. It is therefore of interest to examine the Kremlin's German policy over the years since 1945 and to look at the effect these changes have had on the evolution of the GDR. Basically, the USSR is faced with a dilemma: Are Soviet security interests better served by one Germany or two? This problem has never been satisfactorily resolved.

Varga's Analysis

The Grand Alliance during the Second World War made no impact on Soviet foreign-policy doctrine. The two basic concepts of capitalist encirclement and Lenin's theory of imperialism remained intact. Since state security always take precedence over ideological goals in Soviet foreign-policy decision-making, Moscow was not going to put the hard-won gains of world war at risk without being convinced that its chances of winning, if it did gamble, were very high. Brinkmanship, to use an expression coined later, was not on the Soviet agenda.

Soviet postwar thinking appears to have been influenced by the writings of the economist Eugene Varga. In articles published in late 1944 and 1945, brought together in a book entitled *Changes in the Economy of Capitalism as a Result of the Second World War*, which appeared in 1946, he argued that the war had made capitalism much more complex than in Lenin's day. The intervention of the state in the market economy during hostilities would not cease after the war was over, and this would counter the anarchy of capitalist production. There would be a struggle for markets between the USA, the strongest capitalist power, and Great Britain and France, which would almost certainly lead to armed conflict. Hence Soviet policy should aim at maintaining good relations with the USA, knowing that in the event of an altercation between the Americans and the West Europeans, Moscow could fish profitably in troubled waters. The Americans also wanted amicable relations with the Soviets, but how was Stalin to judge whether this would benefit the USA more than the USSR? The Soviet leader used two criteria to measure the seriousness of US good intentions. Would Washington concede the zone of influence which Soviet military power had won in Eastern and South-Eastern Europe? President Roosevelt had agreed to recognize it, but would his successor, President Truman? After all, Truman had not been party to wartime US diplomatic decision-making. Secondly, would the USA extend large loans and surplus war stock so that the postwar Soviet economy could recover rapidly?

Varga's analysis of capitalism led him to conceive of the postwar world as an interim period between capitalism and socialism, one for which the term 'people's democracy' was coined to demonstrate this evolution in Eastern and South-Eastern Europe.[2] Of the two criteria mentioned above, one was non-negotiable from a Soviet point of view, their zone of influence in Eastern and South-Eastern Europe.

Soviet Conceptions on Germany

Since Germany was the key country in Central Europe, its evolution would have a profound influence on how Western and Southern Europe developed. From Moscow's point of view there were various options concerning Germany. The strategic or long-term goal was a united, socialist Germany in which the leading role of the Communist Party of the Soviet Union (CPSU) was recognized and could be enforced. However, in the meanwhile, tactical or short-term goals suggested themselves: a temporarily divided Germany with Soviet influence predominant in the East and American influence in the West; a unified, neutral Germany, not permitted to enter into any military alliance inimical to Soviet or US interests; a unified Germany under quadripartite control which would permit the USSR to mould developments in its own zone and to influence the evolution of the western zones. A key objective was to prevent the emergence of a military-industrial complex based on the Ruhr which was inimical to Soviet goals and interests. The least advantageous contingency for Moscow would be a divided Germany with a West German state which was hostile to it and which was embedded in a US economic-military alliance. A complicating factor for Soviet decision-makers was the *de facto* division of Germany in 1945. If it cemented into a *de jure* division would this become a threat to Soviet security? In other words, would a divided Germany always be such a potential source of conflict between East and West that a unified Germany, even though it was neutral, be preferable? How many Germanies should there be, one or two?

It took the Soviets ten years, between 1945 and 1955, to accept the reality of a divided Germany. This second-best solution was forced upon them by West Germany entering NATO in 1955. So strong was the West German state regarded and its ties with the USA so strong that Moscow accepted for the time being that two mutually antagonistic German states were unavoidable.

Soviet policy towards Germany in the decade after 1945 was flexible, based on the assumption that a divided Germany was not in the USSR's long-term interests. The aim of trying to prevent the emergence of a separate West German state closely allied to the USA failed because Moscow was not willing to make the concessions which would have secured an all-German state. In other words, Moscow did not believe that this eventuality would be so dangerous as to warrant paying a high price to secure a neutral, all-German state.

It is highly unlikely that the USSR foresaw that two German states would come into existence in 1949. The loss of the raw-material resources of Silesia and the rich farmland of Pomerania were a severe blow to the viability of the Soviet zone. A major Soviet concern was reparations but no precise figure was agreed at Potsdam. Although the Potsdam Agreement provided for the establishment of central German administrations in Berlin they never came into existence due to the conflicting interests of the occupying powers. The French did not want a united Germany and used their veto to telling effect. Britain was concerned about the mounting cost of its zone and had no desire to see a resurgent Germany becoming increasingly competitive in foreign markets. At the London conference of foreign ministers in November–December 1947, the British were very concerned lest the very flexible stance adopted by Moscow lead to a compromise which favoured the Soviets. The Americans wanted a viable German economy which would reduce their occupation costs and permit them militarily to leave Europe.

Communist Failure in West

All the political parties in the Soviet zone wanted a united Germany. After all, each of them included the word 'Germany' in their titles. The desire to establish a united party of the left was strong in 1945 and had it come into being in the Soviet zone it would have exerted a powerful influence on developments in the other three zones. However, the desire of the Soviets to have a communist party which was amenable to CPSU guidance was so strong that this opportunity was allowed to slip away. Moscow feared that a united working-class party would be swamped by Social Democrats, thus making it extremely difficult to mould the policy of the united party according to Soviet wishes. The fusion of the Sozialdemokratische Partei Deutschlands (SPD) and the Kommunistische Partei Deutschlands (KPD), in April 1946, was a setback to Soviet all-German hopes. West German Social Democrats, in the main, refused to follow suit and became increasingly critical of Soviet policies. One of the results of this was that the KPD in the Western zones never attained its pre-1933 influence. The gulf between the Social Democratic leadership in the West and Otto Grotewohl widened at the Bavarian KPD congress in April 1947 when the latter claimed that Soviet policies and Soviet policies alone represented the true interests of Germany. If it is true that communist influence was growing in the Western zones at this time among rank-and-file Social Democrats then Kurt Schumacher, the SPD leader, more than anyone else, countered that influence.

Another reason for the failure of the Communists to make a breakthrough in the Western zones was the fact that not a single high-ranking KPD official, after returning to Germany, was delegated to work in West Germany. As the KPD–SED built up its apparatus, qualified communists from the Western zones were recruited for work in the Soviet zone and Berlin. It had apparently been decided that first priority should be afforded to it, even if this meant that opportunities available in the Western zone could not be fully exploited. First establish firm communist control in the East, then focus on West Germany, appeared to be the plan. Under normal circumstances this might have turned out to be a good decision but the advent of the Cold War in 1947 quickly reduced its chances of success.

The currency reform in West Germany and West Berlin in June 1948 split Germany, but without it economic recovery in the West was not possible. The Berlin Blockade was launched by the Soviets in an attempt to remove the Western Allies from Berlin and also to hold up the formation of a separate West German state. Had it succeeded, the German People's Congress, elected in March 1948, could have convened in Berlin to draft a constitution and appoint a provisional government to represent all Germans. This provisional government would have appealed for German unity and called on all West Germans to halt the move towards a separate state, a move which would cement the division of Germany. However, Stalin was not willing to take the ultimate step to secure his objective: the use of military force. Had he done so in the early stages, the Western Powers, almost certainly, would have retreated from Berlin. Never theless, Stalin was a cautious leader and was unwilling to risk an armed conflict to avert the possible emergence of a separate West German state. It is still unclear why Stalin, once the initial move had failed and the Berlin air lift had proved capable of overcoming the blockade, allowed the exercise to drag on so long. After all, the longer it lasted the more likely it became that a separate West German state would emerge, one which was firmly anti-communist and anti-Soviet. A by-product of the blockade was the insecurity it sowed in Western and Southern Europe. It nourished the fear that the USSR was an aggressive power which, if it won in Berlin, would then march on Western Europe. The West Europeans proposed the formation of a military alliance which would ensure that the Americans remained in Europe to defend it against possible Soviet attack. The Soviets never had any intention of attacking Western Europe, but they permitted the Berlin Blockade to drag on long enough to ensure the emergence of NATO. The blockade was a bad miscalculation and did considerable damage to Soviet prospects in Germany.

The USSR and the Setting Up of the GDR

When the GDR came into existence on 7 October 1949 it declared its goal to be a united Germany and General (later Marshal) Chuikov, commander-in-chief of the Soviet Military Administration in Germany (Sowjetische Militäradministration in Deutschland – SMAD), expressed his full support for this objective.[3] SMAD's functions were passed to GDR ministries and state organs on 11 November 1949. On the same day, the Soviet Control Commission in Germany (SCCG) became the supreme Soviet organ in the GDR. This state of affairs lasted until after the death of Stalin. On 28 May 1953 the USSR Council of Ministers decided to dissolve the SCCG with effect from the following day. The commander-in-chief of Soviet forces was also relieved of his political, economic and social supervisory duties and his competence was restricted to the military command of Soviet troops in Germany. The post of high commissioner was established and Vladimir Semenov appointed. He was to look after Soviet interests in Berlin and was also to represent Moscow in matters of an all-German character in discussions with the Western occupying powers. The extent to which these changes were linked to the attempt of the Soviet leadership, represented in Berlin by Semenov and supported by elements in the SED Politburo such as Zaisser, Minister of State Security and Herrnstadt, editor-in-chief of *Neues Deutschland,* to remove Ulbricht and to slow down the march to socialism can still not be accurately judged. It is tempting to see all these changes as part of a plan to prepare the way for a united Germany. This would have involved meeting the Western Allies at least half way. The uprising of 17 June 1953 and the fall of Lavrenti Beria in Moscow later that month was a mortal blow to such an eventuality. Shortly afterwards, in August 1953, Soviet and GDR diplomatic missions were transformed into embassies and the exchange of ambassadors agreed.

On 25 March 1954 the Soviet government decided to have the same relations with the GDR as with 'other sovereign states'. This affected the high commission immediately. In June 1954 it was reorganized and its personnel sharply reduced. Its representatives in the various GDR *Bezirks* and in Berlin were withdrawn. On 5 August 1954, G. M. Pushkin, Soviet ambassador and high commissioner, informed Otto Grotewohl, GDR Prime Minister, that the high commission staff in Berlin, Karlshorst were being transferred to the embassy in Unter den Linden, near the Brandenburg Gate. All orders and decrees issued by SMAD and SCCG between 1945 and 1953 affecting the political, economic and cultural life of the GDR were declared null and void. The high commission was not abolished until after the signing of the 'treaty on relations between the USSR and the GDR' of 20 September 1955. This treaty finally established the GDR as a sovereign state.

As the USSR moved towards conferring sovereignty on the GDR and thereby acknowledging the division of Germany, a parallel process had been underway, that of promoting German unity. When the GDR came into being its constitution claimed to speak for all Germans. Wilhelm Pieck, the first GDR President, explicitly underlined the desire of all in the GDR for national unity. In 1950 and 1951 the GDR proposed the formation of an all-German Constituent Council. In the latter year the GDR came very close to accepting an all-German electoral law which had been passed by the West German Bundestag. Then came the Soviet note of 10 March 1952 which proposed a unified neutral Germany.[4] After Stalin's death, the 17 June uprising and the fall of Beria made it difficult for the new leadership to make proposals similar to those favoured by Beria. The main stumbling block to an all-German settlement raised by the Western side was that free elections, under international supervision, should be held to elect an all-German assembly. It, in turn, would agree on a government which would be empowered to negotiate a peace treaty with the former belligerent states. The Soviets agreed to all these objectives but reversed the order of priority. They maintained that a provisional government should be formed which would agree on the main points of a peace treaty. When this had been achieved the population could elect a national assembly. The Soviets and East Germans proved inflexible on this point of procedure and by the autumn of 1952 the initiative had run into the sand. However, on 20 January 1955, the Soviets suddenly reversed their position and agreed to free elections under international supervision to elect an all-German national assembly as a first step towards a peace treaty and a united Germany. However, it was too late as West Germany was by then firmly within the Western camp and preparing to enter NATO – the main reason for the communist *démarche*. After the West had shown little interest in the proposal the Soviets reluctantly came to the conclusion that the division of Germany was not going to be temporary. A by-product of this was the Austrian State

Treaty. Until 1955 the USSR had considered the Austrian and German problems together, but the entry of West Germany into NATO uncoupled them. Bulganin, the Soviet Prime Minister, mentioned during the Austrian negotiations that a solution had been found to the German problem which was 'unfortunate'.[5]

Soviet Objectives, 1945–55

It is reasonable to assume that Soviet policy towards Germany and Austria was to ensure that the Western-occupied parts did not coalesce into separate states which slipped into a pro-US military-economic network. This objective was achieved in Austria. Why was it not in Germany?

One way of looking at this problem would be to argue that Soviet policy between 1945 and 1955 had one main objective: the recognition of the sovereignty of the GDR by the Western Powers. If this was the primary objective there was a secondary goal: to hold up the formation of a separate West German state and its integration into a Western alliance system. The longer these phenomena could be delayed the greater the chance they would not come about. Hence all the appeals for German unity by East Berlin, which it knew Bonn would reject, and the Soviet *démarches* were aimed at increasing the legitimacy of the GDR state in the eyes of the East German population. It should be said that the SED's German policy received the whole-hearted support of the population, something which has not happened since 1955. Also each move between 1953 and 1955, ending with the treaty on relations between the USSR and the GDR, was primarily aimed at increasing the standing of the GDR in the eyes of the international community.

There is much to be said for this point of view but it reflects too closely SED interests. Moscow took a wider view of the world and the consequence of West Germany joining NATO was to augment the military threat facing the USSR. It is possible that the USSR did not foresee West Germany joining NATO and hence did not feel constrained to make concessions on free elections under international supervision. Had they done so, the Western Powers might have negotiated seriously on a united, neutral Germany. When Moscow did concede free elections in January 1955 it was too late. It was read by the West as a blatant attempt to prevent West Germany joining NATO. Anyway, by 1955 West Germany was too closely enmeshed with the West for the Western Powers to negotiate seriously on a united, neutral Germany. The note of March 1952 was also too late. Adenauer was strongly against negotiations since he wanted West Germany to become part of the West European defence network. Bonn had been arguing for free elections first ever since March 1950, firm in the knowledge that Moscow was almost certain to say no.

Between 1945 and 1955 the KPD–SED leadership conducted an offensive all-German policy and supported all Soviet initiatives in this direction. Hence, in effect, it was supporting policies which could have resulted in the GDR disappearing from the map. There is no evidence to show that the leadership relished this prospect. Its insecurity was stilled in 1955 when the USSR conferred sovereignty on the GDR and began to integrate it more fully into the socialist commonwealth. However, the SED could not rest secure as long as the GDR was not recognized by the West. The road to recognition was long and can be divided into two periods: 1955–61 and 1962–72.[6]

SED Ideas on Germany

At the Geneva Conference in July 1955 US, British, French and Soviet leaders instructed their foreign ministers to explore the possibility of the unification of Germany by means of free elections. However, on his way home Khrushchev stopped off in East Berlin and declared that there could be no mechanical unification of Germany. The socialist achievements of the GDR would have to be guaranteed in a future all-German state. The SED argued that the German problem could only be solved by the two German states coming closer together. However, the policies pursued by Ulbricht during the second half of the 1950s widened the gap between the two parts of Gemany. One of the arguments advanced by Ulbricht's political opponents in the leadership – all defeated and removed in 1958 – was that his policies made the likelihood of an arrangement with Bonn more remote. The SED was badly shaken by the revelations of Khrushchev at the Twentieth CPSU Congress in February 1956 when Stalin and his whole technique of rule came under bitter attack. However, Ulbricht was skilled enough to ride out the storm partly due to his good relations with Khrushchev.

The SED needed a German policy which would appeal to citizens in the GDR and West Germany. Ulbricht came up with the idea of a confederation in an article entitled 'In the interests of the unification of the working class in the whole of Germany' in *Neues Deutschland* on 30 December 1956. The merit of the concept of a confederation was that the GDR would have equal status with West Germany in a united Germany, even though West Germany was twice as large. It also allowed the SED leadership to present itself to the GDR population as a responsible representative of the interests of all workers and progressives in both parts of Germany. It also provided a channel of contact with the West German working class and progressive elements. Moreover, the USSR was in total agreement with the initiative. The SED leadership was also safe in the knowledge that Bonn would not respond. Hence the failure to reunite the two parts of Germany could be laid at the door of Bonn. The proposal for a confederation remained SED policy until the early 1960s. From the Soviet point of view the plan promised to raise the legitimacy of the SED at home and to make the GDR a more acceptable state to those in the West.

The successful meeting of President Eisenhower and Khrushchev at Camp David in September 1959 when they both agreed to seek solutions to the foreign-policy problems facing them must have caused a flutter in East Berlin. The impetuous Soviet leader was quite capable of devising a solution to the German question which would put the GDR at a disadvantage. Fortunately for the SED the danger passed.

During the 1950s the two German states had been growing apart and the decision to complete the collectivization of agriculture over the years 1959–61 in order to complete the victory of the socialist relations of production – without which a socialist society could not be built – led to a reappraisal of the GDR's position *vis-à-vis* West Germany. Until 1960 the GDR had laid the blame for the division of Germany on the shoulders of the Western Powers. Hence East Berlin's, and Moscow's, policy had been geared to overcoming the unnatural division of the country. In 1960 the GDR began to regard itself as heir to the progressive tradition in German history. The emergence of the GDR was therefore not caused by the policies of the West but was rather part and parcel of the world socialist evolution. The SED prepared three large documents to underline its case: the German People's Plan in 1960, the German Peace Plan in 1961 and the National Document in 1962. The GDR claimed that it was a state in its own right and, moreover, was socially more advanced than West Germany.

The USSR and Germany in the 1960s

After the erection of the Berlin Wall, West Germany decided to try to improve its image in Moscow. In late 1961 and early 1962 the West German ambassador to the USSR, Hans Kroll, presented Bonn's views on the German question and how relations with the Soviets could be improved during several conversations with Khrushchev. By late 1962 the Federal Chancellor, Konrad Adenauer, felt able to offer the USSR a ten-year pact but the Soviet government rejected the proposal. Nevertheless, Bonn's policy remained that of seeking to improve relations with Moscow and trading ties with

Eastern Europe. This development contained dangers from East Berlin's point of view.

Khrushchev's speech to the Sixth SED Congress in January 1963 was disappointing as far as the GDR leadership was concerned. The USSR was no longer bent on seeking a quick solution to the German question either through a peace treaty with both German states or with the GDR alone, and the pressure was taken off West Berlin. Turning it into a demilitarized, free city ceased to be the immediate objective. The SED's goal, announced at the congress, was to transform the GDR into a viable socialist state, one which would serve as a pole of attraction for advanced industrial states in the West. Many political and economic reforms were set in motion, the most important being the New Economic Policy (NES), the blueprint of which was published in July 1963. To enhance its view that East Berlin enjoyed an identity of its own, the GDR negotiated a pass agreement for West Berliners visiting the Eastern part of the city. This was followed in 1964 by a regulation requiring visitors to the GDR to exchange a minimum amount of hard currency daily.

At the same time as it was promoting its own identity, the GDR declared that it was still concerned about a future all-German state. Nevertheless, it set out to establish that Germans living in the GDR were at a qualitatively higher level of social development and hence to widen the gap between the two Germanies. Basing themselves on Marx, GDR specialists claimed that the level of social development was a function of the class nature of the economic structure. The outcome was that from 1964 onwards the GDR spoke of two German peoples and two German states.

In June 1964 the USSR and the GDR concluded the Treaty of Friendship, Co-operation and Mutual Assistance and, in so doing, East Berlin and Moscow undertook to co-ordinate their foreign policies. Other socialist states had already signed similar pacts with the USSR but the agreement was worth waiting for from East Berlin's point of view. It provided the GDR with a formal framework within which it could argue its own understanding of the German question and thereby hope to influence Soviet policy. It is instructive that, at the same time as Khrushchev was putting this pact together, his son-in-law Adzhubei, was acting as his unofficial ambassador in Prague and Bonn. Khrushchev appeared to be seeking an agreement on the German question which might have had far-reaching consequences. In these soundings the Soviet leader went over the heads of his foreign minister and the ministry of Foreign Affairs and dispatched his own envoy. Khrushchev was planning a visit to Bonn when he was removed. This appears to be another example of Khrushchev overestimating his own power, since if he had proposed a novel solution to the German question the foreign-policy establishment would almost certainly have thrown their weight against it. Also in 1964 West German politicians, such as Franz Josef Strauss, were attempting to improve West German–Soviet relations. One proposal was to guarantee that no military or security threat to the USSR would emanate from West German soil. In return, Bonn would expect concessions on GDR–West German relations. Khrushchev's removal came at a time when there could have been movement on the German question. Although the GDR played no part in his removal, the result was of considerable benefit to East Berlin since it removed the risk that a West German–Soviet *rapprochement* could have disadvantageous consequences for the GDR.

As the new Soviet collective leadership needed time to consolidate and to overcome the economic legacy of Khrushchev, the SED was able to take the initiative in German affairs and to launch several initiatives. A State Secretariat of All-German Affairs was established in late 1965 and East Berlin hammered away at the point that the diplomatic recognition of the GDR was necessary to secure the security of Europe. Bonn had to accept that the GDR was a sovereign state. Until it had conceded this GDR – West German relations could not improve. The prickly problem of the German nation was tackled as SED ideologists sought to contest the concept of one German nation.

The establishment of diplomatic relations between Romania and West Germany on 31 January 1967 was a shock and a blow to the GDR. East Berlin had assumed that the Bucharest Declaration of 1966 was binding on all Warsaw Pact states. It had made clear that diplomatic relations could not be entered into with Bonn before the latter had recognized the GDR in international law. Ulbricht reacted furiously and belabored the Romanians in *Neues Deutschland* (3 February 1967), but the Romanians accused the GDR of interfering in their internal affairs. For a while it looked as if other East European states would follow suit, the bait being improved economic relations. However, Ulbricht was strong enough to ensure that the Karlovy Vary conference of European communist parties, in April 1967, reiterated the GDR's view that diplomatic relations with Bonn should follow the normalization of relations between the two German states. This whole episode illustrates the leeway which East European states enjoyed at this time. The GDR needed the backing of the USSR to ensure that its interests took precedence over those of the other East European states.

These moves by the SED underlined its lack of interest in the unification of Germany. At the seventh SED Congress Ulbricht spelled this out by saying that the unification of Germany could only become possible after a democratic revolution in West Germany.

Events in Eastern Europe favoured the SED as Czechoslovakia

engaged in its experiment of socialism with a human face. The GDR's hard line was predictable as East Berlin feared the attractiveness of Bonn's *Ostpolitik*. The invasion of Czechoslovakia meant the end of economic experimentation in the USSR and Eastern Europe, but even more importantly it bound all the states more closely together – the exception being Romania – and it ensured tighter control for Moscow, especially in foreign policy. Defensive solidarity *vis-à-vis* the West became the order of the day. It might appear that East Berlin and Moscow saw eye to eye on the German question but this was not so. The desire of Moscow for *détente* and the material fruits it would bring led to a clash with East Berlin.

Moscow Treaty of 1970

While *détente* was getting underway East Berlin kept up its hard-line policy towards Bonn, and in December 1969 a proposed agreement on the normalization of relations between the two German states was handed to the West German government in Bonn. In this climate the two meetings between the two German heads of government in the first half of 1970 in Erfurt and Kassel, during which the GDR claimed compensation for all the labour lost to West Germany over the years, had little likelihood of success. The meetings occurred on Soviet initiative. Whereas East Berlin feared the corrosive effects of *détente* with Bonn, Moscow did not. As part of the process of *détente* West Germany signed agreements on the renunciation of force with Poland and the USSR in the second half of 1970. In these treaties Bonn made no concessions on the recognition of the sovereignty of the GDR. While in Moscow to sign the treaty, Willy Brandt, the West German Chancellor, pointed out to Leonid Brezhnev, the Soviet party leader, that the treaty stood little chance of being ratified in the West German Parliament if a satisfactory solution to the Berlin question was not found.

The Soviets had never satisfactorily resolved the Berlin problem. Given the fact that they were unwilling to use force to oust the Western Powers only a failure of willpower by the West would have removed them. The GDR needed West Berlin badly. The Achilles heel of the Western case was access to the former German capital. All access routes lay on or over GDR territory. The Soviets argued that therefore the Western Powers should negotiate access with the government of the GDR. However, this would have meant recognizing the GDR. Anyway, Ulbricht was in no hurry to reach an agreement since he was convinced that time was on his side. The Soviets decided that *détente* and the prospects of a conference in Helsinki to confirm the European status quo were too attractive to be put in jeopardy. Hence the Berlin

Agreement fell short of what the GDR believed it could have got. Besides contributing to Ulbricht's downfall it underlined the fact that the GDR's negotiating position *vis-à-vis* the USSR was not as strong as the SED leader had believed. Had the USSR been willing to harass the Western Powers on the access routes to West Berlin there is little the West could have done since no one would have advocated going to nuclear war to secure unmolested access. The West could have sent more by air but this would only have been a temporary solution. The cost of maintaining West Berlin would have become prohibitive. The Soviets may also have calculated that it was in their own interest to keep the Western Powers in Berlin. It underlined the Four Power responsibility for Germany, permitted a Soviet military presence in Frankfurt-on-Main and provided useful leverage when it came to pursuing Soviet interests in the GDR.

Friendship Treaty of 1975

East-West *détente* did not lead to a loosening of the bonds which tied the socialist states together and with the USSR. Indeed, it produced an unparalled increase in agreements and contacts at all levels of political, economic and military activity. For the GDR its culmination was the Treaty of Friendship, Co-operation and Mutual Assistance, signed on 7 October 1975, even before the previous treaty with the USSR had expired. Modelled on similar pacts with the other East European states, it had become necessary partly due to changes in the GDR constitution which took effect on 7 October 1974. The latter had underlined the specifically GDR character of the state and had erased all references to Germany, including the goal of eventual reunification.

The 1970s saw the GDR take its place on the international stage as it joined the United Nations and many other organizations. It also allowed the GDR to escape from the suffocating European environment and expand its influence in Africa and other parts of the Third World. Did this afford East Berlin more room for manoeuvre in its relations with Moscow? Certainly in Africa the GDR played an important role in training troops of the national liberation movements and afterwards in the independent states. The activities of the USSR and the East European states are, of course, co-ordinated – the exception here again being Romania – and a division of labour is evident. The Soviets provide senior military officers and advisers, the Cubans do the fighting and the GDR trains the Africans. Certainly, the East Germans have garnered much experience at the grass-roots level and are in a position to influence decision-making by the socialist camp.

The role of the GDR in Africa may turn out to be significant in the long term. In 1982 the GDR had an estimated 250 troops and military advisers in Algeria; 450 in Angola; 550 in Ethiopia; 125 in Guinea; 400 in Libya; 100 in Mozambique and others in the Middle East.[7] Another aspect has had lasting implications for GDR–Soviet relations, the oil price explosion of 1973–4, followed by other sources of energy and raw materials. Since the price of primary products increased more rapidly than that of finished products and since the GDR is resource-poor, the terms of trade turned against East Berlin. For instance, between 1970 and 1980 the cost of oil rose ten times. About 30 per cent of GDR exports to the USSR in the latter year were needed to cover the cost of imported oil, whereas in 1970 it was only 8 per cent. GDR trade with the USSR as a consequence ran into the red. It rose to an estimated 2,000 million transferable rubles between 1975 and 1979 (approximately £2,000 million). This is roughly equal to the rise in the cost of oil imports. Hence the GDR was only able to import so much due to Soviet credits. The situation would have been more serious had the Soviet price not been lower than the world price.

The GDR and Poland

The crisis caused by the Soviet invasion of Afghanistan in December 1979 gave the GDR pause for thought. As a small power it stood to suffer when relations between the superpowers became strained. Although the GDR identified immediately with the Soviet point of view and eventually provided some medical staff for Afghanistan, it sought to protect one aspect of *détente* from the deleterious effects of international tension. This was its burgeoning relationship with West Germany. When the Polish crisis erupted in August 1980 the GDR became alarmed at the loss of willpower of the Polish United Workers' Party. It advocated military intervention by the Warsaw Pact in December 1980 in order to crush Solidarity and to restore the Communist Party to power. However, the aged Brezhnev was not willing to commit himself to such a move. Intense pressure was applied to the Polish Communist Party to put its own house in order so as to restore the hegemony of communist rule. The GDR must have found the period August 1980–December 1981, when a state of war was declared by General Jaruzelski, very frustrating. The Soviet leadership was old and indecisive and, besides the political crisis, there was the economic burden which Poland was becoming to its partners in Comecon. The GDR provided much needed foodstuffs and consumer goods from time to time but the failure of Polish exporters to fulfil their contractual obligations caused disruption in GDR industry. This obliged East Berlin to import more from West Germany.

During Solidarity's legal existence the GDR wished to maintain its good relations with West Germany and this was made possible by Chancellor Schmidt's understanding attitude. Nevertheless, East Berlin feared the impact of free trade union views and the unrestricted comments of millions of West German visitors. It restricted the import of Polish newspapers and journals and cut the number of West German visitors by stepping up the amount of hard currency which had to be exchanged daily. The policy of the West German government was so conciliatory that Chancellor Schmidt went ahead with his first official visit to the GDR. He was still in the GDR when General Jaruzelski imposed a state of war in Poland in December 1981. This potentially embarrassing situation was circumvented by both German leaders agreeing that the Poles should be free to solve their problems in their own way. It is fair to assume that during the late Brezhnev era the GDR enjoyed considerable room for manoeuvre in its relations with the USSR. The two countries did not see eye to eye on Poland, but here again the USSR had to bear in mind that it was a superpower. Its view of the world was wider than that of the GDR. The pace of East Berlin's *rapprochement* with Bonn was at times a little too rapid for the Soviets. Moscow made clear that it expected more consultation before the GDR entered into important agreements with West Germany. Nevertheless, one can assume that the GDR's main argument was that it was deriving considerable financial advantage from the existing accords with Bonn and wished to grasp all opportunities offered to augment these. In so doing, the GDR leadership was making clear that it had reversed its view on the desirability of closer ties with West Germany. Whereas Honecker was determined to maintain *Abgrenzung* in 1971, he was strongly in favour of expanding contacts a decade later. There is no evidence to show that this change of policy was prescribed from Moscow, rather that East Berlin was able to allay any fears in Moscow that such a move was risky.

Abrasimov Goes

The advent of Andropov saw an important change in East Berlin. The abrasive Petr Abrasimov, Soviet ambassador since 1975, returned to Moscow to become chairman of the state committee for foreign tourism – clearly a demotion. Relations between Abrasimov and Honecker have always been strained and it was even rumoured that towards the end Honecker was refusing to see the Soviet ambassador, partly because of the latter's cavalier attitude to protocol. Honecker may have requested his recall. The new ambassador turned out to be Vyacheslav Kochemasov. A deputy chairman of the Council of

Ministers of the Russian Republic since 1962, his appointment may seem surprising. However, he and Honecker know each other from Kochemasov's days as a Komsomol official and Honecker's days with the FDJ. On his appointment he was immediately co-opted on to the Central Committee of the CPSU. The new ambassador was Andropov's man, but it would appear that when Honecker was on an official visit to Moscow in May 1983 the appointment was discussed. Abrasimov's abrupt manner and regal pretensions contributed some tension to the East Berlin–Moscow relationship. Honecker must be satisfied with the new appointment and it will be instructive to see how the relationship develops. Certainly relations should be smoother.

Honecker Needs Western Trade

The fact that Honecker's hand has remained outstretched since Andropov may be due to several factors. The GDR needs West Germany so badly as a trading partner that political concessions have to be made to maintain this relationship. Moscow wishes to have good relations with Bonn which, in turn, knows that the road to improved inter-German relations runs through Moscow. Hence one reason is economic, the other is diplomatic. Is the trading position of the GDR now so poor that it cannot antagonize West Germany? A pointer in this direction was the course of inter-German trade during the first half of 1983. GDR imports from West Germany increased by 33 per cent compared to the first half of 1982, with agricultural products jumping 69 per cent. The overall result was that in June 1983 GDR indebtedness *vis-à-vis* West Germany was over 4.5 billion VE (1VE=1DM), the highest ever. The large increase in the import of agricultural products was to cover shortages in the GDR. It would appear that the GDR leadership anticipated that these shortages could lead to social unrest. Given an overall hard currency debt of $9–13 billion, the GDR needs international loans to service this debt. The extension of a DM 1 billion loan by West German private banks during the summer of 1983 was therefore very welcome. The West Germans expect a quid pro quo and the freeing of children from the need to exchange a certain minimum of hard currency daily in the GDR is a move in this direction. Honecker was keen to visit West Germany in 1983, but after a visit to Moscow in May he announced that his visit had had to be postponed but was not cancelled. Apparently, Andropov had made clear to the SED general secretary that a visit before December 1983 would appear to condone the installation of Pershing II and Cruise missiles.

What effect will the placement of US missiles have on GDR–Soviet relations? Since Moscow has made clear that this will have a negative effect on its relations with Bonn, the GDR stands to lose since a worsening of relations between the USSR and West Germany would inevitably harm GDR–West German relations. Hence here the interests of the Soviets and the East Germans diverge. What leverage has East Berlin *vis-à-vis* Moscow?

Much will depend on whether the USSR proves capable of resolving its present economic difficulties. If the USSR is successful in its attempt to discipline planners, managers and labour in such a way as to increase efficiency, it will be in a strong position in relation to the GDR. If, however, as appears more likely, the USSR is only able to make minor improvements then East Berlin will be in a position to argue that it needs a closer economic relationship with West Germany since Moscow is not capable of providing the help it needs. This appears to have been the thinking behind Moscow's acquiescence in the GDR's acquisition of a private DM1 billion loan. In this scenario of Soviet economic weakness the GDR has considerable leverage since it can argue that it needs a closer economic association with West Germany. Without it, social unrest would occur due to the inevitable shortages.

From the Soviet point of view the GDR is the most important country in Eastern Europe and West Germany the most significant in Western Europe. The fact that Honecker was the first socialist leader and Kohl the first Western leader to pay official visits to Moscow after Andropov took over underlines this point. During Kohl's visit Andropov spoke of the Germans in the GDR and West Gemany, and the government newspaper *Izvestiya* made the point that not all Germans who look forward to reunification should be regarded as revanchists. The Soviets, as skilled diplomats, can play the all-German card if it suits them. Arguably Moscow has much to gain by cultivating the West Germans. The Soviets can encourage the peace movement and do all in their power to further the leftward shift in the SPD Party. Increasing GDR contacts would provide many opportunities to influence policy and trends in West German society. A future SPD government would be encouraged to abandon NATO in return for the GDR leaving the Warsaw Pact; Soviet troops would leave the East if US and other NATO troops left the West. In effect, West Germany could be nudged in the direction of neutrality in return for a closer GDR – West German relationship. Would the GDR favour this? This resurrects the problem of whether Soviet interests are better served by one Germany or two. Whereas a neutral, unified Germany in the 1950s and 1960s would have inevitably been pro-US and anti-Soviet, this is probably no longer the case. It is possible that such a state in the 1990s would be neutral in the full sense of the word. In a united Germany the SED would not enjoy the power it now exerts in the GDR and hence it can be taken that the SED would view a united Germany with some apprehension. The two German states lie at the heart of Europe. Their relationship may change to such an extent over the next decade as to lead to a Soviet decision to play its all-German card.

Notes: Chapter 10

1 *Deutschland Archiv*, no. 11 (1971), p. 1226.
2 The best treatment of this subject is Heinrich Heiter, *Vom friedlichen Weg zum Sozialismus zur Diktatur des Proletariats Wandlungen der sowjetischen Konzeption der Volksdemokratie 1945–1949* (Frankfurt-on-Main, 1977).
3 On the GDR's foreign policy between 1949 and 1955, see Alexander Fischer, 'Aussenpolitische Aktivität bei ungewisser sowjetischer Deutschland-Politik (bis 1955)', in Hans-Adolf Jacobsen *et al.*, *Drei Jahrzehnte Aussenpolitik der DDR* (Munich, 1980), pp. 51–84.
4 Hans-Peter Schwatz (ed.), *Die Legende von der verpassten Gelegenheit Die Stalin-Note vom 10. Marz 1952* (Stuttgart, 1982).
5 Adolf Schärf, *Die Zununft* (Vienna), no. 4 (1980), p. 26.
6 See Johannes Kuppe, 'Phasen', in Jacobsen *et al.*, *Drei Jahrzehnte Aussenpolitik*, pp. 173–200.
7 International Institute for Strategic Studies, *The Military Balance* (London, 1983), *passim*.

11

The German Democratic Republic and the United States

DAVID CHILDS

When the USA and the GDR agreed to establish formal diplomatic relations, *Neues Deutschland* (5 September 1974), the leading newspaper, announced this on its front page. But the story got slightly less space than the visit of the Communist head of the provisional revolutionary government of the Republic of South Vietnam, Nguyen Huu Tho. On the inside pages of *Neues Deutschland,* a short article emphasized the great interest shown by journalists in Washington in the signing ceremony and the same edition of the SED newspaper contained a brief and factual biography of the new US ambassador, John Sherman Cooper. Cooper, who served between 1974 and 1976, was a former Republican Senator for Kentucky and former ambassador to India. A graduate of the Harvard Law School, he had practised law for many years and after the Second World War had reorganized the legal system in Bavaria. In its account of the event *Time Magazine* (16 September 1974) described how the GDR had been diplomatically isolated. It continued:

> Then five years ago, Chancellor Willy Brandt relaxed Bonn's opposition to the East German regime, and the GDR began its long journey in from the cold. Nation after nation accorded it formal recognition, until last week the most important holdout fell into line. In a three-minute ceremony in Washington, the US became the 110th country to establish diplomatic relations with the GDR.

Time Magazine felt that trade and respectability had influenced the GDR to make concessions to the USA over claims by US citizens against the GDR in respect of property confiscated by the Nazis. The magazine concluded, 'But East Germany may discover that respectability could be slow in coming as long as it remains one of Europe's most repressive police states, still finding it necessary to limit the freedom of its 17 million citizens by walls, barbed wire and the presence of 20 Soviet divisions'.

For its part, the GDR press said little about the USA or the relations between the two states in the days that followed the signing ceremony. The Vietnamese politician's visit and the visit of an SED delegation to Bulgaria, together with the celebrations in connection with the twenty-fifth anniversary of the founding of the GDR, were considered the main news stories by the editors of *Neues Deutschland* in the days following the US–GDR agreement. Had they wanted to follow their traditional 1950s and 1960s line towards the USA, the GDR press could have had a field day on 11 September, the first anniversary of the rightist coup in Chile against the left-wing Allende government. Instead, in its editorial of 11 September *Neues Deutschland* did not mention the USA as being behind the coup. This was more surprising in view of the fact that the GDR had been closely involved with Chile and had given sanctuary to prominent Chilean left-wingers. The anniversary of the coup was marked in the GDR by mass meetings and a delegation of Chilean exiles met Honecker. The USA was not accused of involvement by East German speakers, only by the Chileans and, then, unobtrusively. By 13 September Chile was effectively off the front page of the GDR press. It had been replaced by two world-shattering items. One was the SED's congratulations to Politburo member Friedrich Ebert on his eightieth birthday, the other was an article praising the collective farmers for bringing in the harvest. Solidarity rallies for Chile got only a brief mention on page one or were relegated to page seven (in an eight-page newspaper). During this period the only mention of the USA was the publishing of a letter from the Communist Party of the USA greeting the SED on the establishment of relations between their two states. On 16 September *Neues Deutschland,* on page five, reported briefly on Senator Frank Church's call for an investigation of the CIA's role in Chile. Two days later, page six of the same paper carried a more substantial report of the preparations by US miners for tough class struggles in West Virginia, Pennsylvania and Kentucky. If there had been a diplomatic truce in GDR reporting on the USA 'from a class position' it appeared to be over.

The recognition of the GDR by the USA marked the attainment of the SED's highest policy goal in its relations with the Western 'capitalist states'. The SED knew that many citizens of the GDR were in no way hostile to the USA, and did not see it as an enemy. By recognizing the GDR the SED leaders believed that President Ford and secretary of State Kissinger were helping it to demoralize its internal opponents, encourage its friends, and bolster its image among the mass of Western-oriented, yet apolitical, GDR citizens. Only a tiny handful of Marxist zealots were dismayed by the establishment of better relations with the 'class enemy'. As if to emphasize that this, and other, diplomatic triumphs in the West in no way meant a new orientation in GDR policy the Volkskammer (People's Chamber) voted on 27 September 1974 to amend the 1968 constitution. In a speech proposing the changes, Honecker said, according to *Foreign Affairs Bulletin* (2 October 1974), that the victory of the socialist system in the GDR was irrevocable and final, and the GDR was 'inalienably and for ever allied with the country of Lenin and the other states of the socialist community'. These words became part of the amended constitution. A year later, in October 1975, Honecker signed a new treaty with the USSR binding his state to even closer ties.

Since September 1974 relations between the USA and the GDR have been formally correct, at times cordial, without being of central importance to either side. Ambassador Cooper arrived in the GDR in December 1974. He was received by Honecker on 27 February 1975. (It will be remembered that Honecker was not yet head of state.) The two representatives agreed 'that the speedy extension of the political, economic, scientific and cultural co-operation between the GDR and the USA is in the interest of both states and corresponds to the requirements of peaceful coexistence' (*Foreign Affairs Bulletin,* 11 March 1975). Cooper was able to have talks with Honecker on four occasions during his two years as ambassador which would seem to indicate a reasonable degree of interest on both sides.

Trade Relations

Trade, which was clearly regarded as important by the SED (the GDR's first ambassador to Washington was Dr Rolf Sieber, an economic expert), improved after the establishment of diplomatic relations. The GDR considerably increased its imports from the USA in 1976. At the end of 1975 a GDR delegation headed by Dr Gerhard Beil, state secretary in the Ministry of Foreign Trade, responded to an invitation from the US Department of Commerce. Beil met, among others, Rogers C. B. Morton, US Secretary of Commerce, and David Rockefeller, president of the Chase Manhattan Bank. Other such meetings have taken place since then and there have been discussions on trade between US industrialists and GDR officials at the annual Leipzig trade fairs. From the GDR's point of view there has been disappointment that it has not been able to export more to the USA.

The GDR during this period exported less to the USA than did the other European Warsaw Pact states, with the single exception of Bulgaria. The USA exported more to Poland, Romania and the USSR than it did to the GDR. In 1980 GDR-US trade (see Table

Table 11.1   *US Imports from and US Exports to the GDR, 1970–81*

US imports from the GDR (in million dollars)								
1970	1975	1976	1977	1978	1979	1980	1981	1982
9	11	14	17	35	36	44	48	54

US exports to the GDR (in million dollars)								
1970	1975	1976	1977	1978	1979	1980	1981	1982
33	17	65	36	170	356	479	296	223

Source: *Statistical Abstract of the United States 1984, p. 836.*

11.1) represented 1.6 per cent of the GDR's total foreign-trade turnover. Its trade turnover with such small countries as Austria and Switzerland represented, respectively, 1.6 per cent and 2.1 per cent of total trade turnover. In the same year trade with the USSR and with West Germany represented, respectively, 35.5 per cent and 8.4 per cent of total foreign-trade turnover. Clearly, the GDR hopes for a future improvement in trade with the USA, from whom it would like to import more advanced technological products, as it already does from West Germany and Japan.

Honecker meets Ford

This definite but modest improvement in trade mirrored the more relaxed political relations between the two states. Their leaders met personally at the Helsinki conference on security and co-operation in Europe. As the leaders of thirty-five states, including the USA and Canada, were at the conference, it was relatively easy for Honecker to have brief sessions with many of them. It is interesting that the GDR press gave much publicity to Honecker's encounters with Gerald Ford and Chancellor Helmut Schmidt, rather than to his many other conversations, especially with his political allies. A widely published photograph showed Ford and Honecker smiling broadly and their meeting was described as 'friendly'. This term was not used in connection with the first meeting between Schmidt and Honecker though they, too, were seen smiling (*Der Morgen,* 1 August 1975). Soviet leader Brezhnev was not shown with Honecker on this occasion though they did meet. For Honecker, this brief encounter with the US President must have been a cause for great personal satisfaction. He felt that he had really made it at last! Only his reception by the Emperor of Japan (1981), his meetings with West German chancellors and his trip to Austria (1980) have had similar personal significance. Perhaps, too, but to a much lesser extent, Pierre Trudeau's visit to the GDR (as part of a tour of Eastern Europe) in February 1984 gave

Honecker personal, as well as political, satisfaction. (The two leaders first met briefly in Helsinki in 1975 when they agreed to establish diplomatic relations.) These meetings have been psychologically important for Honecker, an ex-member of the proletariat, at the head of what was certainly a proletarian state. By 'proletarian' I mean that the GDR was excluded, scorned, was materially and psychologically poor and that most of its leaders were indeed of proletarian origin. That this exclusion was keenly felt is indicated by the importance given by the media of the GDR to visits by unimportant foreign dignitaries – something not encountered in West Germany. At the age of 74 (born 1912) one of Honecker's few personal ambitions is likely to be a state visit to the USA. It is important to remember that, for Germans, North America has a peculiar fascination (see below).

Support for American Indians and the Wilmington Ten

Since the heady days of the Helsinki honeymoon, relations between the GDR and the USA have had their ups and downs. In 1976 Jimmy Carter became President and made human rights an important aspect of his foreign relations. The East European leaders felt themselves under attack because of this new concern. This was especially so in the GDR where considerable numbers of people took the Helsinki Final Act seriously and applied to leave the GDR for West Germany. The GDR followed the pattern designed in Moscow for a counter-offensive against the USA (and West Germany) over the issue of human rights. Part of this campaign was to focus attention on the position of Indians, blacks and other minorities in the USA. It also alleged that those 'struggling for peace' were persecuted, revived memories of the McCarthy witch hunts of the 1950s, and drew attention to the more sordid side of the American dream. Russel Means, one of the leaders of the American Indian Movement, was invited to the GDR in 1977 by the Peace Council of the GDR. The council seeks to win support, at home and abroad, for Soviet–SED policies at the non-governmental, non-party political level. *Information*, no. 12 (1977), the Peace Council's bulletin published monthly in German, English, French, Spanish and Italian, explained that Means's visit had to be a short one,

> due to pressure of time: the authorities of the US state of South Dakota had at short notice rescinded their decision to release him on bail. This means that he will have to serve a four-year prison term, because he is a staunch fighter for his people's right to love. He spent the last few hours of his visit to the GDR describing to people the anti-human system of imperialism, which, in institutionalized form, seeks to pursue the genocide of the Indians in North, Central and South America . . . It had

been government policy in the United States since 1972 to sterilize Indian women.

What did Mr Means think of the GDR? 'After what I have seen in your country I find that the lies spread about the Indians are similar to those which are being hammered home to us about the socialist countries. I would be very glad if many United States citizens could come over here to the GDR to pass valid, correct judgment on the spot.' Mr Means had been deeply impressed by a visit to Bautzen where the Slav minority, the Sorbs, live.

In May 1978 *information* devoted nearly one page (out of four) to the case of the Wilmington Ten, 'ten political prisoners in the United States'. The paper claimed that, 'The Peace Council of the GDR received protest resolutions all the time in which citizens of the country call for the release of the prisoners'. It mentioned the GDR Lawyers' Association, the staff of the Guidance Centre for Applied Research and the staff of the administrative headquarters of the Berlin Railway Authority. Of course such resolutions are in no way spontaneous. Citizens of the GDR only hear about such cases, apart that is from West German television, from the GDR media. They are not able to visit the USA and have virtually no opportunity to read American publications or correspond with Americans. Such resolutions are directed from above both to indoctrinate the GDR population and to put pressure on the USA.

An earlier issue of *information*, no. 12 (1975) devoted over a page to an article by Professor Franz Loeser, chairman of the Paul Robeson Committee of the GDR. The professor, a member of the Presidium of the Peace Council, wrote a stirring piece on the Rosenbergs, the Jewish communist couple who were convicted of passing on nuclear secrets to the USSR and who were executed on 19 June 1953. There was much doubt about their guilt and considerable feeling around the world that even if they were guilty they should not suffer the death penalty. Dr Loeser had no doubts about the USA at that time: 'The number of flying saucer take-offs in the United States of America grew proportionally with the number of patients who sought refuge in the country's psychiatric hospitals. Psychosis caused by panic fear of a Soviet nuclear attack and the FBI were the most common diagnosis recorded from the majority of patients.'

The professor also indicted the President:

The President's chair had been occupied by an upstart of Pendergast, one of America's most notorious gangster bosses. He was Harry S. Truman, the very same person who had tried to give military excuses in an attempt to justify the A-bomb drops on Hiroshima and Nagasaki. What had been actually intended by his bombing order was to test the maximum effect of the bomb 'by a real object', the Japanese population, with the view to intimidating the Soviet Union.

The same issue of this bulletin announced that the GDR was represented at the first international conference for solidarity with the independence struggle of Puerto Rico held in Havana. The GDR Peace Council's own second-in-command, Kurt Hälker, was elected a vice-president.

GDR's View on Human Rights

The quality of the argument, and the basic official position of the GDR on human rights, can be summed up by quoting a contribution by Dean Read, 'an American singer, who has been living in the GDR for a number of years, was awarded the Peace Medal by the Peace Council of the GDR'. In *information*, no. 9 (1977) he wrote:

> The Administration of the United States has been talking a great deal of human rights over the last few weeks and months; and it would seem that it has adopted a position of integrity and has the moral right to preach to the world about human rights and denounce certain other countries for 'lack of human rights'. Since I am American, I am especially hurt to see what hypocrisy sprouts from the mouths of some of my fellow-countrymen. E.g. it was only recently that the world learnt about the manufacture by the US military machinery of a neutron bomb which President Carter warns is to be mounted on the war-heads of American missiles. This bomb does not do damage to inanimate objects; it *merely* kills people, but it does not destroy flats, factory buildings or cars. Is not this an important step ahead in the campaign of the US Administration for human rights? A bomb perfected to kill people only! It seems that these people, who preach human rights to the rest of the world, have a complicated and distorted view of these rights.

The GDR also takes the view, like the other Warsaw Pact states, that human rights can only be guaranteed by its socio-economic system.

> As a result of the Great October Socialist Revolution the true implementation of human rights was introduced with the abolition of private ownership of the means of production and the elimination of exploitation of man by man . . . In the GDR too, on the basis of the political power of the working class and its allies as well as of the social ownership of the means of production, respect for the dignity of man is the supreme principle . . . The human rights campaign being waged by forces hostile to détente. This goes for the field of human rights, too. (*Foreign Affairs Bulletin*, 17 January 1978).

More recently Politburo member and chief ideologue, Kurt Hager, made a strong attack on the USA but revealed certain fears as well. He claimed that 'the imperialist propaganda machine is seeking to influence and confuse the public inside the socialist countries'. He further claimed that Secretary of State George Schultz, 'In open disregard of what was agreed upon in Helsinki', had said that it was a moral and strategic task of the USA to back anti-socialist ideologies and groupings in socialist countries through radio broadcasts and other direct means of support.

> The purpose of this ideological strategy is to bring about a change in the socialist countries' social system under the slogan of 'democracy'. Hypocrisy in the extreme, it is representative of a system that denies many millions of people the right to employment, equal educational opportunities, equality in general and the exercise of their democratic rights who, of all people, presume to be crusading for democracy and freedom. (*Foreign Affairs Bulletin,* 20 December 1982)

The GDR and Grenada

The relations between the GDR and the USA have sagged a little due to different approaches to international events, with the GDR, as expected, taking the Soviet line on Poland, Afghanistan, the Middle East, Southern Africa and in the new war of words over the intensification of the arms race. The most recent cause of friction between the two states was the US invasion of Grenada. The GDR, which for some time has pursued active foreign policy in Latin America and the Caribbean area, supporting the rebels in El Salvador and the revolutionary regime in Nicaragua, had close ties with the revolutionary government of Grenada. Maurice Bishop, chairman of the New Jewel Movement and Prime Minister of Grenada paid an official visit to the GDR, 8–10 June 1982. It is significant that Bishop's delegation included his Deputy Minister of Defence, Einstein Louison, and Deputy Minister of the Interior, Liam James. This delegation signed a wide variety of agreements with the GDR putting the Bishop regime well on the road to becoming a mini-replica of the GDR in the Caribbean. I cannot resist the temptation to quote what the two delegations had to say about Poland in the official joint declaration, for it says much about the political maturity of the New Jewel Movement:

> They most vehemently denounce as gross interference in the in- ternal affairs of the Polish People's Republic the massive measures of boycott against that country taken by the USA as well as the attempts to vilify and blackmail Poland's allies, especially the USSR. Both sides note that such a policy poses a serious threat to peace and security and

most emphatically demand an immediate end to that policy. At the same time, they again assure socialist Poland of their unqualified solidarity. *(Foreign Affairs Bulletin,* 23 June 1982)

They also backed Soviet foreign policy from Afghanistan to Kampuchea! The reader will hardly be surprised to learn that the GDR condemned the US invasion of Grenada in October 1983 'most strongly' as a 'crime committed against the Grenadian people' *(Foreign Affairs Bulletin,* 28 October 1983).

'The Splendour of Dresden' in the USA

In spite of these differences the GDR and the USA have sought to have some influence on opinion in each other's country and to have mutually beneficial exchanges. In 1976 astronaut Gerald P. Carr and his wife spent two days in the GDR as guests of the League for Friendship Among the Peoples, the Academy of Sciences and the Astronautical Society of the GDR. Carr spent eighty-four days in space in 1973 as commander of the third team to man the space laboratory *Skylab (Foreign Affairs Bulletin,* 27 July 1976). Carr appeared before carefully selected elite audiences to talk about his mission in space. The GDR did not send its sole cosmonaut, Sigmund Jähn, to the USA, but it did mount a massive art exhibition, 'The Splendour of Dresden'. This was opened, in the presence of the GDR Minister of Culture, Hans-Joachim Hoffmann, on 31 May 1978 in Washington DC. It deserved, and got, a suitable venue, the new East Building of the National Gallery of Art. *Time Magazine* (5 June 1978) commented, 'it is a dazzling show . . . a happy choice to celebrate the opening of the newest and most splendid of the New World's museums'. After its success in Washington it moved to New York's Metropolitan Museum of Art on 18 October. From the USA, in particular from the Philadelphia Museum of Art, an exhibition of 320 pictures by photographer Paul Strand was sent to Berlin's Altes Museum. This opened on 22 March 1978. At the official or semi-official level there have been visits to the GDR by US churchmen – among them Dr Billy Graham – and academics, as well as visits by East German academics to the USA. In 1981 a delegation from the GDR Ministry of Higher and Technical Education had talks with the Irex Board on the exchange of scientists between the two countries. A two-year agreement was signed *(Foreign Affairs Bulletin,* 18 May 1981).

Since the establishment of diplomatic relations there have been a number of official talks between the GDR and the USA. Apart from the conversation between Ford and Honecker, the highest level reached were the talks betwen US Secretary of State Cyrus Vance and GDR Foreign Minister Oskar Fischer in June 1978. These were conducted, according to the GDR version (*Foreign Affairs Bulletin,* 21 June 1978), in an 'open-minded and business-like atmosphere'. What they actually achieved it is difficult to say but, in the nuclear age, probably any talks are better than no talks. On that occasion Herr Fischer also met members of the US Congress. Since President Reagan entered the White House in 1980 the highest level of talks between the two states have been those between Herr Fischer and Richard R. Burt, US Assistant Secretary of State, when Burt visited Berlin. Their meeting was described as 'frank and business-like' (*Foreign Affairs Bulletin,* 28 February 1984). Both expressed the desire for 'further steps towards broadening US–GDR relations'. Mr Burt also had talks with Hermann Axen, a member of the Politburo regarded as close to Honecker.

East German view of the USA

In 1954 the US Census Bureau reported that 21 million of the US population were of German descent. This was out of a population of 151 million. The Germans were the second largest group after the British (52 million) and before the Afro-Americans (16 million). Germans have contributed enormously to the American Dream and the USA figures strongly in the popular consciousness of Germans. Nazi attempts to turn the German people against the USA between 1941 and 1945 did not succeed. For one thing, the Nazis just did not have enough time. Millions of Germans have, at least distant, relatives in the USA (and Canada), thousands have friends there. In the case of West Germany there are many Germans who go to North America as tourists or on educational, business, or military visits. The East Germans have not been as fortunate in this respect. Since 1945 they have been increasingly cut off from the USA and Canada. How are they likely to view the USA today? One would expect that this isolation and the change of generations would mean that GDR citizens are much less aware of, and much less positively disposed towards, the USA and its values than are the citizens of West Germany. The reality is probably far more complicated.

Before drawing any hasty conclusions let us examine the influences which have moulded the attitude of the population of the GDR towards the USA. First, there is the remembrance, handed down from generation to generation, of family members who emigrated to the USA before 1945. Secondly, it is certain that at least a few of the emigrants from Germany to the USA since 1945 are from areas which are now in the GDR. Between 1951 and 1980, 3,450,500 Germans by birth emigrated to the USA (forming the biggest group of European emigrants). Surely some of the 3 million or so GDR citizens who left the republic for the West between 1949 and 1979 must have been among them? They would, in many cases, still have relatives in the GDR. Those left behind would be influenced by the fact of having someone 'over there'. Obviously, since 1961 such emigration has been far more difficult and this must be a factor of declining importance. Another factor, not insignificant but again of declining importance, is the fact that the US armed forces occupied much of the densely populated areas of the southern GDR in 1945 before the Red Army arrived. In large towns such as Magdeburg, Leipzig, Chemnitz (Karl-Marx-Stadt), Jena, Erfurt and Halle the people met the Americans before they met the Russians. Without suggesting that all the Americans who took part in this advance behaved like gentlemen, they made, on the whole, a favourable impression. Certainly there were looters and bullies among them. Certainly there were those who regarded all Germans as Nazi scum and, in some cases, alienated genuine anti-Nazi Germans by their ideas and activities. But the average GI, dressed like an officer and opulent by German standards, impressed the East Germans. The average Soviet soldier who followed him did not. This is not a moral judgement, merely one of fact. Any GDR citizen who was 10 or over in 1945 and who lived in these areas would be likely to remember those events – in other words, a significant minority of the GDR population. Once again such memories are handed down, especially when the media put the official view of 1945. The 1 million East Berliners are in a special category. Daily, busloads of US service personnel and civilians tour East Berlin on sightseeing trips. Individual service personnel are to be seen in uniform in the main streets in the centre of East Berlin. This at least helps to turn the NATO aggressor into a person, and it is more difficult to hate individuals.

As children, many East Germans, like their fathers and grand-fathers before them, will have read the Wild West tales of Karl May or the more recently written, Indian stories of the popular children's writer, Liselotte Welskopf-Henrich, such as *Nacht über der Prärie*. Such books lead their readers to think of the USA as a place of adventure and excitement, if also as a place where sudden death can be a daily occurrence. The very popular books of Jack London lead to the same conclusions. During their school days East Germans will certainly be given a one-sided view of the USA. They will be taught to hate the capitalist system of the USA but not to hate Americans. In fact, the 'other America' of black, communist singer Paul Robeson, black 1960 civil rights activist (and communist) Angela Davis, the legendary union organizer, Joe Hill, and the popularizer of Lenin, John Reed, will be given exaggerated attention. Washington, Lincoln and Roosevelt get favourable mentions.

Perhaps the reader will be surprised to learn that the adult citizen of the GDR has considerable opportunities, provided by the GDR authorities themselves, to gain some impressions of the USA. In recent years the publishing houses, the theatre, the cinema and television have all made a contribution in this direction. This was not always the case. In the 1950s, though the 'other America' was not entirely forgotten, a militant anti-Americanism was peddled by the media. Many American authors, entertainers, artists and musicians who regarded themselves as progressive or liberal, were regarded as decadent by the SED. Among many, one particularly thinks of Hemingway here. Much of this was due to Zhadanov, Stalin's commissar for compulsory culture and his East German lackeys. Some of it was due to the influence of returning communist emigrants who had either not made it in the USA or who were hounded by McCarthy's henchmen, and despaired of that country.

The Hemingway Boom

A big improvement took place in the second half of the 1960s. Why at this time? East German experts such as Eberhard Brüning, a professor at the University of Leipzig, argue that it happened then because socialist conditions had been secured in the GDR and this led to a rise in the 'spiritual-intellectual needs' of the population. Also, with the passage of time, it was easier to look back more objectively at works which had previously been controversial. He mentions in this respect Hemingway's *For Whom the Bell Tolls,* first published in the GDR in 1967. He writes of a Hemingway boom starting in 1966. There is something in this view, in that Ulbricht felt secure enough to experiment a little in the economy and in culture. However, the impulse for this was intimately connected with the 'liberal' mood of the Twenty-Second Congress of the CPSU of 1961. Another fact which Ulbricht had to face was the growing influence of West German television. East German television was forced increasingly to compete with the West, and West German television gave East Germans a greater awareness of American authors, as well as films, theatre, musicals and popular music. In 1958 only 5.1 per cent of GDR households had television, by 1965 the percentage had risen to 48. William Faulkner, another previously despised writer, made his appearance in the GDR in 1967. F. Scott Fitzgerald's *The Great Gatsby* was first published in the GDR in 1968, his *Tender Is the Night* in 1976. John Dos Passos had to wait to the mid-1970s to be discovered, *Manhattan Transfer* appearing in 1975.

John Steinbeck, on the other hand, was banned in 1966 because of his support for the US government's position in the Vietnam War, although he had been popular before this.

Professor Brüning informs us, in an article in *Zeitschrift für Anglistik und Amerikanistik*, no. 4 (1980), that there are twenty 'standard [American] authors' in the GDR: Harriet Beecher-Stowe, Ambrose Bierce, J. F. Cooper, Stephan Crane, Theodore Dreiser, William Faulkner, F. Scott Fitzgerald, Bret Harte, Nathaniel Hawthorne, Ernest Hemingway, O. Henry, Henry James, Washington Irving, Sinclair Lewis, Jack London, Mark Twain, Herman Melville, Frank Norris, E. A. Poe and Thomas Wolfe. Among the many other American authors whose books have been published in the GDR since 1967 are James Baldwin, Truman Capote, Joseph Heller, Norman Mailer, John Updike, Richard Wright and, most recently, Henry Miller (1979).

Those who harbour the 'traditional' Western view of the GDR will be even more surprised to learn that East German publishers now give their readers the opportunity to savour the excitement of American crime writers, especially Raymond Chandler, Erle Stanley Gardner, Dashiell Hammett and Rex Stout. Once again, I believe that spontaneous pressure from the West was a factor, an important factor, but not the only one. Much of this literature also appeared in the second half of the 1960s or later. This was the time when the GDR, as mentioned above, was having to cope with West German television and West Berlin (as well as some West German) visitors. Between October 1964 and June 1966 the frontier had been opened for West Berliners seven times for between fourteen and nineteen days. On these occasions there was an enormous influx of West Berliners. The Berlin Agreement of 1971 and the Basic Treaty of 1972 then brought a steady stream of West German and West Berlin visitors. The SED realized that it would have been too big an undertaking to confiscate all literature carried by Western visitors. It would have also been politically damaging. So to lessen the tendency of East Germans to ask their Western relatives and friends to bring popular books from West Germany to the GDR, the SED decided to publish them in the GDR.

Here it is also worth mentioning that East European publishers publish some American, British and other English-language authors in English. There seem to be two motives here. First of all, this ensures that students of English have a politically suitable supply of books with appropriate editing and commentaries. Secondly, such editions can earn currency by being sold cheaply in Third World states.

American plays in the GDR

The SED could claim with considerable conviction that the theatre-going public has had the opportunity to get acquainted with many American plays. Professor Brüning is once again a useful informant. We are told that between 1950 and 1965 the 'following American plays had their German premières at GDR theatres: *Golden Boy* (1950) by Clifford Odets, *Thirty Pieces of Silver* (1951) by Howard Fast, *Longitude 49* (1951) by Herb Tank, *Merry Go Round* (1953) by Albert Maltz and George Sklar, *The Little Foxes* (1956) by Lillian Hellman, *Look Homeward Angel* (1963) by Ketti Frings, *A Raisin in the Sun* (1964) by Lorraine Hansberry, *Deep Are the Roots* by James Gow and Arnaud d'Usseau'. The latter was a 'heartstirring drama about a black war veteran's experiences after his return to his southern home town'. It became one of the most popular plays of the period. 'More than 60 of the then 71 theatres included it in their repertories.' Arthur Miller's *All My Sons* which 'had openings in at least 35 GDR theatres though banned from theatres in the American Zone. With a total of 95 performances it ranked fifth of all productions of the 1949–50 season'. During this time three American plays had their world premières in the GDR. They were 'Alan Max's and Lester Cole's *Potiphar's House,* . . . in 1956, Barrie Stavis's *Joe Hill – the Man Who Never Died* . . . in 1957, and Howard Lawson's *Parlor Magic* . . . 1963'. These plays dealt with 'racist violence in the South', 'the first proletarian and revolutionary songwriter of the United States who became a working-class martyr' and who was anti-war and anti-thought control. Their authors were all black-listed in the USA (*Zeitschrift für Anglistik und Amerikanistik*, no. 4, 1983). Clearly these plays were unrepresentative of the American stage at the time. They represented what the SED regarded as the 'other America'. By the late 1960s and beyond there occurred 'a remarkable shift of emphasis' in East German productions of American plays. 'There is a much greater interest in plays probing deeper into personal conflicts and psychological problems and offering a more complex approach towards social and cultural phenomena of modern American life' (ibid.). Most American plays are first put on in either Rostock of Leipzig. Perhaps the reasons for this are that both cities are to some extent show-pieces, especially Leipzig with its international fair. Secondly, Rostock is somewhat isolated and therefore can be used to advantage for experimenting. If the effects of a play seem to be undesirable it can be more easily taken off there than in Berlin. Between 1976 and 1978 *Who's Afraid of Virginia Woolf?*, *Sonny Boys, A Touch of the Poet, Our Town* and *Opal,* ' a good mix of light comedy and serious drama', were put on in Rostock. Such progress should not be despised. However, as Brüning admits,

'Eugene O'Neill . . . the most outstanding dramatist of the 20th century American theatre' has had 'very few of his plays produced in the GDR during the last decade' (ibid.).

Although the theatre is probably more important as a mass communicator in the GDR than in the USA it is still a limited vehicle and we must ask what American drama reaches mass audiences in the GDR through television. From 1972 the following plays have appeared on television: *A View from the Bridge* (1972), *Les Blancs* (1974), *The Prisoner of Second Avenue* (1975), *Sweet Bird of Youth* (1976), *Look Homeward, Angel* (1977), *Who's Afraid of Virginia Woolf?* (1977), *A Long Day's Journey into Night* (1980), *Everything in the Garden* (1980), *Mourning Becomes Electra* (1981) and *The Diary of Anne Frank* (1982). Perhaps it ought to be mentioned, in view of the GDR's consistent criticism of Israel and its pro-Arab stance, that *Anne Frank* has been popular as a book as well as a play in the GDR.

Up to April 1984, the most recent première of an American drama in the GDR is Leonard Bernstein's *West Side Story* put on at the Leipzig Opera House.

Robert Redford's popularity

In recent years East German television, and indeed the cinemas, have been screening considerable numbers of American films. Ideally, no doubt, they would prefer to concentrate on socially critical films, but this is not possible. Television, especially, has to be mindful of its West German rivals. This is surely the reason why old Doris Day movies from the 1950s and other films of this genre have been shown in the 1980s. If they were not screened viewers could be expected to watch such films on West German television. In the four weeks from 19 March to 15 April 1984, East German television screened five Soviet feature films, four Italian, two French, three French–Italian co-productions, three Cuban, three British, two Czech, one each from Brazil, the People's Republic of China, New Zealand and Romania, two East German, eight either West German or pre-1945 German, and eight from the USA. Of the American films no less than four featured Robert Redford. These were put on at peak viewing time and in two cases were followed by programmes designed to expose the degradation of daily life under capitalism. Among Robert Redford films exhibited in recent years in the cinemas of the GDR or on television are *All the President's Men*, about the Watergate scandal; *The Way We Were*, the story of communist Barbra Streisand and her compromising, liberal husband; *Barefoot in the Park*, starring Jane Fonda; *Three Days of the Condor*, about bloody and brutal struggles within the CIA; and *Tell Them Willie Was Here,* depicting rough justice for an Indian in pre-1914 America. More recently, on 11 June 1984, K. Costa–Gavras's film, *Missing*, with Jack Lemmon, which deals with the true story of the death of a young American after the right-wing coup in Chile was screened on television. Meanwhile Dustin Hoffmann features in *Tootsie* in the cinema.

The cinemas of the GDR, which cater mainly for young people, exhibited nine Soviet films, plus one Soviet–Czech–GDR production, in the three months from February to April 1984. In the same period DEFA, the GDR film company, was responsible for six movies (three had been shown before), and there were nine others from socialist states (including China). Only two West German films were shown, and one French, one Italian and one Spanish-Italian–American. American films totalled three including *Fame*, about the New York acting school, *On the Golden Pond* with Henry Fonda, Jane Fonda and Katharine Hepburn, and *The Salamander* which featured Franco Nero and Anthony Quinn in a thriller about a neo-fascist plot in Italy.

From this review of the American presence on the East German stage, on the small screen and on the wide screen it can be seen that GDR citizens need not be ignorant of American culture and the American way of life, even if we admit that there is a certain bias towards works which highlight the shortcomings of life in the USA. Most East Germans, however, are not dependent on what the SED chooses to let them see or hear. Apart from small areas around Dresden and Greifswald the other areas of the GDR are within range of West German television. The bulk of the GDR population is able, therefore, to view the USA from the perspective of West Germany.

The Impact of Western Television

What impressions of the USA, its politics, policies and way of life are East Germans likely to get from Western television? There has rarely been a time when a US administration has faced so many critics at home and abroad as the present Reagan administration. Even such staunch allies of the USA as the Conservative governments of Britain and West Germany have dissociated themselves from US policy over Nicaragua and, to some extent, over the Middle East and international trade. On defence, Regan faces a host of critics not normally in the left/pacifist corner. Naturally, all of this is reflected in West German news and current affairs programmes. These programmes also draw attention to the large-scale unemployment and poverty in the USA. At the more popular level, crime of all kinds is an integral part of the American way of life as portrayed by

American television itself. Anyone exposed to American television for any length of time can be forgiven for believing that the USA is a vast battlefield on which is fought a never-ending, never-to-end, war between gangsters, hoods and hoodlums and the tough, yet caring sometimes weary, yet always successful, agents of law and decency. It would be strange if all of this had not dented the image of the USA in Germany as elsewhere. But it would be quite wrong to think that it has produced popular anti-Americanism on either side of the Elbe or the Berlin Wall. West German opinion of the USA and Americans is regularly monitored and the results published. In her *The Germans Public Opinion Polls, 1967–1980,*[1] Elisabeth Noelle-Neumann of the Institut für Demoskopie, found that the West German view of Americans had remained largely favourable between 1958 and 1980. When asked to choose the characteristics of Americans from a list of possibilities, in 1980, 4 per cent of West German interviewees found them false, deceitful, insincere; 12 per cent arrogant; 16 per cent inconsiderate; 25 per cent soft, spoiled. But 37 per cent described them as comradely, eager to help; 41 per cent believed they enjoyed life; and 48 per cent believed they were 'full of initiative'. The four highest scores were efficient, capable in business, 62 per cent; progressive, in step with the times, 58 per cent; mechanically-minded, inventive, 55 per cent; and put personal freedom first, 53 per cent. These scores had not changed dramatically from 1958. West German–American television does not seem to have led to widespread anti-Americanism in West Germany.

Although we have no polls to support us, it seems likely that Western television has not led to anti-Americanism in the GDR either. To be sure there are those who will have had their preju- dices, their Marxist–Leninist convictions strengthened by watch- ing Western television. In my experience this is a small group. Much more significant is the group of those who, although critical or sceptical about various aspects of American society and policies, are impressed by American modernity and democracy, wealth and culture. Contrary to the view often heard in the West, people in the GDR do notice that in Western elections there is controversy, choice and drama. They are well aware that these qualities are absent from elections in the Soviet bloc. Another group of East Germans, a large group in my experience, is made up of individuals who are fascinated by the USA as the land of opportunity, excitement and glamour. They see the USA in terms of *Dynasty* and *Dallas*. They are fascinat- ed by a place they can see but not visit. This mythical world stands out in stark contrast to their own everyday lives. Everyday life in the GDR is one of constant exhortations to produce more, save, work harder, do 'voluntary' gardening, cleaning, maintenance work on the housing estate, in public gardens and buildings. It is a life in which people expect to queue for vegetables, for spare parts for their aging cars (those who have them) and ingratiate themselves with the butcher for some under-the-counter meat. It is a life in which people hope to get a place at a seedy trade union hostel on the Baltic coast for a holiday and hardly expect to manage two weeks at one of the less fashionable Bulgarian resorts where, in any case, they expect to be treated as inferior to the West Germans who have paid less than they have. This is admittedly a one-sided picture of daily life in the GDR, but it is certainly an important part of GDR reality and many East Germans would recognize it as the only reality between the Elbe and Oder. Many East Germans in this category – and they are usually not to be found in the ranks of the dissidents, in the unofficial peace groups, or church groups – are impatient with those who criticize the USA, be they Americans or Germans. They see the shortcomings of their own way of life. They see how their own media seek to gloss over these shortcomings. They see how their own media attack the USA and they believe that if the SED is so much against the USA then it must be a good thing! Perhaps this is part of the reason why the GDR media have been less aggressive towards the USA in recent years.

Reagan versus Honecker

What is true of the USA is true of its leaders. There is nothing like as much opposition to Ronald Reagan in the GDR as we would expect given the opposition to him, the scorn and ridicule, in Western states. The leaders of the USSR and the leading comrades of the fraternal parties pursue the cult of personality. Their pictures are everywhere, their words are quoted by every speaker who raises his voice in public and history is rewritten to do justice to their claims. One example of Honecker's style in this direction will suffice. In its 12 March edition, *Neues Deutschland,* still only eight pages, published no less than forty-three pictures of Erich Honecker in the company of politicians and businessmen at the Leipzig Fair. In 1983 Honecker contented himself with only twenty-six pictures of this event (*Neues Deutschland,* 14 March 1983). Evidently Honecker wanted to let friends, rivals and enemies at home and abroad see that he is in full control and let his people see how important is their leader and their state. The pictures were all of the standard variety which the East German public know so well. Honecker receiving foreign delegations, making speeches, inspecting well-drilled troops or well-drilled workers, offering advice (gratefully accepted) to artists, writers, doctors, enterprise directors and collective farmers. There are virtually no pictures of the general secretary and chairman of the Council of State relaxing, taking a walk, pottering in his garden (does he have one?), enjoying a hobby, resting his weary feet. What is true of Honecker is even more true of his colleagues in the Politburo. If they have private lives, they remain very private. These comrades give the impression of being, as Robert Conquest described Lenin, 'Little more than a sort of animated political machine'. For this reason, if for no other, US presidents appear more likeable. We see US presidents stumble as they emerge from planes; jogging; on the farm, ranch, homestead; facing hostile as well as respectful questioners; dancing the night away; happy, perplexed, dejected; in victory and defeat. We see the US President ducking to avoid the assassin's bullet. He gains our sympathy, we think we know him a little. If an attempt is made on the life of a Soviet bloc leader it is never reported. Any sign of opposition is feared, so is any sign that the leaders are mortal. Of campaigner Reagan in the 1970s, Jules Witcover said that he, 'demonstrated a talent for answering the easy questions with great verve and detail, and for finessing the tough ones. As theater the perfomance was excellent; as information it left much to be desired.' He noted Reagan's 'on-camera skills' which 'thrived in the press-conference format' and 'the retentive mind of the actor, and the actor's ability to speak with conviction, whether he meant it or not'.[2] Because they have never had to compete in elections Soviet bloc leaders do not have such skills. Edmund Wilson wrote of Lenin that 'the repetitiousness of his polemical writing and his monotonous addiction to a vein of rather flat-footed Marxist invective show a clumsiness which is never present in even the rancorous hair-splitting Marx'.[3] The SED leaders are degenerate Leninists, lacking both the master's ideas and his style! There really is not much of a contest between US presidents and their adversaries in the GDR and elsewhere in Eastern Europe.

English for You

Another surprising fact about East German television is the opportunity it gives its viewers to learn English. *English for You* has been running regularly since 1966. There are, including repeats, no less than eight half-hour programmes weekly. The series is intended for use in schools as well as by interested adult viewers. English is the second foreign language in the GDR after Russian. The reasons for this happy state of affairs are that the late Walter Ulbricht's advisers knew that English was widely used in the Third World (a target of GDR interest), that a knowledge of English was important for specialists wishing to read American technical and scientific works, and that there was a strong interest in it among those aspiring to be educated. Once again, opportunities to learn the language from the Western media must have also been a consideration.

An elementary knowledge of English makes it easier for East Germans to listen to the American Forces Network (AFN) and the British Forces Network (BFN). These stations have had many listeners since the early days after the war (English had been widely taught in the Third Reich and Weimar Germany). Later, many, who could not speak English, listened to the pop music provided by these stations. This helped to force a more tolerant attitude to such music on East German radio. These additional windows on the world have also helped, therefore, to give the people of the GDR a more sophisticated view of the USA than they would have otherwise had.

Western Contacts

Very few East Germans get the chance to meet Americans face to face. Those who do have in most cases been vetted. Apart from Foreign Ministry officials and a few businessmen, they are selected academics and artists, hotel staff and officials of the mass organizations. In many cases, they will be individuals trained to deal with the English-speaking world. As one would expect, they are usually courteous, sometimes charming and are allowed to be a little more flexible in their answers to questions about the GDR. Even so, 'awkward' questions can throw them badly. Encounters with such official individuals can bring mutual respect, better understanding and occasionally sentiment, but genuine friendship is virtually impossible. An official of, say, the East German CDU, a trade union, the Peace Council or an institute specializing in family problems are all, strange as it may seem, regarded as *Geheimnisträger* (holders of official secrets) and therefore ineligible to have contacts with Western foreigners outside their official duties. Individuals having such contacts are usually those who have given up the rat race, those in the private sector, certain students who are allowed to have pen friends to improve their English, a very few, very privileged individuals and those who have supervised friendships (which could be useful to the regime). Not too long ago I was told by a casual acquaintance, a student, that he had a pen pal in the USA but that he always put the party line in his letters, though he did not believe it. He did so because he presumed his letters would be read by the State Security Service (SSD). Was his American friend hoodwinked? Churchmen make a partial exception to these categories.

Coverage of the 1984 US Presidential Contest

Recently the GDR media, despite all the huffing and puffing about US rockets introducing a new ice age, have treated the USA relatively mildly compared with their attitude in the past. As there was (relatively speaking) much interest in the 1984 US presidential election, this was explained to the East Germans. One example of the treatment it was given were the articles published in *Der Morgen*, the daily paper of the Liberal Democratic Party of Germany (LDPD). On 20 March, Peter Fischer started his series with a fairly straightforward account of the primaries. In his second contribution on 27 March he dealt with election financing explaining that 'candidates of both parties of the ruling class' needed not only to use a considerable personal fortune but needed 'the monopolies' behind them as well. Herr Fischer's third contribution concentrated on scandals, 'a traditional part of any election'. On 10 April he (rightly) pointed out that Ronald Reagan was elected in 1980 by roughly 25 per cent of the potential electorate (as he received 51 per cent of the votes cast by the 52.3 per cent of the electorate who voted). Fischer explained that the low turnout resulted from the residence laws in some states which keep potential voters off the register, literacy tests in certain states and, more importantly, by apathy. According to Fischer the apathy was born of the knowledge that it did not matter which of the candidates of the two *Monopolparteien* won. Like other writers on the USA, Fischer commented on the fortunes of the tiny Communist Party. He avoided exaggerating its importance, confining himself to naming the candidates, Gus Hall for the presidency and Angela Davis as his running mate. But he did mention the difficulty the party has in even getting on the ballot paper. Any party needs 20,000–50,000 signatures of voters supporting its application to be included on the ballot paper. In 1980 it was on the ballot paper in twenty-four states and the District of Columbia. A more optimistic look at the Communist Party of the United States appeared in *Neuer Weg* (January 1984), the journal aimed at SED functionaries. It was reporting on the Communist Party's Twenty-Third Congress held in Cleveland in November to which the SED sent a delegation. *Neuer Weg* recorded that the party had gained 1,000 new members in the last six months and that the party paper, *Daily World*, had doubled its circulation in the last two years. What it did not tell its readers was that *Daily World* probably has more readers in the Soviet bloc and among the FBI than among politically aware Americans. Rightly, the magazine mentioned that it is not easy to be a communist in the USA.

The GDR also faced elections in 1984. In May elections were held for local government assemblies. In their case the term *Monopolparteien* was even more apt than in the US case. After many months of campaigning the electors were, as usual, faced with a single list of candidates. All they had to do at the polling station was to fold their unmarked ballot papers and drop them into the box. In theory they could cross out the names of any candidates they did not approve of, but East Germans assume that such an act would automatically get them on to a list of troublemakers and ruin their careers. They know their protest would change nothing. Abstention would have the same results. Most East Germans are fully aware of their situation. Even convinced supporters of the GDR among them are saddened, sickened and/or embarrassed by such 'elections'. They feel they are unworthy of the great ideal of socialism and unworthy of what they regard as the GDR's achievements. Most East Germans look with a certain envy when West Germans go to vote. It is felt that something nearer the West German system would suit them better than the US system. But despite the shortcomings of the US system they certainly do not despise it.

One curious aspect of the GDR press in 1984 has been the way the Soviet connection has been played down, relatively speaking, and the way contacts with West Germany, Austria, Japan, Sweden and the USA, among others, have been given prominence. Why was this? Clearly there have been policy differences between the GDR and the USSR from at least the time of the abrupt departure of the Soviet ambassador in 1983. It looks as though Honecker was trying to take advantage of the relatively weak and divided Soviet leadership to gain a little more elbow room for the GDR in the Warsaw Pact. He knows of the dissatisfaction at the grass-roots level, and the continuing popularity of West Germany and the USA, among others, compared with the USSR. The Soviet criticisms both of his *Westpolitik* and his moves for better relations with West Germany, which led to the cancellation of his visit to Bonn in the summer of 1984, have increased rather than lessened the tensions between East Berlin and Moscow. It is to be hoped that State Department analysts are recording these differences and that their masters are quietly putting out feelers in the interests of peace, understanding and *détente*.

Notes: Chapter 11

1   Elisabeth Noelle-Neumann, *The Germans Public Opinion Polls, 1967–1980* (Westport, Conn., 1981).
2   Jules Witcover, *Marathon: The Pursuit of the Presidency, 1972–1976* (New York, 1977), pp. 92–3.
3   Edmund Wilson, *To the Finland Station* (London, 1970), p. 386.

Selected Bibliography

The emphasis in this bibliography is on recent books about the GDR under Honecker, especially those relevant to the chapters in this volume. Inevitably, not all fit into these categories. Some sources used by the contributors are not included.

Ansorg, Linda, *Kinder im Ehekonflikt. Ratgeber für Eltern* (East Berlin, 1983).

Anweiler, Oskar, and Knebart, Freiderich, *Bildungssysteme im Osteuropa – Reform oder Krise?* (West Berlin, 1983).

Arbeitskreis für Wehrforschung, *Die Nationale Volksarmee der DDR* (Munich, 1980).

Ash, Timothy Garton, *'Und Willst du nicht mein Bruder Sein . . .' Die DDR heute* (Reinbek bei Hamburg, 1981).

Assmann, Walter, and Liebe, Günter, *Kaderarbeit als voraussetzung qualifizierter staatlicher Leitung* (East Berlin, 1972).

Bahro, Rudolf, *Die Alternative Zur Kritik des real existierenden Sozialismus* (Cologne, 1977).

Bartram, Graham, and Waine, Tony (eds), *Culture and Society in the GDR* (Dundee, 1984).

Baylis, Thomas, *The Technical Intelligentsia and the East German Elite* (Berkeley, Calif., 1974).

Beeston, T., *Discretion and Valour* (London, 1974).

Blumenthal-Barby, Kay, *Betreuung Sterbender* (East Berlin, 1982).

Böhme, Irene, *Die da drüben* (West Berlin, 1983).

Brandt, Hans-Jürgen, *Die Kandidatenaufstellung zu den Volkskammerwahlen der DDR* (Baden-Baden, 1984).

Bruns, Wilhelm, *Deutsch-deutsche Beziehungen* (Opladen, 1982).

Bund der evangelischen Kirchen in der DDR, *Kirche als Lerngemeinschaft* (East Berlin, 1981).

Büscher, Wolfgang, *et al.*, *Friedensbewegung in der DDR* (Hattingen, 1982).

Bussiek, Hendrik, *Notizen aus der DDR* (Frankfurt-on-Main, 1979).

Calleo, David, *The German Problem Reconsidered* (Cambridge, 1978).

Childs, David, *The GDR: Moscow's German Ally* (London, 1983).

Croan, Melvin, *East Germany: The Soviet Connection*, Washington Papers, vol. 4, no. 36 (Beverley Hills, Calif., 1976).

Dähn, H., *Konfrontation oder Kooperation?* (Opladen, 1980).

Dasbach-Mallinckrodt, Anita, *Propaganda hinter der Mauer* (Stuttgart, 1971).

Deutsches Institut für Wirtschaftsforschung, *DDR Wirtschaft Eine Bestandsaufnahme* (Frankfurt-on-Main, 1974).

Diehl, Ernst, *et al.*, *Geschichte der SED Abriss* (East Berlin, 1978).
Döbert, Hans, and Scholz, Günter, *Ordnung und Disziplin an der Schule* (East Berlin, 1983).
Dohlus, Horst, *Der Demokratische Zentralismus – Grundprinzip der Führungstätigkeit der SED bei der Verwirklchung der Beschlüsse des Zentralkomitees* (East Berlin, 1965).
Franke, Konrad, *Die Literatur der Deutschen Demokratischen Republik* (Zurich and Munich, 1974).
Fricke, Karl Wilhelm, *Politik und Justiz in der DDR* (Cologne, 1979).
Fricke, Karl Wilhelm, *Opposition und Widerstand in der DDR* (Cologne, 1984).
Fricke, Karl Wilhelm, *Die DDR Staatssicherheit* (Cologne, 1984).
Gransow, Volker, *Kulturpolitik in der DDR* (West Berlin, 1975).
Griffith, William, *The Ostpolitik of the Federal Republic of Germany* (Cambridge, Mass., 1978).
Günther, Karl-Heinz, and Lost, Christine, *Dokumente zur Geschichte des Schulwesens ind er DDR*, part 3: *1968–1972/3* (East Berlin, 1974).
Hager, Kurt, *Beiträge zur Kulturpolitik* (East Berlin, 1981).
Heinze, C., *et al.*, *Recht im Dienste des Volkes* (East Berlin, 1979).
Helwig, Gisela, *Frau und Familie 'in beiden deutschen Staaten* (Cologne, 1982).
Helwig, Gisela, *Jugend und Familie in DER DDR* (Cologne, 1984).
Henkys, R., (ed.), *Die evangelischen Kirchen in der DDR* (Munich, 1982).
Henrich, Wolfgang, *Das unverzichtbare Feindbild* (Bonn, 1981).
Honecker, Erich, *From My Life* (Oxford, 1981).
Jäckel, Harmut (ed.), *Ein Marxist in der DDR* (Munich, 1984).
Jacobsen, H., *et al.*, *Drei Jahrzehnte Aussenpolitik der DDR* (Munich, 1980).
Jäger, Manfred, *Kultur und Politik in der DDR* (Cologne, 1984).
Kiera, Hans-Georg, *Partei und Staat im Planungssystem der DDR* (Düsseldorf, 1975).
Knauft, W., *Katholische Kirche in der DDR* (Mainz, 1980).
Knecht, Willi, *Das Medaillenkollektiv* (West Berlin, 1978).
Krause, Udo, *Erziehungsrecht – Erziehungspflicht* (East Berlin, 1983).
Kuhrig, Herta, *et al.*, *Zur gesellschaftlichem Stellung der Frau in der DDR* (Leipzig, 1978).
Leiter, Olaf, *Rockszene DDR – Aspekte einer Massenkultur im Sozialismus* (Reinbek, 1983).
Lekschas, John, *et al.*, *Kriminologie Theoretische Grundlagen und Analysen* (East Berlin, 1983).
Lieser-Triebnigg, Erika, *Recht in der DDR* (Cologne, 1984).
Lippmann, Heinz, *Honecker and the New Politics of Europe* (New York, 1972).
Loeser, Franz, *Die unglaubwürdige Gesellschaft* (Cologne, 1984).
Loest, Erich, *Der Vierte Zensor* (Cologne, 1984).
Luchterhandt, O., *Die Gegenwartslage der evangelischen Kirche in der DDR* (Tübingen, 1982).
Ludz, Peter, *Die DDR zwischen Ost und West* (Munich, 1977).
McCardle, Arthur, *et al.*, *East Germany: A New German Nation under*

Socialism? (Washington, DC, 1984).

McCauley, Martin, *Marxism–Leninism in The German Democratic Republic* (London, 1979).

McCauley, Martin, *The German Democratic Republic since 1945* (London, 1983).

Mampel, S., *Die sozialistische Verfassung der Deutschen Demokratischen Republik* (Frankfurt-on-Main, 1982).

Mannschatz, Eberhard, *Einfuhrung in die sozialistische Familienerziehung* (East Berlin, 1971).

Merkl, Peter, *German Foreign Policies, West and East* (Santa Barbara, Calif., 1974).

Moeller, Karl-Heinz, *ABC des Jugendklubs Hinweise und Empfehlungen für Jugendklubs der FDJ* (Leipzig, 1983).

Moreton, Edwina N., *East Germany and the Warsaw Alliance: The Politics of Détente* (Boulder, Colo., 1978).

Müller-Römer, Dietrich, *Die neue Verfassung der DDR* (Cologne, 1983).

Nagel-Dolings, Ursula, *Möglichkeiten und Grenzen eines Verleichs der Lebenshaltung in beiden deutschen Staaten* (Frankfurt-on-Main, 1984).

Nawrocki, Joachim, *Bewaffnete Organe in der DDR* (West Berlin, 1979).

Neuner, Gerhart, *et al.*, *Allgemeinbildung – Lehrplanwerk – Unterricht* (East Berlin, 1973).

Noll, F. Uber, *Schwerter und Pflugscharen* (Plambeck-Neuss, 1983).

Otto, Elmar Dieter, *Nachrichten in der DDR* (Cologne, 1983).

Poppe, E., *et al.*, *Grundrechte des Bürgers in der sozialistischen Gesellschaft* (East Berlin, 1980).

Roggermann, Herwig, *Die DDR-Verfassungen* (West Berlin, 1980).

Ruban, Maria Elisabeth, *Gesundheitswesen in der DDR* (West Berlin, 1981).

Sandford, John, *The Sword and the Ploughshare* (London, 1983).

Schneider, Eberhard, *Die DDR* (Stuttgart, 1975).

Schomann, Friedrich-Wilhelm, *Operationsgebeit Bundesrepublik Politik, Wissenschaft, Wirtschaft Die Spionage der DDR* (Munich, 1984).

Sontheimer, Kurt, and Bleek, Wilhelm, *The Government and Politics of East Germany* (London, 1975).

Spanger, Hans-Joachim, *Die SED und der Sozialdemokratismus Ideologische Abgrenzung in der DDR* (Cologne, 1984).

Staritz, Dietrich, *Geschichte der DDR 1949–1984* (Frankfurt-on-Main, 1984).

Starrels, J. M., and Mallinckrodt, A. M., *Politics in the German Democratic Republic* (New York, 1975).

Steele, Jonathan, *Inside East Germany* (New York, 1977).

Thalheim, Karl C., *Die wirtschaftspolitik der DDR im Schatten Moskaus* (West Berlin, 1979).

Thalheim, Karl C., *Die wirtschaftliche Entwicklung der beiden Staaten in Deutschland* (Opladen, 1981).

Voigt, Dieter, *Soziologie in der DDR* (Cologne, 1975).

Weber, Hermann, *DDR Grundriss der Geschichte 1945–1981* (Hanover, 1982).

Weber, Hermann, *et al.*, *DDR–Bundesrepublik Deutschland* (Munich, 1980).

Westen, Klaus, and Schleider, Joachim, *Zivilrecht der DDR im Systemverg-*

leich (Baden-Baden, 1984).

Wettig, Gerhard, *Die Sowjetunion, die DDR und die Deutschland Frage 1965–1976* (Bonn, 1976).

Wilkens, E., *Christliche Ethik und Sicherheits politik*, Frankfurt-on-Main, 1982).

Wonneberger, Günther, *et al.*, *Köperkultur und Sport in der DDR* (East Berlin, 1982).

The Authors

Dr David Childs is Reader in Politics at Nottingham University and chairman of the Association for the Study of German Politics. He has been visiting the GDR for over thirty-three years. Among his eight earlier books are: *The GDR: Moscow's German Ally; Germany since 1918, West Germany: Politics and Society* (with Jeffrey Johnson); *East Germany* and *Marx and the Marxists.*

Dr Inge Christopher is principal lecturer in German at Ealing College of Higher Education.

Stephen F. Frowen, M.Sc.(Econ.), Senior Lecturer in Economics at the University of Surrey, was formerly a research officer, National Institute of Economic and Social Research, an economic adviser, Industrial and Commercial Finance Corporation (ICFC) and editor of *The Bankers' Magazine* (now the *Banking World*). His publications include *Economic Issues; Framework of International Banking; Monetary Policy and Economic Activity in West Germany* and *Controlling Industrial Economies*. He has also published many articles in leading financial and economic journals. He is Visiting Professor at the University of Würzburg, and frequently lectures at other European universities and at the European Forum Alpbach.

Dale R. Herspring is a Foreign Service Officer of the US State Department. The author of *East German Civil–Military Relations*, his next book is *The Soviet Union and Strategic Arms* (with Robbin Laird). His contribution first appeared in *Problems of Communism* (USIA), January–February 1984.

Dr Martin McCauley lectures in Soviet studies at the School of Slavonic and East European Studies (London University). He is author of *The German Democratic Republic since 1945; Marxism–Leninism in the German Democratic Republic; The Soviet Union since 1917; The Stalin File; The Origins of the Cold War*, and other works.

Dr John Page is Principal Lecturer at Birmingham Polytechnic. He completed his PhD at Nottingham University on education and politics in the GDR. He is author of the *Penguin German Reader*.

Dr J. H. Reid is Reader in German at Nottingham University. Among his publications are *Heinrich Böll Withdrawal and Re-emergence; Critical Strategies. German Fiction in the 20th Century* (with E. Boa); and articles on German literature in the annual *Britannica Book of the Year, Modern Languages Review* and other publications. He is a former secretary of the Conference of University Teachers of German in Great Britain and Ireland.

Dr Roland Smith is Senior Lecturer in German at Bradford University.

Professor Hermann Weber, University of Mannheim, is author of *Die Wandlung des deutschen Kommunismus; DDR Grundriss der Geschichte 1945–1981; Kleine Geschichte der DDR; SED Chronik einer Partei 1971–1976,* and other works.

Dr Roger Woods is Lecturer in Area Studies at the University of Aston. His contribution first appeared in *Survey.*

Index of Persons

General Index